PETER VINEY

With contributions by Bernard Hartley

DIRECTIONS

An intensive English course for
upper intermediate students.

Oxford University Press

Learning languages

Interview another student and complete this form for him/her.

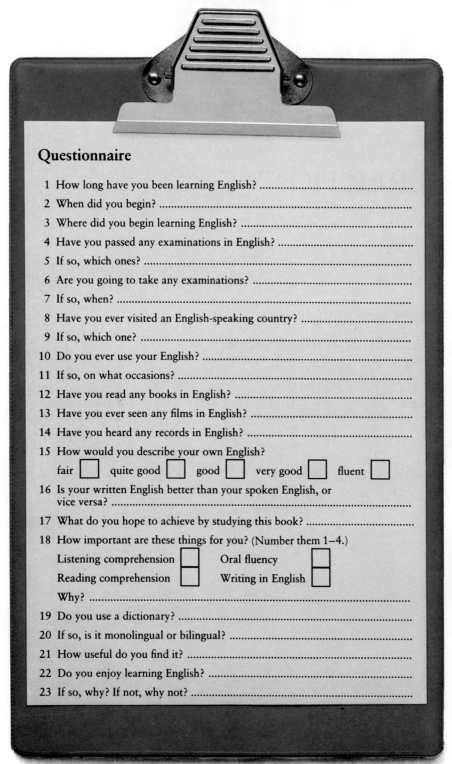

Questionnaire

1 How long have you been learning English? ....

2 When did you begin? ....

3 Where did you begin learning English? ....

4 Have you passed any examinations in English? ....

5 If so, which ones? ....

6 Are you going to take any examinations? ....

7 If so, when? ....

8 Have you ever visited an English-speaking country? ....

9 If so, which one? ....

10 Do you ever use your English? ....

11 If so, on what occasions? ....

12 Have you read any books in English? ....

13 Have you ever seen any films in English? ....

14 Have you heard any records in English? ....

15 How would you describe your own English?

   fair ☐   quite good ☐   good ☐   very good ☐   fluent ☐

16 Is your written English better than your spoken English, or vice versa? ....

17 What do you hope to achieve by studying this book? ....

18 How important are these things for you? (Number them 1–4.)

   Listening comprehension ☐   Oral fluency ☐

   Reading comprehension ☐   Writing in English ☐

   Why? ....

19 Do you use a dictionary? ....

20 If so, is it monolingual or bilingual? ....

21 How useful do you find it? ....

22 Do you enjoy learning English? ....

23 If so, why? If not, why not? ....

Listening

You're going to hear four people talking about their experiences of learning English. Listen to them, and complete the spaces.

Which of them had experiences of learning English most like yours?

Compare your experiences with three other students.

Name _____
Place of birth _____
When started _____
Residence now _____

Name _____
Place of birth _____
When started _____
Residence now _____

Name _____
Place of birth _____
When started _____
Residence now _____

Name _____
Place of birth _____
When started _____
Residence now _____

'While we must accept that there is no single "best method" (of learning a language), we must allow that not all methods are of equal value. There are many roads to Rome, but some are more direct than others and quite a number never arrive at all.'

L. G. Alexander

Exercise

You have a friend who has never studied English.

Which ten words or expressions would you advise your friend to learn before visiting an English-speaking country for a holiday? Make a list.

Compare your list with another student's. Give reasons for your choice.

Reading

This passage is from *Weep Not, Child* by N'gugi (Heinemann African Writers, 1964).

Read it quickly. Discuss the problems the children have with their English classes.

Lucia, Mwihaki's sister, taught them. They all sat expectantly at their desk with eyes on the board. A knowledge of English was the criterion of a man's learning.

Teacher I am standing. What am I doing?
Class You are standing up.
Teacher Again.
Class You are standing up.
Teacher (pointing with a finger) You – no – you – yes. What's your name?
Pupil Njoroge.
Teacher Njoroge, stand up.

He stood up. Learning English was all right but not when he stood up for all eyes to watch and maybe make faces at him.

Teacher What are you doing?
Njoroge (thinly) You are standing up.
Teacher (slightly cross) What are *you* doing?
Njoroge (clears his throat, voice thinner still) You are standing up.
Teacher No, no! (to the class) Come on. What are *you, you* doing?

Njoroge was very confused. Hands were raised up all around him. He felt more and more foolish so that in the end he gave up the very attempt to answer.

Teacher (pointing to Mwihaki) Stand up. What are you doing?
Mwihaki (head bent on to one shoulder) I am standing up.
Teacher Good. Now, Njoroge. What is she doing?
Njoroge I am standing up.

The class giggled.

Teacher (very annoyed) Class, what is she doing?
Class (singing) You are standing up.
Teacher (still more angry) I am asking you . . . What is *she* doing?
Class (afraid, quietly singing) You are standing up.
Teacher Look here you stupid and lazy fools. How long do you take to catch things? Didn't we go over all this yesterday? If I come tomorrow and find that you make a single mistake I'll punish you all severely.

With this sharply-delivered threat, she walked out. Njoroge, annoyed with himself at his poor showing, could now be heard trying to re-establish himself by telling them that they ought to have answered, 'She is standing up.' But one boy (the most stupid in the class) rebuked him. 'Why didn't you speak up when she was here, if you're so clever?'

After some more weeks of anger and threats the children managed to glean something of which they were very proud. Njoroge could now sing.

I am standing up.
You are standing up.
She is standing up.
He is standing up.
We are standing up.
You are standing up.
They are standing up.
Where are you going?
I am going to the door.
We are going to the door.

Point to the blackboard. What are you doing?
I am pointing to the blackboard.

Shark attack!

Death traps of the sea

"I was just inches from the monster's mouth"

California lifeguard Casimir Pulaski (above) was paddling with his surfboard in the Pacific Ocean off San Luis Obispo when a shark attacked him.

He says: 'I had swum about 13 miles and I was about a mile and a half out when suddenly something came straight up out of the water, knocking me off my surfboard and into the air.

'I didn't know it was a shark until I surfaced again. Then I saw this big fish swimming around with my surfboard in its mouth.

'I could see its long grey dorsal fin and I thought, "Oh, my God, it's a Great White Shark." The next thought was, "Nobody gets this close to a Great White and lives to tell the tale."

'You just don't know what you're going to do in a situation like mine. I saw the shark coming towards me with my surfboard in its jaws. I grabbed the tail of the surfboard and climbed back on it. I don't know why. Then I was afraid that if the shark let go of the board he'd go for me.

'I got on my knees on the tail of the board, trying to keep my balance because all the time he's shaking the board – trying to get me off it.

'I was starting to fall back in the water – where I'd be easy meat for him – so I moved up to the centre of the board where I could hold on to the rail.

'But I slipped back two or three inches. And that's when I whacked him on the nose. I just open-handed slapped him on the nose.

'It was more an automatic reaction than a deliberate slap. It was like something was taking over my body.

'I was just six inches away from his teeth, but it was the eyes I remember most. It seemed as though he wasn't looking at anything when he was looking at me.

'Anyway, I just went for him and whacked him – and about two or three seconds after I hit him he went.

'For a minute I really thought I'd had it – I might have seen my life pass in front of me a little bit – and after he went I started paddling back to the beach. But I was waiting for him to come back again.

'They were the worst moments. Then I kind of knew he wasn't coming back, and I managed to get to the beach. I stood up and looked at my hands and feet – practically counted my fingers and toes – to make sure everything was intact. I couldn't believe I got away without a scratch.

'When I recovered my surfboard later, it had big teeth marks in it. A biologist, who investigated, said the bite mark was probably from a Great White about 18 feet long.

'I had nightmares that night, but the next day I was back in the ocean. I love it. Even before the attack I'd reckoned it was silly to worry about sharks because attacks are so rare. I still feel that.'

TV TIMES MAGAZINE 8–14 January 1983

TV TIMES MAGAZINE 8–14 January 1983

Exercise 1

1 What was he doing when the shark attacked him?
2 How far had he swum?
3 How far was he from the shore?
4 When did he realize it was a shark?
5 What did he do when it came towards him?
6 When did he hit the shark on the nose?
7 What did he do after it went?
8 Why did he check his hands and feet?
9 What did he see when he recovered the surfboard?
10 How long was the shark?

Exercise 2

Find words which mean:
hit (two words)
to come from under the water
took hold of   bad dreams
still in one piece   mouth

Language study

The simple past (*I did it*) and the past continuous (*I was doing it*).

1   He *was paddling* on his surfboard *when* the shark attacked him.
     (when → the same time)
2   *When* the shark attacked him, he *fell off* his surfboard.
     He *fell off* his surfboard *when* the shark attacked him.
     (when → just after)
     Note: At the time of the attack, he was on the surfboard.
3   *When* he *fell off* his surfboard, the shark attacked him.
     Note: At the time of the attack, he was in the sea.
4   The shark attacked him *while* he *was paddling* on his surfboard.
     While he *was paddling* on his surfboard, a shark attacked him.
     (while goes with the past continuous.)
5   (It seemed as though) he wasn't looking at anything | *when* / *while* | he *was looking* at me.

The Great White Shark
(*Carcharodon carcharias*)

Length: 5–12 metres
Weight: 2000–5000 kg
Colour: Grey/blue on top, white underside.
Habitat: All tropical, sub-tropical and moderately warm seas.
Largest specimen captured:
11.27 metres, June 1930, White Head Island, New Brunswick, Canada.

Perhaps no creature on land or sea inspires so much terror as the Great White Shark. Great Whites are surface hunters, swift and powerful swimmers which will attack and try to eat anything. They only attack man occasionally, but the attacks are sudden, deadly and dramatic. One bit a man in two, another six-metre specimen died after trying to swallow a man whole. In 1916 a Great White killed four bathers off a New Jersey beach. Sharks circle their prey, appearing from nowhere, and frequently approaching from below. A Great White has been known to part a wire rope with a breaking strength of 2000 kilograms.

Most attacks occur in shallow water, where the surface temperature is between 16°C and 21°C, usually between 10 a.m. and 6 p.m. 70% of shark-attack victims die, largely due to blood loss and shock. Sharks are single-minded, and will usually ignore rescuers; they concentrate on their original victim. In Australia shark nets are used to protect beaches, and in other parts of the world there are look-out towers, bells, sirens or electric fences.

The book and the film, *Jaws*, which tell the story of a shark cruising off a New England beach, created mass fear of bathing. In the book a shark attacks and sinks a small boat, and there are several recorded cases of Great Whites sinking boats. However shark attacks are extremely rare. There is more chance of being struck by lightning.

Shark attacks always hit the news. Here are two stories from summer 1983.

One is from *The Times*, a 'serious' newspaper. The other is from the *Daily Express*, a 'popular' newspaper. Which is which?

Shark kills two off Barrier Reef

Melbourne – The skipper of a prawn trawler, wrecked off the North Queensland coast near the Barrier Reef on Sunday night is recovering in hospital after a 36-hour ordeal during which his two-member crew, one a woman, were taken by a shark as the three clung to wreckage.

Mr Ray Boundy, aged 33, skipper of the New Venture, said that after the shark attacked Dennis Murphy, aged 24, taking off his leg, Mr Murphy swam clear to draw the shark away. He was not seen again. Also killed was Linda Horton, aged 21.

● JAWS is dead. The incredible monster of the deep who has been terrorizing America's Eastern Seaboard was killed in a terrifying battle. And it was just like a scene from the famous horror movies.

● It happened in Eastern Long Island Sound, 10 miles from the coast. Boat captains Gregory Dubrule and Ernie Celotto waited patiently for 10 hours alongside a dead whale they used as bait for the monster. Suddenly, Jaws reared up from the ocean and Dubrule harpooned him.

● "The line went out like mad and he dragged the huge flotation balls under," Celotto said. "Then he headed full speed for Greg's boat and we harpooned him again. There wasn't time to be scared."

● For six hours the skippers, from Mystic, Connecticut, fought on. Finally they killed the 17ft 3,000lb Great White, with two shot-gun blasts.

The yellow bulldozer

The house stood on a slight rise just on the edge of the village. It stood on its own and looked out over a broad spread of West Country farmland. Not a remarkable house by any means – it was about thirty years old, squattish, squarish, made of brick, and had four windows set in the front of a size and proportion which more or less exactly failed to please the eye. The only person for whom the house was in any way special was Arthur Dent, and that was only because it happened to be the one he lived in.

On Wednesday night it had rained very heavily, the lane was wet and muddy, but the Thursday morning sun was bright and clear as it shone on Arthur Dent's house for what was to be the last time. It hadn't properly registered yet with Arthur that the council wanted to knock it down and build a bypass instead.

At eight o'clock on Thursday morning Arthur didn't feel very good. He woke up blearily, got up, wandered blearily round his room, opened a window, saw a bulldozer, found his slippers, and stomped off to the bathroom to wash.

Toothpaste on the brush – so. Scrub.

Shaving mirror – pointing at the ceiling. He adjusted it. For a moment it reflected a second bulldozer through the bathroom window. Properly adjusted, it reflected Arthur Dent's bristles. He shaved them off, washed, dried, and stomped off to the kitchen to find something pleasant to put in his mouth.

Kettle, plug, fridge, milk, coffee. Yawn.

The word *bulldozer* wandered through his mind for a moment in search of something to connect with. The bulldozer outside the kitchen window was quite a big one.

He stared at it. 'Yellow,' he thought and stomped off back to his bedroom to get dressed.

Passing the bathroom he stopped to drink a large glass of water, and another. He began to suspect that he was hung over. Why was he hung over? Had he been drinking the night before? He supposed that he must have been. He caught a glint in the shaving mirror. 'Yellow,' he thought and stomped on to the bedroom.

He stood and thought. The pub, he thought. Oh dear, the pub. He vaguely remembered being angry, angry about something that seemed important. He'd been telling people about it, telling people about it at great length, he rather suspected: his clearest visual recollection was of glazed looks on other people's faces. Something about a new bypass he'd just found out about. It had been in the pipeline for months only no one seemed to have known about it. Ridiculous. He took a swig of water. It would sort itself out, he'd decided, no one wanted a bypass, the council didn't have a leg to stand on. It would sort itself out.

God what a terrible hangover it had earned him though. He looked at himself in the wardrobe mirror. He stuck out his tongue. 'Yellow,' he thought. The word *yellow* wandered through his mind in search of something to connect with.

Fifteen seconds later he was out of the house and lying in front of a big yellow bulldozer that was advancing up his garden path.

The Hitch-Hiker's Guide to the Galaxy
Douglas Adams.

Exercise 1

Find the words which mean the following:

1 a large tractor with caterpillar tracks and a broad blade in front, used for moving earth
2 a mental picture, a memory
3 a flash of reflected light
4 facial hair on a man who usually shaves
5 a new wide road taking traffic round a town or village
6 to stamp, to walk very heavily
7 a large mouthful (of a drink)
8 the feeling when someone has drunk too much alcohol the night before
9 a 'glassy-eyed' look, when people have stopped focusing their eyes because of boredom or incomprehension
10 a small hill

Exercise 2
What do these phrases/sentences mean?

1 'It had been in the pipeline for months.'
  a It had been forgotten about for months.
  b They had started laying pipes months ago.
  c It had been planned and due to happen for months.

2 'The council didn't have a leg to stand on.'
  a The council didn't know what to do.
  b The council had ignored the rules, and wouldn't be able to justify their action.
  c The council hadn't chosen a place to begin.

3 'It hadn't properly registered with Arthur that the council wanted to knock it down.'
  a Arthur had not been told formally, in writing.
  b The council had not put their plans on the official register, and had not informed him.
  c Although Arthur did know, he hadn't realized that it really would happen.

4 'It would sort itself out.'
  a If he waited, the problem would resolve itself.
  b The council would prosecute itself.
  c The council workmen would fight each other.

5 'of a size and proportion which more or less exactly failed to please the eye.'
  a the size, shape and position never displeased people.
  b the size, shape and position were very average.
  c the size, shape and position were ugly.

Language study (1)

He shaved, washed, dried and stomped off to the kitchen ...
In many European languages, verbs like *shave, wash, dry,* and so on are reflexive.

In English they can be reflexive, but they usually aren't. We can say *He shaved himself, washed himself, dried himself ...* but we wouldn't bother unless it was unusual, or done with difficulty. Verbs like *feel, think* and *concentrate* are never reflexive.

Reflexive pronouns (or emphatic pronouns)

myself	*itself*	*themselves*
yourself	*oneself*	
himself	*ourselves*	
herself	*yourselves*	

Exercise 3
In which of these sentences would you use a reflexive pronoun?

1 After the accident she was in plaster for three weeks. It was a great thrill when she was able to wash _____ again.
2 Hold on, I won't be long, I've just got to shave _____ before we go out.
3 You're soaked! You'd both better hurry and dry _____ There's a cold wind, and we've only got a small towel.
4 After a long journey, I'm always dying to have a shower and get _____ clean.

Language study (2)

Informal, spoken style   *The only person the house was special for was Arthur.*
The only person that the house was special for was Arthur.

Formal, written style   *The only person for whom the house was special was Arthur.*

Exercise 4
Transform these sentences into a more formal style.

1 He's the man I bought it from.
2 The person I spoke to was very rude.
3 I bought a carton of eggs, and six were bad.
4 The people who the police brought charges against had long criminal records.
5 Here's the book that I found the quotation in.
6 Douglas Adams is the man the extract was written by.
7 It's something that I know nothing about.
8 She's the woman I was telling you about.
9 The goods, which I sent you a cheque for, have never arrived.
10 She's a person who we rely on very much.

The RUMOUR

Man: Is Mr Joyce here?
Secretary: No, he's gone to the hospital.
Man: Oh? He wanted me to wash his car.
Did he leave the keys?
Secretary: His car isn't here, I'm afraid. The police towed it away.

Man: Did you hear that Mr Joyce had gone to hospital?
Woman: No, what happened?
Man: A car crash, I think. Anyway, the police have towed away the wreckage.
Woman: Oh, dear. I saw an ambulance on my way to work.

Man: Has anyone told you about Mr Joyce?
Woman: No . . . what about him?
Man: He crashed his car. It's a complete write-off. He's in hospital . . . intensive care, I heard.
Woman: Are they going to operate?
Man: Well, I'm not sure. I heard that he's got a lot of allergies.

Man: Do you know how Mr Joyce is?
Woman: Oh, you've heard too. Bad news travels fast. I hear that he needs to see a Swiss specialist.
Man: That's going to be expensive.
Woman: Yes, but there are 3,000 people working here. Let's have a collection to raise the money!

Woman: We're collecting for Mr Joyce.
Man: Who's he?
Woman: He works in the Accounts Department. He had an awful crash. They're flying a surgeon in from Geneva. He'll never work again.
Man: Oh dear . . . well, here's a pound

Mr Joyce: Hello, where is everyone?
Secretary: I've got no idea, Mr Joyce. How was your grandmother?
Mr Joyce: Oh, she was fine. It wasn't a heart attack – just indigestion, that's all. I'd better go and collect my car from the police station. You know, I only parked on a double yellow line while I was getting her some flowers and they towed it away . . .

Unit 4

The wrong sentence

Stanley's first teaching job was at the local prison. He was very nervous when he arrived for the first lesson. He looked around the room at the prisoners. Some of them were in prison for robbery, others were there for crimes of violence. One or two were in prison for murder. He coughed, and said, 'Good morning. I am your new English teacher. Let's begin with grammar. I suppose you all know what a sentence is?'

Where was Stanley's first teaching job?
Why were the prisoners in his class in prison?
Why did Stanley say the wrong thing?
What are the two meanings of 'sentence'?

Note: at *the* prison/in prison

The accident

Jim's father was driving him to school when the accident happened. They were waiting to turn into the road that led to the school when a lorry hit them. They were both rushed to hospital, and taken to the operating theatre. The doctors called a famous surgeon, who hurried to the hospital. The surgeon walked into the operating theatre, stopped, and said, 'I can't operate. That's my son on the operating table!'

Where was Jim's father driving him?
Which road were they waiting to turn into?
Where were they rushed to?
Who did the doctor call?
What did the surgeon do?
Why couldn't the surgeon operate?
How is this possible?

Note: to school/to *the* school/to hospital/to *the* hospital.

Language study

1 The ambulance took them *to hospital*.
The doctors hurried *to the hospital*.
Their relatives went *to the hospital* to visit them.

The criminal was sentenced to five years *in prison*.
His wife went *to the prison* to see him.

The students go *to school* every day.
I always go *to the school* to collect my daughter.

Students/pupils	go to	school.
	are at	college.
		university.

Everyone else, including teachers, go to *the* school.

Criminals	go to	prison.
	are in	jail.
		court.

Everyone else, guards, visitors, etc., go to *the* prison.

| Patients | go to | hospital. |
| | are in | |

Everyone else, doctors, visitors, cleaners, delivery men, go to *the* hospital.

2 The congregation/the priests go *to church*. They are *in church*.
Sailors go *to sea*. They are *at sea*.
Workers go *to work*. They are *at work*.
When we are tired, we go *to bed*. We are *in bed*.

3 He was rushed to hospital *by ambulance*.

Note: by bus/by car/by taxi/by tube/by plane/by ship/by hovercraft/
by road/by sea/by air
on foot/on horseback

'I came to work by bus. I couldn't get on *the* first bus. I had to wait for *the* second. *The* second bus was late.'

Exercise 1

Make up a story about someone in the class, or someone you know. Say when something happened, what happened, who was there, and what was said.

Use these phrases to help you:
Did you hear that ...?   *Did you know* | *that ...?*
                                                 | *about ...?*

Have you heard about ...?   *Someone told me ...*
I was told that ...
Has anyone told you about ...?
I heard that ...

Whisper the story to someone else, who will whisper the story to a second person, who will pass it on to a third person. When the story has passed on through the group, the last person reports it aloud. Is the story still the same?

Exercise 2
Have you ever overheard something that you weren't meant to overhear?
What was it?
How did you feel?
What did you do?

Two-word verbs

News of the Globe

All the World's News – every Sunday

Talks break down

Africa: Mandanga broke off diplomatic relations with Zaspal yesterday when talks between the two countries over a border dispute broke down. Fighting broke out in the area two months ago after a Mandangan plane was shot down.

'FLU BREAKTHROUGH

Help is on the way for sufferers from the 'flu epidemic which broke out before Christmas. IDC announced a new 'flu treatment, Influprin, last week. It has been hailed as a major scientific breakthrough.

Sarah's Surprise

Shapely Scottish singing sensation, Sarah Sownes, broke off her engagement with American transport millionaire, Laurie Van Truck, yesterday. Sarah has been seeing Laurie since her marriage to film star, Steve Newman, broke up two years ago. She said, 'I've decided to break with Laurie completely. I don't love him. He was helping me to break into the film industry, but nothing's happened.'

MYSTERY SOLVED !

The man responsible for more than 30 burglaries in the Bingley area was finally caught last night. Police caught him breaking into a house in Warwick Street. He broke away from his captors, but they gave chase and saw him . . . climbing over the wall into Bingley prison! The man, who was serving a 10 year sentence for burglary, had broken through his cell wall, and had been breaking out of prison twice a week to break into local houses.

Rocket breaks up

The American rocket, Columbus XIV, broke up and fell to Earth yesterday after the cooling system broke down and the engines overheated. There was no danger as the sections broke into small pieces and burnt up when they hit the atmosphere.

...and the rest of the news

● World War III broke out on Thursday, see p.17.
● Fire broke out and destroyed half of New York on Saturday, see p.6.
● Prince George has broken with family tradition by getting engaged to a shop assistant, see p.22.
● Fighting broke out at the England-Scotland Football match, see p.26.

Language study

Two- and three-word verbs

In English, there are many two- and three-word verbs, such as *go against, go for, go into, go back* and *go along with*. Sometimes it is easy to guess the meaning, because you know the **verb** and the **preposition** or **adverb** it is combined with.

In other cases the meaning of the compound may seem unrelated to the two parts. Water (H_2O) is a compound of hydrogen (H) and oxygen (O), but is quite different from either of them. So you might guess the meaning of '*Go back* and get another coffee, John's just arrived', but you might have trouble with 'I'm afraid I can't *go along with* the plan' or 'Business is very bad. Unless things improve, the whole company will *go under*.'

A **break in**[1] [A1] interrupt. **S:** speaker, critic. **A:** sharply, abruptly, excitedly □ '*But what's going to happen to us?*' *one of the miners* **broke in**. □ normally precedes or follows direct speech.

B **break in**[2] [B1i pass] accustom to new discipline, make docile; make soft and pliable. **S:** trainer, drill sergeant. **O:** horse, mount; recruit, novice; pair of boots □ *Petrucchio* **broke in** *a shrewish wife.* □ *New recruits are often* **broken in** *by repeated drilling on the barrack square.*

C **break in/into** [A1 nom A2 pass adj] force an entry (into), force one's way in(to). **S:** burglar, intruder. **o:** shop, private house, warehouse □ *Tell them that those inside need protection against desperate characters who are trying to* **break in** *from outside.* TBC □ *There was a* **break-in** *at Smith's warehouse.* □ *Stores were* **broken into** *and looted during the riots.*

D **break in on/upon** [A3 pass emph rel] interrupt, disturb. **S:** noise, voice. **o:** thinking, meditation, conversation □ *A sudden noise from outside* **broke in upon** *his day-dream.* □ *Their meeting was* **broken in upon** *by the arrival of a group of petitioners.*

E **break into**[1] [A2] suddenly change from a slower to a faster pace. **S:** horse, elephant, herd. **o:** ⚠ a run, trot, canter, gallop □ *As soon as they scented water, the whole herd* **broke into** *a gallop.* □ '*I shall be late*' — *she was on the point of* **breaking into** *a run.* PW

F **break into**[2] [A2] suddenly begin to laugh etc. **S:** audience, crowd. **o:** (loud) laughter, song, cheers □ *As the President's car appeared, the waiting crowds* **broke into** *loud cheers.*

G **break into**[3] [A2 pass] take time from, encroach on/upon (q v). **S:** overtime, extra duties, night-work. **o:** evenings, leisure time □ '*I can't take on any extra overtime: my weekends have been* **broken into** *far too much as it is.*'

H **break into**[4] [A2 pass] use a high-value note or coin to buy an article costing less. **S:** customer, purchaser. **o:** pound note, ten-dollar bill □ '*I can't give you the forty pence I owe you without* **breaking into** *a five-pound note, so do you mind if I pay you back tomorrow?*'

I **break into**[5] [A2 pass] open and consume (sth held in reserve for emergency use). **S:** garrison, beleaguered population, expedition. **o:** (reserve stocks of) water, food, ammunition; iron-rations □ *The stranded party* **broke into** *their emergency supplies of food and water.*

J **break into**[6] [A2 pass adj] force an entry into. ⇨ break in/into.

The most important thing for you to know when you are learning two-word verbs is whether they are **separable** or **inseparable**.

These sentences give examples of a separable two-word verb.
> I must *think over* your suggestion.
> I must *think* it *over*.
> I must *think* your suggestion *over*.

In this sentence the two-word verb is inseparable.
> I can't come out. I've got to *look after* my little brother.

The combinations of **verb + preposition**, and **verb + adverb + preposition** are inseparable. The difficulty comes with the **verb + adverb** combinations. Here are a few simple rules:

1 If there is no object, then of course there is no problem!
(e.g. Go away! Go back!
Go forwards!)

2 If the object is *me, you, him, her, it, us,* or *them,* then the phrasal verb will always be separated.
(e.g. It brings *me* down, I want to give *it* up.)

3 If the object is a noun or a word like *someone, everything,* we can

use either the order:
> **verb + noun + adverb** (I'll *send* my answer *back* soon)
or
> **verb + adverb + noun** (I'll *send back* my answer soon)

Exercise 1
Read through the newspaper page. Note down all the two-word verbs with *break*.

Break

'Break' forms several two/three-word verbs. Above is an extract from the *Oxford Dictionary of Current Idiomatic English: Volume I*: This extract looks at uses of 'break' with 'in' and 'into'. Only 'break in[2]' (B) is separable.

Exercise 2
Read these sentences, and note which meaning (A-J) you think is being used.

1 New shoes are often uncomfortable until you've broken them in. ☐

2 'Hold on, I'll just find some change. I don't want to break into a ten pound note.' ☐

3 'Come back tomorrow and ...' 'I can't wait that long,' broke in Mark, 'I've got to see him today.' ☐

4 I was trying to keep a straight face, but when he fell over the wastepaper bin I just broke into roars of laughter. ☐

5 I was trying to work, when the noise of a cassette-player blasting out music broke in on me. ☐

6 When they saw the bus coming, they broke into a run. ☐

7 Look, I know you're busy. Do you mind if I just break in on you for a moment? ☐

8 They broke in through an upstairs window which the owners had forgotten to close. ☐

9 'We've run out of milk. We'll have to break into the reserve supply again.'
'But we keep that for an emergency!' ☐

10 That's the trouble with the night-shift. It breaks into your private life too much. ☐

The explorer

Good evening, and welcome to the *Patrick Logan Show*. On tonight's show we're going to meet Broderick Foyle, the scientist who believes influenza comes from outer space; Moira Robinson, the author of *Super Housewife,* and we're going to hear the latest song from 'Shining Teeth'. Our first guest needs little introduction from me. He has climbed Mount Everest, gone down the Amazon by canoe, and crossed the Sahara Desert on foot. Ladies and gentlemen ... it's Richard Mills!

Patrick Richard, welcome. You've been everywhere and you've done everything, and now your latest book has just been published, hasn't it?

Richard That's right, Patrick. It's called *Miles of Sand.*

Patrick I've been reading it this week, and there are some pretty fantastic stories in it.

Richard They're all true, Patrick, all true.

Patrick I'm sure they are. I particularly liked the story of your 'rescue'. Could you tell us that one?

Richard Yes. I was crossing the Sahara on foot when it happened. I had a small radio, but it packed up after ten days or so, and I just kept on going. Obviously, when I didn't call in, people began to worry, and they sent out a search party. Now, I was travelling at night and sleeping during the day. On this particular morning I had set up my tent and just crashed out. I'd been sleeping for a couple of hours when the search party arrived, and I didn't hear their truck. What happened was I woke up and heard these voices outside the tent. Someone said, 'I had a look, he's dead, I reckon!' 'Who? Me?' I shouted and popped my head out of the tent. You should have seen their faces! They were even more surprised when I refused a lift from them ... but they did give me a new radio.

Patrick So, what are you doing at the moment, Richard?

Richard I'm keeping pretty busy. I'm writing a book about the Everest trip, and I'm preparing for my next expedition.

Patrick The next one? You mean, there's somewhere you haven't been?

Richard Oh, yes. I'm planning to walk across the polar ice-cap, via the North Pole.

Patrick You're going to walk?

Richard That's right. I'm still looking for sponsors at the moment. It's going to be pretty expensive.

Patrick It sounds like a very ambitious project to me.

Richard Yes, it is. The most difficult yet. You see, the temperature goes down to minus 75° centigrade, and at that sort of temperature metal freezes to the flesh. And of course I'll be walking across the sea ... on ice.

Patrick How are you preparing for that?

Richard I train every day. I run ten miles, and do weight training. I shall have to be very fit indeed.

Patrick What sort of problems are you anticipating?

Richard First there's navigation. Compasses don't work near the poles, so I'll be using satellite navigation throughout the trip.

Patrick Say you have equipment problems ... like the radio in the Sahara.

Richard I'll have a sextant to navigate by the stars, but it'll be plastic of course.

Patrick Ah, yes. You said metal freezes to the flesh.

Richard Yes.

Patrick How long will it take?

Richard At the beginning I'll be covering ten miles a day. I won't be able to keep that up all the way, but I'll have reached the Pole by mid-July. By then I'll have been walking for six weeks. Say three months for the whole journey.

Patrick One thing that interests me, you always have such wonderful photographs in your books. Will you be taking photos on this trip?

Richard I'll be filming myself during the entire trip.

Patrick But how will you manage that?

Richard I'll simply put the camera on a tripod.

Patrick And food. Will you be trying to shoot polar bears?

Richard I certainly hope not. An aircraft will be dropping supplies to me at regular intervals ... if the weather's good enough, that is.

Patrick Rather you than me, Richard. Can we look forward to a book about this trip?

Richard I hope so.

Patrick Any ideas about a title? *Miles of Snow* perhaps?

Richard Actually that's a possibility.

Patrick Thank you for talking to us, Richard. I hope you'll come back and tell us about the trip. And we'll be back after the break ...

Language study

	Past perfect	Past	Present perfect	Present	Future perfect	Future
Simple	I had done. I hadn't done. Had I done?	I did. I didn't do. Did I do?	I've done. I haven't done. Have I done?	I do. I don't do. Do I do?	I'll have done. I won't have done. Will I have done?	I'll do. I won't do. Will I do?
Continuous	I had been doing. I hadn't been doing. Had I been doing?	I was doing. I wasn't doing. Was I doing?	I've been doing. I haven't been doing. Have I been doing?	I'm doing. I'm not doing. Am I doing?	I'll have been doing. I won't have been doing. Will I have been doing?	I'll be doing. I won't be doing. Will I be doing?

Exercise 1

This is an extract from one of Mills' early books, *Miles of Jungle*. Put the verbs in brackets into their most appropriate form.

I _____ (explore) remote places for the last 20 years. This _____ (happen) when I _____ (travel) by canoe along the Amazon. I _____ (travel) for 12 days and I _____ (stop) at a small clearing for the night. I _____ just _____ (go) to sleep when something _____ (wake) me. I _____ (open) my eyes and there it _____ (be)! It _____ (be) a boa constrictor and it _____ (come) into the tent, well, about a quarter of it _____ (come) in, the rest was outside. I could _____ (see) it in the light of my camp fire. It _____ (be) the longest snake I _____ ever _____ (see) in my entire life. I _____ never _____ (be) so scared. It _____ (crawl) right through the tent and out of the other side. I _____ (jump) to my feet, and _____ (pick up) my gun, but when I _____ (run) outside, it _____ already _____ (go).

Exercise 2

Mills is planning to leave from Spitzbergen on April 15th. He hopes to reach the Pole by mid-July, and then continue to Point Barrow in Alaska. A plane will drop supplies on April 25th, May 5th, May 15th, May 25th, and June 4th. For each date, ask and answer:
How long will he have been walking by April 25th?
If he manages ten miles a day, how far will Mills have walked by April 25th?

Exercise 3

Make conversations from the prompts below.

film myself during trip/put camera on tripod

A *I'll be filming myself during the trip.*
B *How will you do that?*
A *I'll put the camera on a tripod.*

1 navigate by stars/use plastic sextant
2 check my position/use radio for satellite navigation
3 travel 10 miles a day throughout trip/walk
4 talk to my wife every Saturday/use radio link
5 eat very well during journey/plane drop supplies every 5 days

Describing a picture

Listen to people talking about each
picture. Then discuss them yourself.

What kind of picture?

a photograph	black and white colour
a painting	oil watercolour
original	reproduction
a print	limited edition
a drawing/a sketch	pencil ink crayon
an engraving an etching a poster	
an illustration	photographed painted drawn designed

What's the subject? What's it of?
What's it about?
What's the title? What's it called?
Who was the artist/photographer?
Who painted/drew it?

How do I feel about it?

I (like/love/loathe/hate/dislike/can't
stand) it.
It does (nothing/something to/for)
me.
It (appeals/doesn't appeal) to me.
I don't think much of it.
I think it's (great/a load of rubbish/
awful/marvellous).
It's not my (kind of thing/taste/style).
I prefer something more (modern/
traditional/realistic/abstract).

Unit 7

The Corn Harvest

Summer!
the painting is organized
about a young

reaper enjoying his
noonday rest
completely

relaxed
from his morning labors
sprawled

in fact sleeping
unbuttoned
on his back

the women
have brought him his lunch
perhaps

a spot of wine
they gather gossiping
under a tree

whose shade
carelessly
he does not share the

resting
center of
their workaday world

William Carlos Williams

Exercise 1
Match the poem with one of the
pictures.

Exercise 2
Write the poem out in prose.

The British royal family

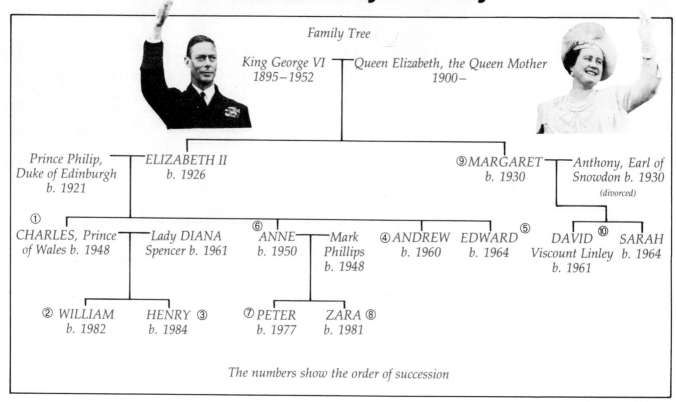

Family Tree

King George VI
1895–1952 ┬ Queen Elizabeth, the Queen Mother
1900–

Prince Philip, ┬ ELIZABETH II
Duke of Edinburgh   b. 1926
b. 1921

⑨ MARGARET ┬ Anthony, Earl of
b. 1930   Snowdon b. 1930
                (divorced)

①
CHARLES, Prince ┬ Lady DIANA
of Wales b. 1948   Spencer b. 1961

⑥
ANNE ┬ Mark
b. 1950 Phillips
         b. 1948

④ ANDREW   EDWARD ⑤
b. 1960   b. 1964

DAVID ⑩ SARAH
Viscount Linley b. 1964
b. 1961

② WILLIAM   HENRY ③
b. 1982   b. 1984

⑦ PETER   ZARA ⑧
b. 1977   b. 1981

The numbers show the order of succession

The Queen meets thousands of people every year. She has to shake hands with each of them, and she has to find something interesting to say. If you meet the Queen you should call her 'Your Majesty', then 'Ma'am'. The other Princes and Princesses are 'Your Highness', then 'Sir' or 'Madam'.

When she wants to end a conversation, she takes a half step backwards, smiling broadly, then moves on.

Here are some favourite royal conversation starters.

1 'How long have you been waiting?' (The Queen).
2 'What exactly are you doing?' (Prince Charles).
3 'How long have you been working here?' (Princess Anne).
4 'Keep you busy, do they?' (Prince Charles).
5 'What's your job?' (Prince Philip). At the reply: 'I'm a postman,' he will say: 'Oh, you're a postman, are you?'
6 'Where have you come from?' (The Queen).
7 'Pay you enough, do they?' (Prince Charles).
8 'Have you done this sort of thing before?' (Princess Anne).

The basic facts

The British monarchy is an enormously popular institution. This is largely due to the fact that it does not actually govern. Government is the task of ministers, who are responsible to the House of Commons, which is elected by the people. Although the Sovereign has very wide theoretical powers, they are seldom, if ever, used. The Queen is really a figurehead representing the country, but she has the power to prevent any politician establishing a dictatorship. The Queen and her family are a symbol that people can identify with. The British public is obsessed with the details of royal family life, and when people feel that the Queen has problems with her children, or her sister, they see her as a 'real person' with the same worries and anxieties as themselves.

The monarchy has not always been popular. During the late 19th century there was a growing republican sentiment, but the personality and family image of the Queen, her father and grandfather have removed that feeling. The Queen is probably the wealthiest woman in the world, most of the money coming from family investments rather than the state. Her state salary (the Civil List) pays for her servants and transport. In recent years the Queen has become a roving ambassador for Britain, and if we calculate the increase in trade after a royal visit abroad, the nation probably makes a profit from her activities, and that does not take into account the income from tourism in Britain generated by the monarchy and great state events such as royal weddings.

Just how popular is she? In the late 1970s a newspaper conducted an opinion poll. People were asked, 'If there were no monarchy, who would you vote for as President?' More than 80% chose the Queen. Prince Charles came second, closely followed by his father, Prince Philip. The prime minister of the day was fourth – with 2% of the votes.

Ten things the Queen could do by using the royal prerogative

1. Dismiss the Government
2. Declare war
3. Disband the Army
4. Sell all the ships in the Navy
5. Dismiss the Civil Service
6. Give territory away to a foreign power
7. Make everyone a peer
8. Declare a State of Emergency
9. Pardon all offenders
10. Create universities in every parish in the United Kingdom.

Eleven things the Queen takes on journeys

1. Her feather pillows.
2. Her hot water bottle.
3. Her favourite China tea.
4. Cases of Malvern water.
5. Barley sugar.
6. Cameras.
7. Her monogrammed electric kettle.
8. Her toilet soap.
9. A special white kid lavatory seat.
10. Jewellery associated with the countries she is visiting.
11. Mourning clothes and black-edged writing paper in case of bereavements.

The Queen's particular likes

Yellow Submarine: Favourite film

1. Horse racing ('Were it not for my Archbishop of Canterbury, I should be off in my plane to Longchamps every Sunday').
2. Scottish country dancing.
3. Jigsaw puzzles.
4. Long-stemmed, deep-pink carnations.
5. Champagne.
6. Deerstalking.
7. Quiet evenings at home watching television with her supper on a tray.
8. Crossword puzzles.
9. Bright red dresses.
10. The Beatles film, *Yellow Submarine*.
11. Sandringham.

Dislikes of the Queen

1. Ivy.
2. Snails ('How can you like those beastly things?'she asked Prince Philip).
3. Tennis, including Wimbledon.
4. Milk pudding.
5. The cold.
6. Grouse.
7. Any talk of Edward VIII.
8. Charles Dickens.
9. Dictating letters.
10. Laying foundation stones.
11. Cigar smoke.
13. Sailing.
14. Listening to after-dinner speeches.

Royal facts

Exercise 1
Work with another student, and list ten things you would take on a journey (not including clothes).

Exercise 2
Now work with another student, and make a list of each other's likes and dislikes.

Exercise 3
Find these things in the lists.
1 The name of a famous French horse-racing track.
2 The name of the Queen's country house in Norfolk.
3 The title of the head of the Church of England.
4 The name of the sport of hunting deer.
5 A green plant which grows on the outside walls of houses.
6 A bird which is shot, and eaten, mainly in Scotland.
7 The name of the Queen's uncle, who gave up the throne to marry a divorced American woman.
8 The name of a famous nineteenth-century British writer.
9 The name of the first stone in a new building.

Exercise 4
The Royal Family often has problems with the media. This is a typical story from *The Sun* (3rd January 1984).

Read it quickly.
Why was the Queen angry about the photo?

QUEEN IN PHOTOS FURY

SIXTEEN Pressmen were withdrawn from Sandringham yesterday after the Queen made a plea for privacy.

The plea, in a letter to Fleet Street editors, complained of "continual harassment".

It came as the Royals began their New Year riding and shooting holiday on the vast Norfolk estate.

In line with other national newspapers, The Sun withdrew its own reporter and photographer.

The message was drafted within days of:
● The Queen being incensed by photographs of a Royal shooting party, some showing Master Peter Phillips swinging a dead pheasant round and round by the neck:
● A security scare over a middle-aged "royal nut" grabbed by police outside the gates of Sandringham House:
● Rumours that bachelor Princes Andrew and Edward were expecting girlfriends to join them for the festive break.

A Buckingham Palace spokesman said: "The Queen and her family are angered by the feeling that nobody can move without being seen."

Expressing your feelings

Which of your feelings do you let other people know about? Which do you keep to yourself?

Sometimes it's a good thing to say what you feel. At other times it's better to keep quiet about your feelings. Sometimes it's hard to know exactly what it is you do feel. At other times feelings are so strong they seem to overwhelm you. How often do you express what you feel?

Controlling or letting feelings out

The stereotype of the English is that they are cold, reserved and unemotional. Compared with the extravagant French or the explosive Italians the English are an uptight lot. If they do feel anything they're not likely to let you know. It's a caricature but it has some truth in it.

We grow up in a culture which tells us that it's good to control our feelings. We learn that it's best to restrain our warmth, our tears, our anger. We learn that it's better to be rational. But is it? What happens to feelings you don't express? Many people argue that they don't just disappear. They continue to exist under the surface and affect the way you feel and behave.

Anger that you don't express to others can become anger that you turn against yourself. Fears that you don't talk about may make you timid in all things. You may put on a brave front but inside you're fearful and anxious. Hurts and disappointments that you've never cried over may make you protect yourself hard against any possible new hurt and become over-cautious about getting close to others.

How do you show your feelings?

The following quiz looks at some feelings that are common to us all and some of the different ways that people react to them.

Reactions can range from expressing the feeling spontaneously and directly to finding some way of denying that it exists at all.

For each section circle the answer that is most often typical of you.

1 Anger
When you feel angry, which of the following reactions would be most typical of you?
a Raising your voice or shouting at the person you're angry with
b Explaining quietly why you're angry
c Trying not to be angry (perhaps because you think it's wrong or unfair)
d Telling yourself you're not really angry or that you've not really got anything to be angry about

2 Feeling sad or upset
When you feel sad or upset, which of the following reactions would be most typical of you?
a Crying about it to someone else
b Talking to a friend about what's upset you
c Going away and crying on your own
d Telling yourself you don't really feel upset or sad or that you don't really have anything to feel upset or sad about

5 Feeling happy
When you are feeling happy, which of the following reactions would be most typical of you?
a Laughing and smiling, telling someone how you feel
b Analysing to yourself or others the reasons why you're happy
c Going around with an inner glow
d Telling yourself this can't last, it's not really true or it's not right to be happy when others aren't

6 Feeling disgust or dislike
When you feel disgust or dislike, which of the following reactions would be most typical of you?
a Screwing up your face, grimacing as you say what you feel
b Telling a friend how much you dislike or feel disgust about something or someone
c Controlling your disgust or dislike
d Pretending that nothing's happened, ignoring the things or people that make you feel this way

3 Feeling frightened or worried

When you feel frightened or worried, which of the following reactions would be most typical of you?

a Trembling, shaking or crying as you tell someone how you feel

b Talking to a friend about the things that are frightening or worrying you

c Going away on your own and crying about it or feeling bad

d Telling yourself you don't really feel frightened or worried or that you don't really have anything to feel frightened or worried about

7 Feeling warmth or affection for others

When you feel warmth or affection for others, which of the following reactions would be most typical of you?

a Touching, holding, embracing, kissing other people

b Talking to a friend about the way you feel

c Deciding not to express how you feel, perhaps because you're afraid you might get hurt

d Telling yourself it's sloppy and sentimental to feel like this about people and pushing the feelings away

4 Feeling embarrassed or ashamed

When you feel embarrassed or ashamed, which of the following reactions would be most typical of you?

a Laughing in embarrassment as you try to explain to someone why you feel embarrassed or ashamed

b Telling a friend later about how you felt embarrassed or why you felt so ashamed

c Swallowing hard and wishing the floor would open so that you could disappear from sight

d Pretending you're not in the least embarrassed or ashamed and putting an arrogant or cocky face on it

Do you ...

Express feelings directly?

The **a** statements show ways in which feelings can be expressed directly. You feel something and you show it.

Talk about them?

The **b** statements show ways in which feelings can be partially expressed by talking about them. Talking about your feelings can help you get clear about what you feel. You can get support. You may start to build up the confidence to express feelings more directly.

Keep them to yourself?

The **c** statements are about trying to control your feelings. Sometimes you may feel it's best to keep quiet about what you feel. You may not want to make yourself vulnerable before others. Or you may decide that expressing your feelings would be destructive to someone else. If you *always* keep your feelings to yourself, however, you may find that they start to come out in other ways.

Deny them?

The **d** statements are about ways of denying your feelings altogether. You may think they're not nice. Or you may be frightened of their strength. Again, these denied feelings may emerge in other ways.

Exercise

Look through the following list of feeling words and count how many you regularly use.

Pleasant	Unpleasant
amazed	afraid
amused	angry
astonished	anxious
calm	bored
confident	broken-hearted
contented	depressed
cool	disappointed
delighted	distressed
enjoyment	frightened
enthusiastic	frustrated
excited	furious
fascinated	guilty
friendly	hate
grateful	helpless
happy	hurt
hopeful	impatient
interested	jealous
loving	lonely
optimism	mean
peaceful	miserable
pleasant	sad
proud	sorry
quiet	surprised
satisfied	terrified
sensitive	tired
surprised	troubled
tender	uncomfortable
thankful	unhappy
touched	upset
warm	worried

How do I get to ...?

Listening

You are going to hear six people asking for directions. Listen to all the conversations, and match them with the plans. Listen again and find the starting points on the maps. Follow their routes.

Exercise

In pairs, ask each other for directions using the maps.

Amsterdam Schiphol Airport

Helpful information for transfer and arriving passengers

A smooth transfer

If you're continuing your journey by air from Amsterdam you should go to the nearest transfer desk after entering the airport. The desks are easy to find (just follow the yellow TRANSFER sign) and there's one in each of the four arrival piers.

After you've checked in for your connection you'll be given a boarding pass, which tells you the pier, departure gate and boarding time of your flight. (By this time your baggage will have been transferred automatically.)

All the arrival and departure gates are on the same level and you don't have to go through customs for a second time.

To find your new departure gate, just follow the signs showing pier letters and gate numbers. Getting there is no problem either – moving walkways take you there quickly and effortlessly.

The main facilities of the airport, which are located in the central lounge, are shown.

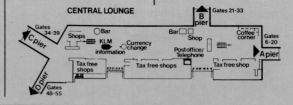

Trouble-free arrival

To get to the main airport building from your arrival pier follow the yellow EXIT signs. You'll pass through the passport check on your way to baggage claim and customs.

If you need to change any currency you'll find two bank offices in the baggage claim area.

After you've claimed your baggage and cleared customs you enter the public section of the Arrival hall. There you'll find some more helpful features of Schiphol such as: KLM's hotel reservation desk, Car Rental desks, Airport Authority Information desk, check-in for NLM-CityHopper's domestic flights, etc.

In front of the Arrival hall is everything you need to continue your journey. There's a taxi rank, a shuttle bus to the nearby airport hotels and regular KLM coach services to Amsterdam (Central Station) and Utrecht.

The railway station is also in front of the Arrival hall, and is best reached by an underpass from the hall itself. From there you can go direct to the Amsterdam RAI (Congress) Station, Leiden, The Hague, Rotterdam, Delft and Dordrecht. The trains run every 15 minutes to Amsterdam/RAI and Leiden and every 30 minutes to the other cities.

Good connections put practically the whole of the south of Holland, Belgium and Luxembourg within easy reach.

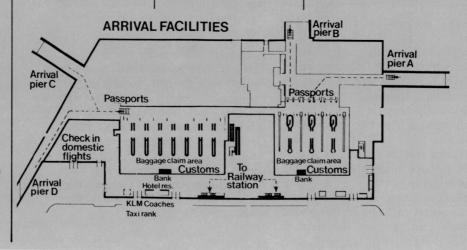

From 'Holland Herald', KLM In-Flight magazine

Unit 10

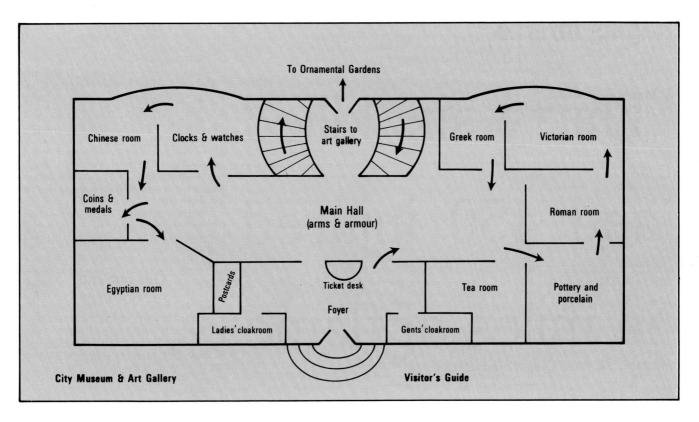

City Museum & Art Gallery

Visitor's Guide

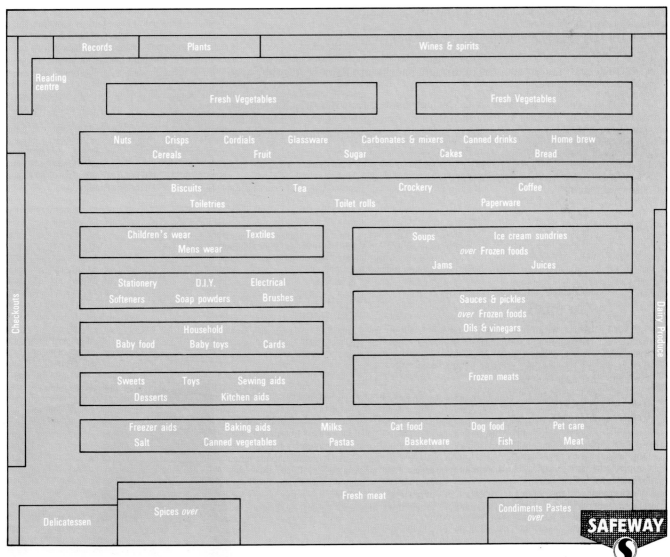

SAFEWAY

Raging inferno

Thirty-six killed and 450 injured in miles of flame

FROM
RICHARD SHEARS
IN MELBOURNE

AT LEAST 36 people, including a family of five in a car, were burned to death within hours yesterday as vast tracts of the southern part of Australia, parched by months of drought, burst into flames. Another 450 people were injured.

Uncontrollable bush fires fanned by high winds engulfed nearly 300 houses in the states of Victoria and South Australia. And such was the fear, that 50 people evacuated from threatened or dying towns waded into the sea to evade walls of flame.

Five small towns in Victoria were destroyed and ten others evacuated. Several towns in South Australia were also evacuated.

'This is a black, black day for Australia,' said Victoria's Police Minister, Mr Race Mathews, as, tears in his eyes, he followed the example of South Australia and declared a state of disaster.

Choking clouds of smoke

Last night, with hundreds being treated for burns and smoke inhalation at make-shift medical centres, more than 600 troops were being rushed to help 4,000 fire fighters already in action.

Both Melbourne in Victoria and Adelaide, 400 miles away in South Australia, were ringed by fires.

Small holiday towns along the coast west of Melbourne — Lorne, Torquay, Anglesea — were evacuated. A thousand people were driven away into the choking smoke from Lorne alone.

Communications were cut, telephone poles crashed in flames. 'It's as if the earth just wants to burn itself out and Mother Nature is doing her best to stop us inter-

fering,' said one tired fire fighter, watching a huge freak dust cloud blot out the late afternoon sun.

Smoke and dust clouds were so thick above Melbourne that airports were closed indefinitely.

Children crying on the phone

Other fires engulfed homes south and north-east of Adelaide. Burned-out cars were found abandoned on steep, wooded hills. Police fear the occupants fled into the scrub for safety only to meet a wall of fire. Three firemen died, trapped by the flames they were sent to fight.

At the German settlement of Handorf, 50 patients were evacuated from a nursing home which was destroyed by the rapidly moving fire. And at Greenhill, about nine miles from Adelaide, staff at the fire headquarters heard women and children screaming and crying over the phone as local newsmen and volunteer firefighter Murray Nichol telephoned for help. All the residents were safely evacuated but 16

homes were lost. One resident who lost his home, Peter Cox, smeared with black ash, told a firefighter: 'You just don't know when to leave.

'You see flames where you don't expect to see them. I went back for a television set, and when I came out flames were everywhere. I thought this is it, I've left it too late.'

Estimates put the damage caused by the fires blazing over several hundred square miles in the two states at around £50 million.

'Get out and get out fast'

Weary firemen said last night that they had feared the worst would happen. After months of little rain in South Australia and Victoria, temperatures in parts soared to 112 degrees Fahrenheit. The raging inferno followed.

Police in both states were investigating reports from firemen that some of the fires were started deliberately.

The first emergencies began in Adelaide yesterday as flames swept the Adelaide hills. Later police broadcasts warned people living in the hills not to try to get to their houses from work. Those already home were told: 'Get out—and get out fast!'

Some didn't make it. At Mount Gambier near South Australia's border with Victoria, a family of five were burned alive when their car was trapped.

Sergeant Paul Seeboham of Mount Gambier police said from the burning town last night: 'Things here are pretty bloody grim. Everything's burning.'

AUSTRALIA
SOUTH AUSTRALIA
ADELAIDE VICTORIA
MELBOURNE
FIRES RAGING HERE

Exercise 1
The newspaper report on the left is long and detailed. Write a short, one-paragraph report on the fire for a local newspaper in your country.

Exercise 2
Find as many examples as you can of past passive verbs in the newspaper story opposite.

Listening

Adelaide radio journalist Murray Nicoll provided the country with a graphic report when he described the destruction of his own home live on radio. Listen to the recording of his broadcast.

Exercise 3
1 How long had the journalist lived in his house?
2 What happened to the roof?

Exercise 4
These are pages from a journalist's notebook. Complete the notes.

Australian fire

Number killed : 36
Firefighters in action : 4,000
: 600
Numbers evacuated : 50
: 450
: Lorne, Torquay, Anglesea
: Family of five
: 3
: 50 Hahndorf
: 16 homes Greenhill

: £50 million
Name of journalist : Murray Nicoll
: Peter Cox
: Race Matthews
: Paul Seeboham
: 112°F
Possible title for article :

Language study

In the newspaper article there are a number of examples of verbs in the passive form of the past tense, for example, _were burned, were injured._ Read this extract from Thomson and Martinet, _A Practical English Grammar_ to remind yourself of the use of the passive.

Use
The passive voice is used in English when it is more convenient or interesting to stress the thing done than the doer of it, or when the doer is unknown:
My watch was stolen is much more usual than _Thieves stole my watch._
Note that in theory a sentence containing a direct and an indirect object, such as _Someone gave her a bulldog,_ could have two passive forms:
She was given a bulldog.
A bulldog was given to her.
The first of these is much more the usual, i.e. the indirect object becomes the subject of the passive verb.

Exercise 5
Find words which mean the following:
1 walked through water
2 continuous period of dry weather, causing distress
3 the powder that is left after something has been burned
4 hide from view
5 surrounded by
6 hot, dry and without water
7 removed from an area because of danger
8 injury caused by breathing smoke into the lungs (2 words)
9 covered or marked with streaks of something dirty
10 impossible to control

Exercise 6
Complete these sentences with expressions from the list below.
1 Although she _____ her hardest, she failed the exam.
2 I never look my _____ at night.
3 There was no news for several hours after the boat was lost in the storm, and we began to _____ the _____.
4 'All right,' said the manager, 'They've a better team, but just go out and _____ your best.'
5 'I'm an optimist. I always _____ for the best.'
6 He's a wonderful person. He always thinks the _____ of everyone he meets.

7 'Leave him alone, he's _____ his _____.' 'Yes, I know, but his best isn't good enough!'

to do your best
to fear the worst
to try your hardest
to look your best/worst
to feel your best/worst
to think the worst/best of ...
to hope for the best

Exercise 7
Try and tell the story of a natural disaster that you have heard about: a flood, earthquake, famine, volcano, tidal wave, hurricane, typhoon, or tornado.

Assess yourself

Look at the chart. Look at the first line. You have to assess yourself. If you think you're very generous, circle the number 3 on the left, quite generous circle 2, a little bit generous 1, neither generous nor mean, 0. If you think you're a little mean, circle 1 on the right, fairly mean 2, very mean 3. Only circle one number in each line.

How did you get on? Find out from your partner how he/she assessed themselves. Say how you assessed yourself. Discuss.

Generous	3	2	1	0	1	2	3	Mean
Hard-working	3	2	1	0	1	2	3	Lazy
Careful	3	2	1	0	1	2	3	Reckless
Considerate	3	2	1	0	1	2	3	Thoughtless
Optimistic	3	2	1	0	1	2	3	Pessimistic
Light-hearted	3	2	1	0	1	2	3	Serious
Quick-tempered	3	2	1	0	1	2	3	Calm
Relaxed	3	2	1	0	1	2	3	Nervous
Extroverted	3	2	1	0	1	2	3	Introverted
Helpful	3	2	1	0	1	2	3	Unhelpful
Polite	3	2	1	0	1	2	3	Impolite
Talkative	3	2	1	0	1	2	3	Taciturn
Strong-willed	3	2	1	0	1	2	3	Easily-led
Uncompromising	3	2	1	0	1	2	3	Flexible
Courageous	3	2	1	0	1	2	3	Timid
Honest	3	2	1	0	1	2	3	Dishonest

Exercise 1
Look at the list again. Which qualities do you think of as 'positive', and which as 'negative'? Why?

Exercise 2
Write down five things that you like about yourself, and five things that you don't like about yourself.

Exercise 3
Compare your list with other students'. Comment on their lists. You might use these expression to disagree.

Oh, I don't think you're ...
You don't seem ... to me.
I've never thought of you as ...
What makes you feel you're ...?
I wouldn't say you were ...

Exercise 4
Write down five things that you would like to learn. Write down five things you think you could teach somebody. Find out if you could teach something that another student might like to learn.

(Don't forget it might be as simple as how to mend a plug, or how to sew on a button, or as complicated as a foreign language, or motor vehicle maintenance.)

Choose a simple item from your 'teach' list. Try and explain it to another student. If possible, choose a student who has the same thing on their 'learn' list.

Games

Bingo is a very popular indoor gambling game in Britain. In many towns and cities several old cinemas have been converted into Bingo Halls. It's a simple game. You have a card with numbers on. The 'caller' takes ping-pong balls with numbers on from a machine, and calls the numbers out. The first person to be able to cross out all the numbers on his/her card is the winner, and shouts 'Bingo!' The caller tries to make a joke for many of the numbers, for example 'Legs-eleven'.

Exercise 5

What numbers do you think these calls represent? (Answers below.)
Two fat ladies
Prime Minister's Den
Key of the door
Unlucky for some
Sunset Strip
Doctor's orders.

Answers 88 10 21 13 77 99

Exercise 6

This is *People Bingo*. It's a competition. You have to ask other students the questions in the boxes, until you find someone who answers 'Yes'. Then you put a tick (√) in the box and move on to another question. The first person to tick all the boxes is the winner.

Exercise 7

In this game, one student goes to the front of the class, and shouts out a number between 1 and 17. The class have their books closed, except for one person, who reads out the appropriate question in the list below. The student in front must answer honestly, and is then replaced by whoever he/she has named.

1 Who is the happiest?
2 Who's the best at English?
3 Who's the tallest?
4 Who would you most like as brother or sister?
5 Who's the strongest-willed?
6 Who's the most impatient?
7 Who's the most discontented?
8 Who's the most kind-hearted?
9 Who sits nearest to you as a rule?
10 Who's the most talkative?
11 Who's the calmest?
12 Who's the hardest-working?
13 Who's the most serious-minded?
14 Who's the nicest?
15 Who's the most polite?
16 Who lives nearest to you?
17 Who's the most practically-minded?

Did you go out last Saturday evening?

Do you like sugar in your coffee?

Can you play any musical instruments?

When you dream, do you dream in colour?

Were you born in the first half of the year? (i.e. before July 1st)

Have you ever been abroad? (If you're studying abroad, don't count the country you're studying in.)

If there were a football match on television this evening, might you watch it?

Would you normally drink orange juice with your breakfast?

Are you able to speak three languages?

Will you still be studying English in six months' time?

Did you have a pet when you were a child?

Have you ever had a tooth extracted?

The language of advertising

Here are some methods used in persuasive advertising. Read them quickly. Decide which appeal to you and which don't.

Now think of an example for each type from your country.

Persuasive advertising

1 Repetition The simplest kind of advertising. A slogan is repeated so often that we begin to associate a brand name with a particular product or service.

2 Endorsement A popular personality is used in the advertisement.

3 Emotional appeal Advertising often appeals to basics such as mother-love, sex, manliness, femininity.

4 Scientific authority Sometimes the advert shows a person in a white coat (i.e. a scientist) telling us about the product. More often it mentions 'miracle ingredients' or 'scientific testing' to persuade us.

5 'Keeping up with the Jones's' An appeal to pure snob value. You want to appear to be richer or more successful than your neighbours.

6 Comparison The advert lists the qualities of a product in direct comparison with rival products.

7 An appeal to fear or anxiety This type is similar to 3, but works on our fears.

8 Association of ideas This is usually visual. Until it became illegal in Britain, cigarette advertising showed attractive, healthy people smoking in beautiful rural situations.

9 Information If a product is new, it may be enough to show it and explain what it does.

10 Special offers/free gifts This is a very simple and direct appeal – it's half price!

11 Anti-advertising This is a modern version which appeals to the British sense of humour. It makes fun of the techniques of advertising.

Exercise 1
Listen to the advertisements on the recording. Complete the chart with the types of persuasion you think they are using. Write one number in each box, or two numbers if you feel an advertisement is using two types of persuasion.

A	B	C	D	E	F	G	H	I	J

Exercise 2
Discuss in groups what these advertisements are selling. Who might they appeal to?

Exercise 3
Some advertisements use little stories and dialogues. Work in groups to prepare an advertisement like this. Act it out.

Reading

The Advertising Standards Authority controls advertising in Britain. Read this extract from their *Code of Practice*.

Appendix M
Advertising of cigarettes and hand-rolling tobacco

RULES

2.1 Advertisements should not exaggerate the attractions of smoking or otherwise seek to persuade people to start smoking.

2.2 Advertisements should not seek to encourage smokers to smoke more or to smoke to excess or show a cigarette left in the mouth.

2.3 Advertisements should not exploit those who are especially vulnerable, whether on account of their youth or immaturity or as a result of any physical, mental or social handicap.

2.4 Advertisements should not claim directly or indirectly that it is natural to smoke, or that it is abnormal not to smoke.

2.5 Advertisements should not claim directly or indirectly any health advantage of one brand over other brands except on evidence which has been accepted by the health authorities.

2.6 Advertisements should not claim directly or indirectly that smoking is a necessity for relaxation or for concentration.

2.7 Advertisements should not claim directly or indirectly that to smoke, or to smoke a particular brand, is a sign or proof of manliness, courage or daring.

2.8 Advertisements should not include or imply any personal testimonial for, or recommendation of the product by any well-known person of distinction in any walk of life, nor should they claim directly or indirectly the recommendation of a particular brand by any group or class of people engaged in an activity or calling which particularly attracts public admiration or emulation.

2.9 Advertisements should not include copy or illustrations which are sexually titillating or which imply a link between smoking and sexual success, nor should any advertisement contain any demonstration of affection in such a way as to suggest romantic or sexual involvement between those portrayed.

2.10 Advertisements should not claim directly or indirectly that it contributes significantly to the attainment of social or business success to smoke, or to smoke a particular brand.

2.11 No advertisement for cigarettes should appear in any publication directed wholly or mainly to young people.

2.12 Advertisements should not feature heroes of the young.

Exercise 4

The ASA is also concerned with the use of language in advertising. The use of the words 'free' and 'guaranteed', for example, are strictly controlled. The authority however admits that words like 'best' and 'finest' have become so devalued that they can be used in advertising. Imagine you are creating an advertisement. Which words would you choose for these sentences?

1 The lipstick is
  a cherry red
  b crimson
  c blood red.

2 The eye-shadow is
  a black diamond
  b coal black
  c sooty.

3 The cigar has a strong
  a aroma
  b smell
  c odour
  d stink.

4 This jacket is especially suitable for men who are
  a fat
  b stout
  c well-built.

5 The new alcoholic drink is
  a sharp-tasting
  b acid
  c dry.

Exercise 5
Look at these advertisements. Find abbreviations for the following: central locking/situated/cloakroom/ electric windows/decorative/entrance/ lounge/stainless steel/gas-fired/ double/electric aerial/registration/ central heating/power assisted steering/automatic/excellent.

Exercise 6
Now write a newspaper advertisement for:
1 a house
2 a car
3 a job

684391
MAX FACTOR & CO, incorporating Gala Cosmetics and Fragrances Ltd. Secretaries are required to work jointly for two Product Group Managers and four Assistant Managers. Accurate shorthand and typing essential, should also be numerate. We also have a vacancy for a Secretary to the Export Area Manager. Hours of work 9 a.m. - 5.25 p.m., Monday-Thursday, 9 a.m. - 12.55 p.m. Friday. — Applicants should telephone Zena Hoar, Senior Personnel Officer: Bournemouth 524141 Ext. 115, for an application form.

JAGUAR XJ6 4.2 auto, PAS, e/win, c/lock, Brg/beige leather interior, e/aerial, new battery, new s/s exhaust, 55,000 miles only, R Reg, immaculate throughout £2,700. — Tel. Bournemouth 295725 (9-6 pm). C17/19

SPACIOUS FAMILY HOUSE BEARWOOD

Sit. on this popular estate close schools, local shops and bus routes to Bournemouth and Poole. GF c/h, cavity wall insulation. Exc dec order. Ent porch, hall, clkrm. Attractive lng 23ft 6in × 18ft overall, dng rm, well fitted kit, 4 dble beds, bath. Garage. Garden. Now reduced to £43,000 for quick sale. Ref. 11472.

Subscribe!

Exercise 1
Jane Grant received the following letters. Perhaps wisely, she decided not to reply to any of them. Compose the shortest and simplest reply to each one.

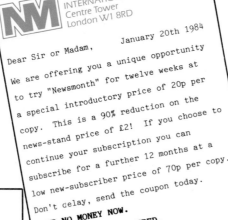

NM "NEWSMONTH"
INTERNATIONAL
Centre Tower
London W1 8RD

Dear Sir or Madam,   January 20th 1984

We are offering you a unique opportunity to try "Newsmonth" for twelve weeks at a special introductory price of 20p per copy. This is a 90% reduction on the news-stand price of £2! If you choose to continue your subscription you can subscribe for a further 12 months at a low new-subscriber price of 70p per copy. Don't delay, send the coupon today.

SEND NO MONEY NOW.

NO POSTAGE STAMP NEEDED.

Name (Mr/Mrs/Miss) ....
(Delete as applicable)
Address .... postcode ....

Signature ....
(I am over 18)

NM "NEWSMONTH"
INTERNATIONAL
Centre Tower
London W1 8RD

Ms. J. Grant   February 1st 1984
28 Highland Rd
Tadworth TW4 7JQ

Dear Madam,

We note that you have not yet taken up our offer for "Newsmonth" magazine. Printed below is a lucky number. If you subscribe before February 28th, your name will go into our lucky draw. First prize is a BM Calypso 4-door saloon. Imagine, Ms Grant, driving down Highland Road in your new Calypso. Subscribe today and it could be yours.
Yours faithfully

D. Tyler

D. Tyler
Subscription Manager

YOUR LUCKY NUMBER IS 0732294158607

NM "NEWSMONTH"
INTERNATIONAL
Centre Tower
London W1 8RD

Ms. J. Grant   February 12th 1984
28 Highland Rd
Tadworth TW4 7JQ

Dear Ms Grant,

We wonder if you would be kind enough to assist us. We are conducting Market Research on our campaign for "Newsmonth" We see that you have not replied to our previous communications. We are trying to find out why. Do you simply throw away all publicity material? Did you read it? Do you know how good "Newsmonth" is? If you will reply, we will send you a **FREE** sample copy. We enclose an SAE.
Yours sincerely

Dennis Tyler

Dennis Tyler
Subscription Manager

NM "NEWSMONTH"
INTERNATIONAL
Centre Tower
London W1 8RD

February 19th 1984

Dear Miss Grant,

I am so sorry to trouble you again. We really are unable to understand why you haven't replied. We have been waiting all week to hear from you. We are convinced that "Newsmonth" is right for you.
We have decided to offer you 8 weeks, free subscription without obligation. All you have to do is reply. Please do.
Yours sincerely

Dennis Tyler

Dennis Tyler
Subsription Manager

Miss J. Grant
28 Highland Rd
Tadworth TW4 7JQ

NM "NEWSMONTH"
INTERNATIONAL

Jane Grant
28 Highland Rd
Tadworth TW4 7JQ

Postage
will be
paid by
Licensee

Do not affix Postage stamps if posted in
Gt. Britain, Channel Islands, N. Ireland
or Isle of Man.

BUSINESS REPLY SERVICE
Licence No. WD 2823

NEWSMONTH
Centre Tower
London W1 8RD

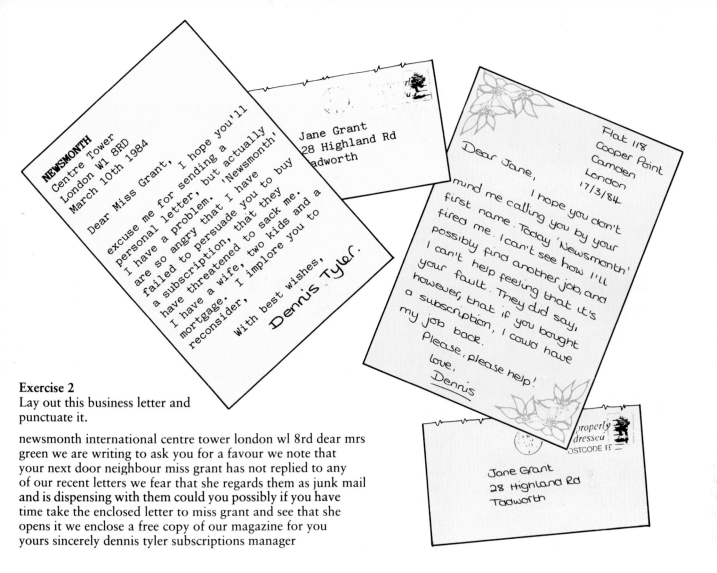

NEWSMONTH
Centre Tower
London W1 8RD
March 10th 1984

Dear Miss Grant, I hope you'll
excuse me for sending a
personal letter, but actually I
have a problem. 'Newsmonth'
are so angry that I have
failed to persuade you to buy
a subscription, that they
have threatened to sack me.
I have a wife, two kids and a
mortgage. I implore you to
reconsider,
With best wishes,
Dennis Tyler.

Jane Grant
28 Highland Rd
Tadworth

Flat 118
Cooper Point
Camden
London
17/3/84

Dear Jane,
I hope you don't
mind me calling you by your
first name. Today 'Newsmonth'
fired me. I can't see how I'll
possibly find another job, and
I can't help feeling that it's
your fault. They did say,
however, that if you bought
a subscription, I could have
my job back.
Please, please help!
love,
Dennis

Jane Grant
28 Highland Rd
Tadworth

Exercise 2

Lay out this business letter and punctuate it.

newsmonth international centre tower london wl 8rd dear mrs green we are writing to ask you for a favour we note that your next door neighbour miss grant has not replied to any of our recent letters we fear that she regards them as junk mail and is dispensing with them could you possibly if you have time take the enclosed letter to miss grant and see that she opens it we enclose a free copy of our magazine for you yours sincerely dennis tyler subscriptions manager

Language study

Formal and business letters

Addressed to:	Beginning	Ending
The Personnel Manager, Forest Insurance Co.,	Dear Sir, Dear Madam, Dear Sir or Madam,	Yours, Yours faithfully, (GB) Yours truly, (US)
The Sales Manager, Southern Computers Ltd,		
The Managing Director, Hampton plc		
Natwest Bank PLC	Dear Sirs, (GB) Gentlemen. (US) Dear Sir or Madam,	
Wessex Transport		
Messrs Smith and Jones*		
Mr M. Smith/Michael Smith M. Smith, Esq., (GB formal)	Dear Mr Smith,	Yours sincerely, Yours,
Mrs Smith/Miss Smith/ Ms Smith/Jane Smith	Dear Mrs Smith, Dear Miss Smith, Dear Ms Smith,	

* 'Messrs' is an old-fashioned term. It is used when the names of two or more people make up the name of the firm.

It is not used for limited companies (Ltd) or public limited companies (plc).

Abbreviations

Here are some common abbreviations. Do you know what they mean?

A/C	inc.	ref.
advt.	info.	RSVP
approx.	jnr.	snr.
a.s.a.p.	km.	st.
Bros.	lb.	tel.
cf.	Ltd.	UK
Co.	max.	VIP
c/o	min.	vs.
COD	misc.	w.p.m.
cont.	NB	Xmas
dept.	OHMS	yr.
enc.	para.	
etc.	PLC	
fwd.	pp.	
govt.	p.p.	
HQ	p.w.	
hr.	recd.	

Britain from the air

Listening

Look at the picture of Salisbury. Listen to the description of the town. Listen again and look at the notes below. Use the notes to write a short paragraph for a guide book on Salisbury.

new town – 1st
1220, replace O.Sarum – 3m. N.
O.S. – Roman, Saxon
Important C12 & C13, but water problem
So – moved. Rivers join, R. Avon
Cath 1220 – 1258 most beaut. ⍺ Evr?
Spire 404 ft. tallest G.B. 1334
Cath 473 ft.
Market town. agric. area + milit.
    bases. N. of city.
tourism – Cath, old town + STONEHENGE,
    10m, NNW
Cent. S. Eng, 30m. coast,
    83m. W. of Lond.
Ring road (E of cent.)

Note-taking

Think about making notes in English. How would you write abbreviations for these words? Match them with the abbreviations in the box below.

south east	therefore
population	bigger than
miles	to, towards, led to
feet	and, as well as
near	increased to
approximately	decreased to
19th century	born in
around (1471)	died in

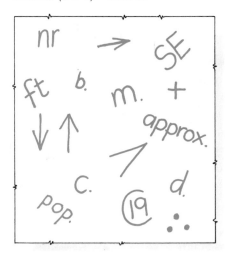

Remember, how you take notes is up to you. Do as you would in your own language – use your own abbreviations, use your own language's abbreviations if it helps.

Exercise 1

Look at the town in the upper right-hand picture on the page opposite. Listen to the description. Make notes. Listen again, correct your notes.

Exercise 2

Say as much as you can about the town in the lower picture on the page opposite. Mark four things with a cross (X) that you would like to hear more about. What do you think they are?
Now listen to the description and make notes.

Exercise 3

Look at the town in the upper left-hand picture on the page opposite. What can you say about it? Describe it. What would you like to see if you went there? Where would you like to walk?
Now listen to the description and make notes.

Writing

You are a journalist. Describe each town in one paragraph for a magazine.
Write a similar description of your own town.
Write a final paragraph comparing your town with the three on the right-hand page.

△ Liverpool

△ Caernarfon

△ Durham

The Town That's Going To Die?

The National Coal Board today announced the forthcoming closure of the Llanbevan Mine in Tredowy, South Wales.

The mine, which will close next year, employs nearly 2000 men. Although there is plenty of coal left underground, the mine is unsuitable for modern equipment, and is uneconomic. Losses last year totalled £5,420,000. At present, a government enquiry is taking place into plans to build a massive nuclear reactor two miles north of the town. It is hoped that the construction of the reactor will create jobs in an area already hard-hit by closures in the steel industry, and

TREDOWY Gwent Map 12F
Pop: 13,100 Abergavenny 15, London 161, Brecon 13
Merthyr Tydfil 10, Tredegar 6, Newport 27
EC Wed. MD Mon. See Wesley Gardens, Green Rock.
  Duke of Monmouth. 16 bedrs, 3 priv. bat. CH.
BB £14. DB £23. Tel: 2730.
  Jones' Autos, Prince St. Tel: 2618

Listening

Listen to the recording and find the site of the nuclear reactor on the map.

Exercise 1
In pairs, use the map and give directions:
a to the mine.
b from Caerdowy to Hill Farm.
c from Glenclower Farm to Caer Farm.

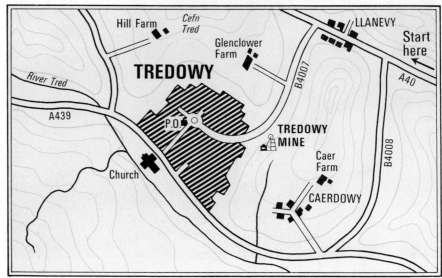

Language study

The nuclear power station will open (in 8 years).
It will employ 60 men.

Both of these sentences are about future time. When we put them together, the new sentence is:

When the power station opens, it will employ 60 men.

When introduces a time clause.
There are four tenses we can use in time clauses:

Simple present (*it employs*)
Present continuous (*it is employing*)
Present perfect (*it has employed*)
Present perfect continuous (*it has been employing*)

A We will be building it for 5 years. We will need 400 men.
We will need 400 men *while* we are building it.

B We won't begin. We will have had a full enquiry.
We won't begin *until/till* we've had a full enquiry.

C It will create jobs. It will have been operating for a few months.
It will create new jobs *when* it has been operating for a few months.

D The coal mine will close. People will leave Tredowy.
People will leave Tredowy *as soon as/immediately/once* the coal mine closes/has closed.

Exercise 2
Combine these sentences with the words in brackets.
1 People will leave the area. Property values will fall. (*once*)
2 The reactor will begin operating. It won't need many workers. (*when*)
3 They will be building the reactor. The area will be very busy. (*while*)
4 They will have finished the reactor. They will need specialist workers. (*when*)
5 They will be training workers. They will be building the reactor. (*while*)
6 We won't know how many they will need. They will have finished the plans. (*until*)
7 The nuclear waste will be dangerous. Our grandchildren will be old. (*until*)
8 We'll be worried about accidents. The reactor will open. (*as soon as*)
9 We'll have a protest meeting. The enquiry will begin. (*immediately*)
10 The coal mine will have closed. 2000 men will be unemployed. (*after*)
11 The reactor will have opened. 60 men will be employed. (*once*)
12 Many will have left Tredowy. The reactor will open. (*before*)

Exercise 3
How do you think these people might complete these sentences. Look at the examples to help you.
1 (man, 65) I'll stay in Tredowy until ...
2 (woman, 3 children) I'll move somewhere safer before ...
3 (miner, 36) I'll look for a job in Cardiff when ...
4 (farmer) I hope I'll be able to sell my land once ...
5 (man, 19) I'll work for the construction company while ...
6 (girl, 20) I'll leave town after ...
7 (pub owner) I'll sell very little beer as soon as ...
8 (estate agent) Nobody will be able to sell houses when ...
9 (woman, 40) This town will die once ...
10 (woman, 25) There'll be protests immediately ...

Exercise 4
Read through the exercises to get more information about the closure. Read through the information about four people from Tredowy.
In groups of three, four or five conduct an enquiry. One person is the government representative; the others live in Tredowy.

MINER (MINER'S WIFE)
- AGE 48
- 34 YEARS IN MINE
- LITTLE CHANCE OF WORK ON CONSTRUCTION
- I CHILD AT COLLEGE LOCALLY. OTHER MARRIED – SAFE LOCAL JOB. I GRANDCHILD
- FEELS MINE COULD SUPPLY AS MUCH ENERGY AS REACTOR – MORE SAFELY
- TRADE UNION MEMBER
- FEELS MINE CLOSURE WILL CREATE UNEMPLOYMENT IN ALL LOCAL INDUSTRIES

FARMER
- AGE 50
- HIS/HER FARM MIGHT BE BOUGHT FOR SITE – OR NOT
- MIGHT SELL PART OF LAND FOR ROAD
- IF NOT, SHEEP WILL BE FRIGHTENED BY NOISE OF CONSTRUCTION
- WILL FIND IT DIFFICULT TO SELL PRODUCE
- FAMILY HAS OWNED FARM FOR 200 YEARS

YOUNG UNEMPLOYED PERSON
- AGE 19
- DIDN'T WANT MINE WORK ANYWAY
- SCARED AT IDEA OF 2000 MORE UNEMPLOYED
- WILLING TO RETRAIN FOR REACTOR WORK
- NOT AFRAID OF NUCLEAR ENERGY
- EXCITED BY IDEA OF NEW TECHNOLOGY
- OLDER BROTHER KILLED IN MINE ACCIDENT – AS 37 OTHERS WERE. CAN REACTOR BE **MORE** DANGEROUS THAN THAT?

PARENT WITH 3 SMALL CHILDREN
- AGE 34
- BELIEVES NUCLEAR POWER IS DANGEROUS – NOW & FOREVER
- CHILDREN'S SCHOOL ONLY 2 MILES FROM REACTOR
- WASTE WILL TRAVEL THROUGH THE VILLAGE
- WORRIED ABOUT WATER SUPPLY
- DOES NOT WANT TO MOVE – AND IS NOT EMPLOYED IN THE MINE

Collector's corner

What *is* a collector? After all, people collect a wide variety of things, from the obvious ones like stamps, coins or autographs, to the less common ones, such as beer bottle labels, bus tickets or gramophone-needle tins. The economies of several small countries rely heavily on the sale of colourful stamps. Some collectors spend hours looking through junk shops and build up a collection for a few pence per item, while collectors of antiques, fine china or paintings might spend thousands of pounds on a new acquisition. Some people collect as an investment, but most do it for fun. Collecting is basically illogical. If you simply want to listen to Elvis Presley's first record, you can get a copy at most record shops. A collector, however, will want to own an original 1955 disc, complete with its original sleeve and label, and will be willing to pay for it.

What makes an item valuable? Rarity and condition are the most important factors. A coin or stamp which is worth hundreds in mint condition might be worth only pence in average or poor condition.

What should you collect? Most collectors begin acquiring things which interest them, and as the collection grows, knowledge of the subject grows. If you want your collection to grow in value, it is probably best to avoid things which are sold especially for collectors. Nearly everybody who buys a set of new coins or stamps will preserve them in perfect condition, so that a mint set will never become rare. The most valuable items are often things which were widely available, but which were usually thrown away after use, such as Coca-Cola bottles or toy cars. An interesting collection can be started very cheaply.

One collector has started a collection of 1950s and 1960s ball-point pens ('biros'). At the moment it's worth nothing, but she predicts it will one day be valuable. Ball-points were widely available, and were made in a large range of colours and styles. They were often designed to be thrown away when they were empty. Many people are reluctant to throw away used pens, and put them in a drawer or box, perhaps hoping they might work again one day. So it is possible to find unusual examples, made thirty years ago or more, for nothing. As she says, it's no crazier than collecting barbed wire of the American West, and there's a club with its own magazine for barbed-wire collectors.

Listening

Read the questions below. Listen to the recording, and then answer the questions.

How many bottles has Adrian got?
How long has he been collecting bottles?
What was he doing when he found the first one?
Who did he show it to?
What was he offered for it?
How much is it worth now?
Where does he look for bottles?
How much has he spent on his collection?

Exercise 1
It's a shop. You can buy bottles there.
It's a shop *where* you can buy bottles.

Now join these sentences in the same way.
1 My mum told me about a shop. She'd seen bottles in the window.
2 You should look under bridges. People throw bottles away there.
3 You should look in rubbish dumps. People used to bury their rubbish there.
4 Old people can remember the places. People used to throw old bottles away.
5 I never buy them from specialist shops. Some collectors buy bottles there.

Exercise 2
Have you collected any of the things in the pictures? Why might people want to collect them? Have you collected anything else?

Language study

She has been collecting | *for* a year/twelve months.
| *since* this time last year/January 1984.

She will be collecting | *for* another three years.
| *until* January 1988.

She will have completed the set *by* January 1988.

She won't have completed the set *until* January 1988.

In January 1988, she will have been collecting *for* four years.

Exercise 3
Answer the following questions:
1 How many models will she have collected by January 1986?
2 What about January 1987?
3 How long will she have been collecting in January 1986?
4 What about January 1987?

Exercise 4
Complete these sentences with *for, since, by, until*.
1 Call me back at six. I'll have finished the report ... then.
2 At Christmas, we'll have been living here ... exactly ten years.
3 Sorry. I can't meet you at 5.30. I'll be busy ... six.
4 I won't know the answer ... the post arrives.
   I've had this car ... 1984.
6 I'm exhausted. It's nearly 8, and by 8 I'll have been working ... 12 hours without a break.
7 I won't have completed it ... this time next week.
8 I hope to have the answer ... Saturday next.

Exercise 5
collect   *collection*
acquire   *acquisition*

reserve   *reservation*
alter   *alteration*

Now make nouns from these verbs:

connect
inform
predict
expand
cancel
admit
oppose
qualify
subscribe
combine
persuade
pronounce

Life in zero g

Some facts

- Objects you throw go in an exactly straight line until they hit something.
- Water floating in mid-air forms itself into a perfect sphere.
- Heavy objects can be lifted or moved with one finger.
- Small objects are dangerous — they float all over the place.
- There is no 'up' nor 'down'.
- Astronauts sleep in zip-up bags hung from the walls. One astronaut slept 'upside down' because of a draught.
- Salt and pepper have to be mixed with water and squirted on to food.
- Food is easier to eat on vertical plates than horizontal ones. You have to eat everything. Left-overs are too difficult to clear up.
- Washing your hands is difficult— if not impossible.
- Astronauts use special electric razors which suck in the whiskers. (Otherwise the cabin would be full of whisker dust.)
- Magnetic soap holders, and velcro pads are needed to keep everything in place.
- There were 20,000 items stored on Skylab — and they all had a labelled place. This was a problem — how do you read if you are upside down or sideways.

Think of some of the problems of living in a confined space in zero g. Make a list and compare it with another student's.

Food

On Skylab and the Space Shuttle, astronauts had nearly normal food. (Although food in tubes was the rule for earlier missions.) Each astronaut had to make a 6-day menu of three meals a day for himself — then eat his choice for two or three months. No departure from the cycle was permitted.

Make up a menu for yourself. Would you like to stick to it strictly for 3 or 4 months? Why/Why not?

The human body in space

The Space-Shuttle is designed to sustain 7 people in orbit for 30 days. The earlier Skylab space-station was inhabited for 171 days. What happens to the human body in that time?

- Space sickness. About 50% of astronauts experience this for a few days. It feels like travel sickness.
- Blood moves out of the legs towards the head. It feels like hanging upside down. After a few days astronauts lose fluid — the equivalent of a wine-bottle-full from each leg. Astronauts find it difficult to walk for a few days after returning to Earth. This might get worse with longer stays in space.
- The blood cells change in shape. They grow spikes and protrusions. There is no evidence that this is harmful — yet.
- Calcium is lost from the bones and after 8–12 months they might become very fragile.
- Spaceships have windows which seriously weaken their structure. Outside TV cameras would do the same job, but Skylab proved that astronauts had a psychological need for a window. Some spent 10 or 12 hours a day gazing at Earth.

In the future astronauts may be expected to spend great lengths of time in zero g. Their bodies may change permanently. Ed Gibson, an astronaut, said, 'The body does a great job of adjusting to zero gravity. It does just what it should to adjust to the new environment. What we worry about is what happens when you come back.'

Language study

Look at this

The exercise	lacks is without is devoid of	a	point.	We	've run out of 're (right) out of could do with some need some can't do without	flour.
	has no					
	is pointless				're short of	

If I were abroad, I'd miss English breakfasts.
When I'm abroad, I miss English television.

Exercise 1
Don Cooper was an astronaut. Complete the spaces below:

'In space I suppose my biggest fear was of being unable to return to Earth. The spacecraft had plenty of food and water, and if it had got stuck out there I think the _____ of human company would have been worst. Then the food would begin to _____ _____ . If you're _____ of food, you can live for some time, but you can't do _____ water, and you can't _____ _____ air. I used to think about it, imagine you survived the shortage of food, and imagine you were rescued after several months. After all that time in a spacecraft totally _____ of gravity, would you be able to survive on Earth?'

Exercise 2
If you were going to live in a totally different country, which things from your culture could you do without? Which things couldn't you do without? Which things would you notice the lack of? Which things would you miss?

Sequences

Talking about sequences

There are natural sequences, like the inevitability of infancy followed by childhood, adolescence, maturity and old age. Can you think of any other natural sequences? Try to make a list.

In language we can express sequences both by our choice of tenses, and by our choice of sequence words and phrases.
Look at the chart on the right.

Exercise 1
Brian decided to buy a new car. He first studied the car magazines, then took a test drive.

Which of these cars do you think he chose, and why?

Quick tests

BM Calypso/5 dr/1250cc. Our initial impression was average. It looked like so many small hatchbacks. After having driven it for a week though, we began to appreciate its performance and comfort. In addition, the digital instruments and 'speaking voice' computer impressed us. **To sum up**: A good all-round small car. Unexciting, but well-built. £5,335.

Euro Carnival, 5 dr/1149cc. We immediately liked the futuristic styling, and, having taken it at high speed to Scotland, we also gave good marks for speed and handling. Some drivers found it rather small. **To sum up**: An unusual car, overall less impressive than it looked. £4,930.

Cord Festivity/3 dr/998cc. Our first thought was that Cord should have made a 5-door version. Furthermore, they should have made a bigger engine available. It was ideal in town, but a nuisance on long journeys. **To sum up**: A good 'shopping' car; easy to park. Not for long distances. £4,875.

* *secondly, thirdly* are used, and occasionally *fourthly* and *fifthly*, but it would be very unusual to add *-ly* after five in a sequence. You use *sixth, seventh,* and so on.

General words Informal style	Formal style	Making a speech, arguing a point in a text
first	initially	first of all to begin with let us begin by
second/secondly* next then	subsequently	in addition also following (on from)
before	formerly/previously	
after/afterwards		furthermore
last lastly finally	ultimately	last of all last but not least to sum up in conclusion

Car wash

Brian was extremely proud of his car. It was his first new car after years of second-hand disasters, and he had saved long and hard to get it. He remembered the day three months previously when he had walked into the showroom to order it. The salesman had been helpful and friendly and Brian had enjoyed every detail of the transaction. Having had a test drive he had sat for over an hour, poring over the list of options. Yes, he would have metallic paint; no, he wouldn't bother with an electric aerial or electric windows, certainly not at a cost of £350. Yes, he would have the de luxe sheepskin seat covers and so on. When it was eventually delivered gleaming to his door, he had been almost afraid to drive it. That was three weeks ago, and the gleam had gradually become dulled by dust. (It was the hottest summer in living memory.) It was time for its first wash.

Brian drove carefully to the automatic car wash at a nearby service station. He was sure that passers-by must be admiring his beautiful machine. He drove in, got his token and joined the queue. At last it was his turn, and he pushed the token into the slot, and carefully positioned the car in the centre of the car wash. He felt a bit apprehensive when he looked at the huge green brushes, but he wound down his window again and firmly stabbed the start button. There was a loud whirring noise as the brushes descended and the spray began. Brian tapped his fingers in time with the song on his stereo FM radio. The radio ... it was working ... that meant the aerial was up. Brian turned to look ... too late, there was nothing he could do. Wait ... better close the window quickly. Brian grabbed at the winding handle in panic. There was a slight cracking noise and Brian found himself staring down at the handle. It had broken off in his hand – with the window open. He felt the first, fine spray on his face, and he had time for one last, longing look at his sheepskin seat covers before the deluge of detergent and water hit him.

Exercise 2

Look at these instructions for using an automatic car wash. Put them in the correct sequence by numbering them 1–8.

Write a paragraph (using link words) explaining how to use the car wash.

- Press button to start machine.
- Place token in box.
- Move slowly forward.
- Stop and apply handbrake when start button is at shoulder level.
- Close window securely.
- Stop when token box is at shoulder level.
- Obtain token from cashier (£1).
- Remove sun visors/roof racks. Check for loose chrome trims. Retract aerial fully into body.

Language study

a When I *got* to the airport, my flight *had gone.* (i.e. I missed it.)

b When the Queen *arrived*, the flight *left.* (i.e. it waited for her.)

c My flight $\begin{vmatrix} left \\ had\ left \end{vmatrix}$ before I arrived.

d I arrived after my flight $\begin{vmatrix} left. \\ had\ left. \end{vmatrix}$

Note: In c and d, the sequence words make the meaning clear, so we often would not bother to use the past perfect.

DIPLOMATIC APPOINTMENTS

Mr Mark Richards has been appointed Ambassador to Rome. Mr Richards, who was formerly the head of British Motors, will take up his appointment in the autumn. Mr Richards has had a long and distinguished career in industry, beginning with his success as legal adviser to the British Gas Corporation. He subsequently became Managing Director of North Oil, and later held a similar post with European Telecommunications before joining BM. It came as a surprise to many of his colleagues when he accepted the diplomatic post in Rome, but following his success in so many fields, observers feel that he will ultimately move into the top diplomatic post at the Washington Embassy.

The present Ambassador to Rome, Sir James Campbell, who was appointed by the previous government, will be retiring after his 63rd birthday in September.

Exercise 3

Mark Richards has had four important jobs. His next job is mentioned, as well as one that he might get one day. Put the six jobs in sequence and number them.

Exercise 4

Underline all the sequence words in the text.

Exercise 5

A friend of yours wants to know something about the new ambassador. Read the newspaper article again and use it to write an informal letter.

Exercise 6

Which number should come next in these mathematical sequences? Explain carefully *why* you think it comes next.

a 1 4 7 10 13 –
b 20 22 26 28 32 –
c 3 9 27 81 –
d 3 5 7 11 13 17 –
e 25 5 16 4 9 –

Exercise 7

Read the following passage, and put the verbs in brackets into the most appropriate tense.

The Burglar Alarm
There ... (be) several burglaries in my neighbourhood, and although my house ... (be) pretty small, and I haven't got anything to steal, I ... (not want) all the fuss and mess of a burglary. So I ... (decide) to buy a burglar alarm. They ... (come) in all shapes and sizes, from the simplest, a simple, empty red metal box ... (label) 'burglar alarm', to elaborate systems which ... (have) infra-red and body heat sensors and a direct connection to the police station. I ... always ... (believe) in buying the best, and once it ... (be) installed I ... (relax). A few weeks later, while I ... (be) at work, I ... (have) my first burglary.

The police ... (wait) for me when I ... (get) home from work. Fortunately the burglars ... (take) only one thing, my burglar alarm system. As the police ... (say) it ... (be) the most valuable thing in the house.

Urban legends

Have you heard any of these stories before?

The hook

(Told by a student from Albuquerque, 1960)

A boy and girl were sitting in a parked car late one evening listening to the radio.

... over the radio came an announcement that a crazed killer with a hook in place of a hand had escaped from the local insane asylum. The girl got scared and begged the boy to take her home. He got mad and stepped on the gas and roared off. When they got to her house, he got out and went around to the other side of the car to let her out. There on the door handle was a bloody hook.

The vanishing hitch-hiker

(Told by a teenager in Toronto, Canada, 1973)

Well, this happened to one of my girlfriend's best friends and her father. They were driving along a country road on their way home from the cottage when they saw a young girl hitch-hiking. She told the girl and her father that she just lived in the house about five miles up the road. She didn't say anything after that but just turned to watch out the window. When the father saw the house, he drove up to it and turned around to tell the girl they had arrived – but she wasn't there! Both he and his daughter were really mystified and decided to knock on the door and tell the people what had happened. They told them that they had once had a daughter who answered the description of the girl they supposedly had picked up, but she had disappeared some years ago and had last been seen hitch-hiking on this very road. Today would have been her birthday.

The mouse in the bottle

Two old ladies stopped at a restaurant to have lunch. They ordered their lunch, and asked for two bottles of a well-known soft drink while they were waiting. The bottles were made of green glass, and they each poured themselves a glass. They were chatting away and drinking and one of them finished the first glass and poured another. She noticed something in the bottom of the bottle, but couldn't make out what it was. She tried to get it out and finally succeeded. It was a decomposed mouse. They both fainted and had to be revived. Anyway they sued the soft drink company and got thousands of dollars.

Exercise 1
How much truth do you think there is in the stories?
Have you heard any similar stories?
How true do you think they are?

This is what Jan Harold Brunvald says in the introduction to his collection of urban legends:

'In common with age-old folk legends about lost mines, buried treasure, omens, ghosts and Robin Hood-like outlaw heroes, urban legends are told seriously, circulate largely by word of mouth, are generally anonymous, and vary constantly in particular detail from one telling to another, while always preserving a central core of traditional elements or 'motifs'. To some degree – again like much other folklore – urban legends must be considered false, at least in the sense that the same rather bizarre events could not actually have happened in so many localities to so many aunts, cousins, neighbours, in-laws, and classmates of the hundreds and thousands of individual tellers of the tales.'

Exercise 3
Look at story 3. Write an alternative version about bananas and a poisonous spider in a market in some docks. Use the phrases in the table to help you.

Exercise 2
When someone tells one of these stories it sounds interesting because of the details. They tell you:

When it happened, who it happened to, where it happened, how people felt, what they were wearing, etc.

Here are some examples of the 'central cores' of some urban legends. Re-tell the story, but add this kind of detail. Pretend that it is a true story. Compare your version with other people's in the class. Then write out an 'urban legend' that you have heard.

1 Left on the road
A couple were on holiday, either in a car with a caravan or a minibus. One (*which?*) decided to sleep, got into (the caravan) and got changed for bed. For some reason (*what?*) the vehicle stopped or started suddenly. The person in the back was standing against the door and either (a) fell out, or (b) got out to see what was wrong. The vehicle drove away, leaving him/her in the middle of the road, wearing (*what?*). (*What happened next?*)

2 The cat in the package
A cat died. The owner lived in a flat. The owner wanted to dispose of the body and put it into a shoe box (or wrapped it in brown paper). For some reason (*what?*) there was nowhere to get rid of the package.

The owner stopped somewhere and put the package down. It was stolen. The thief was found. (*how? why?*) (OR)

The package was put down in a shop. The owner picked it up again, went home, and opened the package. It was the wrong package. The package now contained a leg of lamb.

3 The bite
Someone was shopping in a discount store. They started to examine an item of clothing (*what?*), when they felt a sudden, sharp prick on the hand. They thought it was a pin or needle, but when they got home their hand was swollen and blue. A doctor was called (or they rushed to hospital). It was a snake bite. They returned to the shop. A snake (or several snakes) were found in the lining of the item of clothing, which had come from a tropical country (*which one?*).

4 Long-distance
A person was going away on business for (*how long?*). Just before leaving, they had a row with (*Who? A cleaner? A husband or wife? Someone else who had keys to the flat or house?*) It was a serious row. The person left, saying, 'And when I get back, you'd better have gone … and don't come back!' After the business trip, the person returned to the flat. As they opened the door, they heard 'at the tone the time will be 3.53 and forty seconds'. It was the telephone. It was off the hook. The voice was the Speaking Clock from New York, 3000 miles away. Before leaving, the other person had called the Speaking Clock. The telephone bill arrived some time later. It was (*how much?*).

Language study

When did it happen?	Who did it happen to?	Where did it happen?
Once … /One night …	A friend of mine …	In (Toronto) …
A few (years) ago …	A friend of a friend …	In / Near my home town …
In 1984/in April/ in the summer	Someone at work … / I know … / I met …	On the way home (from X) … / On the road from X to Y …
On Tuesday/the 12th of November/my birthday …	A relative … (cousin, aunt, uncle, niece, nephew …)	At a cinema …
At Christmas/ Easter …	An acquaintance …	In a park/wood/forest …
During the holiday …	A schoolmate …	On a beach …
Last (month) …	A fellow (student) …	
	My cousin's wife's brother-in-law's boss …	

Prejudice

North and South

In every country there are regional differences. People living in one region make jokes about the characteristics (real or imagined) of people living in another. Television is breaking down regional differences, but the jokes and comments continue. In Britain there are many jokes which begin 'There was an Englishman, an Irishman, a Scotsman and a Welshman, and ...'. In England itself there are myths about every region, but the broadest differences are those between the North and the South. There are real geographical and economic variations; the North can be characterized as more industrial, cooler, hillier and more working-class, the South as middle-class, more suburban, flatter and wealthier. There are also the often irrational things the English say about each other. Several people were asked to comment on the differences. Perhaps the most interesting comment was made by a woman from Lancashire (in the North), who said: 'Southerners? I can't stand them. They're stuck-up and snobbish. But at least they're not as bad as bloody Yorkshiremen!'

As Yorkshire is also in the North, it shows that the most violent prejudices are very localized.

Here are some of the comments we collected.

What some Northerners say:
'If you go into a pub in the South, everybody ignores you. The North is much more direct and friendly. We're real people.'

'You know the old saying ... people in the North earn the money, people in the South count it.'

'As you go North, the beer gets better.'

'I think there's more sense of community. Perhaps we interfere more — but we help each other too.'

'Southerners? They don't like getting their hands dirty. They stand around in wine bars, covered with talcum powder and after-shave, talking posh.'

'I was born in Manchester, but I live in the South. You know, I think things are better in the South for women. Northern men seem to want to get down the pub on their own and avoid women. Men in the South help more in the home — that's a statistic. Northern men are more ... more macho.'

'They think they're better than us — just because they talk posh. They're a load of snobs.'

'In Yorkshire we say what we mean. Southerners think we're bloody rude, but we're more blunt and honest. They smile in your face and stab you in the back.'

'If you go to London, keep your hand on your wallet. They'd rob their own grandmothers.'

'Liverpudlians are the funniest people in the country. They've got this marvellous natural sense of humour.'

'The North may be dirtier — but don't forget "where there's muck there's brass".' (i.e. where there's dirt, there's money.)

Listening

Perhaps there isn't such a thing as 'standard English'. For many years though the English used on television, spoken by ex-public school boys and taught to foreigners, was based on a southern model. British TV stations now tend to use more and more regional accents. Listen to a few examples of regional accents.

Exercise 1

What kind of regional prejudices do you have in your country?
Do you think there's any truth in them?
Are there prejudices about different towns?
What do people in towns say about people in the country?
What do people in the country say about people in towns?
[Town/Country prejudices are very similar all over the world.]

Exercise 2

Prejudice can be:

national
regional
religious
racial
social
sexual
political
based on appearance
based on intelligence/or ability

Can you think of examples of each type of prejudice?
Can you think of any other types of prejudice?

Exercise 3

What prejudices do *you* have?

For example:
Would you give a job to a man with an earring/a woman with pink hair/a man with very long hair/a woman in very modern clothes? Why/Why not?

What would you/your family think about you marrying a foreigner/a person of a different race or religion/someone much poorer/richer than you?

Do you think someone's clothes/appearance tells you anything about them? What?

What some Southerners say:
'Actually some of my best friends are Northerners, but of course they're not typical Northerners, if you know what I mean.'

'The North? A load of men with heavy colds, standing round in pubs wearing cloth caps, swilling beer and playing darts.'

'They spend their money on beer and Bingo. We probably earn less, but we spend it on our houses. When they come down here, they think we're all rich. We're probably worse off than them.'

'I used to work in Yorkshire. They're all bloody rude, and bloody mean.'

'They live on sticky buns, tripe and black pudding. The food's much more varied down here.'

'I really think the North's more conservative ... I'm not talking about politics, but their attitude to life. Things change more here.'

'They say we "talk posh" – we just speak better English, that's all.'

'There's more equality of the sexes in the South. Northerners treat women like doormats. Mind you, the women go round in curlers all day on Saturday – or they used to ten years ago.'

'They've got a massive inferiority complex. They imagine that we're all either stockbrokers, or country bumpkins with straw in our mouths. The prejudice comes more from them. They don't see that we're just like them.'

'I'm a Southerner – but I do find the North much warmer ... the people, that is, not the weather ... and friendlier ... more genuine, I think.'

Making your point

Exercise 1
Listen to part of the marketing meeting in progress.

Exercise 2
Read the survey on coffee makers.

GB Electrics is a small company specializing in household appliances, with a range of products that includes irons, toasters and kettles as well as a series of filter coffee machines. They have developed an espresso coffeemaker, the GB Express. It is similar to Italian machines and makes a strong cup of real espresso coffee. Before putting it on the market they are holding a marketing meeting to decide:

a whether to sell it at all
b if they sell it, which people it would appeal to
c how to advertise it.

Five reports have been prepared. Two of them use an advertiser's classification of the population, which divides the country into six groups.

Coffee makers

JUG METHOD – simple and cheap. Put ground coffee into a jug, pour on boiling water, stir, leave to settle, pour through a strainer.

PERCOLATOR (electric or heated on a cooker) – heated water circulates through the coffee until it is strong enough.

FILTER MACHINE – cold water is heated, filters through coffee and drips into a jug which is kept hot by an electric hot plate.

VERDICT — percolators and filters keep coffee hot. Percolators are difficult to clean. Filters need filter paper and are bulky. The latest method, from Italy, uses steam not hot water – the espresso method.

Group	Description	Examples
A	Professional, higher managerial	Doctors, accountants, company directors
B	Junior managerial	Managers, civil servants, teachers
C1	'White-collar' workers	Clerks, typists
C2	'Blue-collar' workers (skilled)	Skilled manual workers
D	'Blue-collar' workers (unskilled)	Unskilled manual workers
E	Not usually significant for advertisers	Old-age pensioners, students, the unemployed, the aristocracy

Market Research Doc. 1
Coffee-making habits

	Groups A/B	Groups C/D/E
Instant	70%	87%
Real coffee: Jug/non-electric percolator	7%	2%
Filter machine	19.5%	8%
Electric percolator	3%	3%
Espresso machine	0.5%	0

Market Research Doc. 3
Consumer reaction to machine

Excellent, easy to use & clean	21%
Good, but took time to use & clean	19%
Fair, took too long to use & clean	30%
Poor, too awkward to use & clean	20%
No definite reaction	10%

Advertising Department
Review of media for GB Express adverts

Note: 100 = cost of campaign in popular newspapers

	Group reached	Cost of campaign
Popular newspapers	B,C,D,E	100
Serious newspapers	A,B,C	80
Popular magazines (e.g. Radio Times)	A,B,C,D,E	85
Selected quality magazines	A,B	50
TV – ITV	A,B,C,D,E	250
TV – Channel 4	A,B,C	125
Local radio	A,B,C,D,E	60

Market Research Doc. 2
Consumer reaction to coffee made in GB Express

Too strong, would not use	75%
Might use after a special dinner party	10%
Might use occasionally	13%
Would use frequently/all the time	2%

Sales Division
Price Survey

	Cost of machine	Cost per cup
Instant	—	2½–3p
Coffee bags	—	6p
Filter cups (bought individually)	—	15p
Filter machine	£15–30	7p
Jug	£2–5	7p
Electric Percolator	£10–15	6p
GB Express	£70	5p

The marketing meeting

At the marketing meeting the following people will be present:

The Managing Director

You can hear her opinion in the listening exercise (1).

The Design Manager

Has to report on Market Research document 3. Planned the machine, and feels very strongly that GB can sell a lot of machines over a 5-year period. After all, they are very popular in Italy and the USA. Feels the public will need to be educated to like 'real coffee'. Compares it with sales of mineral water – which have more than doubled each year since 1976.

Market Researcher A

Has to report on Market Research document 1. Thought the survey should have separated casual cups made during the day from a cup after a main meal, or a dinner party, when a much larger proportion served real coffee. Points to huge success of filter machines over a ten-year period. Reckons the espresso machine will take over, and that filter users are the best market. Thinks small figure for espresso is encouraging. It leaves more people to buy them.

Market Researcher B

Has come to the conclusion that most British people don't really like coffee (after preparing Market Research document 2). Thinks the machine is too up-market and that sales will be limited to the well-off. Favours small-scale advertising campaign, concentrated on expensive food/homes type magazines. Wouldn't oppose scrapping the whole project.

The Sales Manager

Has price survey to report. Is optimistic about price per cup, but pessimistic about capital outlay involved in purchasing machine. Notes that 'milk boiler' device on the machine saves a lot on electricity/gas, and also uses less milk to make white coffee. All in all, thinks it's worth trying, but doesn't expect volume sales.

Language study

Expressing an opinion	Pros and cons		Explanation
In my opinion ...	The (main)	advantage disadvantage is ..	i.e.
The point is ...			in other words ...
I'd just like to say that ...	... against which ...		that is to say ...
Don't you think that ...	... besides (which) ...		by which I mean ...
From my point of view ...	... on the other hand ...		
As I see it ...	... from another point of view ...		

Additions	Proposals		Conclusion
Also ...	We should/ought to/ 'd better do this.		To sum up ...
In addition ...			
Furthermore ...	If we do this,	that will happen.	Finally ...
What is more ...	If we don't do it,		
... as well as ...	Unless we do it,		

Exercise 3

Each student should work in a group of 4, 5 or 6 with the roles outlined above. Each has to make a report on one of the documents, and give an opinion. Try to balance the 'pros and cons' while making your points. Open up into a discussion, and decide what to do about the machine. Each group should then report its conclusions to the class. Use the language below.

Exercise 4

Change to a different role, and write a report from that point of view on GB Express.

Teletext

TELETEXT

Teletext is a British success story. The teletext services carried on Ceefax (BBC) and Oracle (ITV) were developed in the UK.

That's all very well, you say – but what can teletext do for me?

More perhaps than you think is the answer – the teletext services bring you a wealth of news and information – all at the touch of a button.

WHAT IS TELETEXT AND WHAT CAN IT DO FOR YOU?

Teletext is the transmission of pages of text and drawings alongside the normal television programmes on BBC and ITV. Teletext is continuously transmitted at all times when regular television programmes are broadcast. It is a free service, available to anyone who has a teletext set which can be bought or rented at TV trade outlets all over the UK.

At present there are four teletext channels – the Ceefax service on BBC1 and BBC2 and Oracle on ITV and Channel 4.

Each page of information has its own number. All you have to do is press the appropriate number on the remote control keypad and the page you require will appear on screen.

You can switch from text to television pictures at will – you can even have the text superimposed on the picture if you wish, as seen in the sub-titling and newsflash services.

A million teletext sets are already in use in the UK – so don't you think its time you found out what teletext can do for you?

HERE'S HOW TELETEXT CAN BENEFIT YOU

Teletext offers something for everyone – parents, teenagers, young children and special groups such as those with hearing or sight difficulties – teletext covers their special interests.

Exercise 1
Describe briefly what you would expect to find on Oracle, pages 101, 203, 300, 304.

Exercise 2
Write tomorrow's Teletext weather summary for your own country.

Exercise 3
Look at the headlines. Try to write out the stories 'behind the headlines' as one page of Teletext each.

Exercise 4
Two men had their arms sewn back on. Which one had an accident first? What did he do?
Are the details of his accident given in the papers, or on the teletext news for 29th June?
Where did the second man have an accident?
What was his job?
What happened to him?
Where was he operated on?
What other stories have you heard about limbs being sewn back on?

P100   ORACLE
100   Wed29   Jun   ITV   1026:28

ITV ORACLE ITV

CURB CHEQUE-BOOK JOURNALISM CALL . . . 206

101 TV GUIDE	201 NEWS HEADLINES
	250 Newsflash
150 Alarm Clock	290 Newsfile
155 ADVERTISERS	203 BUSINESS NEWS
190 A–Z INDEX	300 YOUR REGION
	303 WEATHER INDEX
202 SPORTS NEWS	304 TRAVEL INDEX

LEISURE, KIDS PAGES & CHANNEL 4 GUIDE
ARE ON CHANNEL 4 – PAGE 400

P198   CEEFAX 166   Wed 29   Jun   06:09:01

WEATHER EYE

Forecast for 6am to midnight today:
Scotland and N Ireland
will have sunny intervals and showers.

N Wales and N England
will start cloudy with hill fog and outbreaks
of rain. Brighter weather will follow.

S Wales and S England
will be rather cloudy with occasional rain.

Outlook for Thursday and Friday:
rather cool, sunny intervals and
showers, mainly in north and east.
Mostly dry and warmer on Friday.

P198   CEEFAX 136   Wed 29   June   06:10/15

BBC
NEWS   SUMMARY

COMMONS Angry scenes as Heseltine
accuses Labour over nuclear arms

WARSAW PACT summit calls for
East–West weapons freeze

PEERAGES Foot and Thatcher clash

SURGEONS fight to replace severed
arm of factory worker

REAGAN denies he saw secret Carter
campaign documents

HOUSING Building societies report
huge demand for home ownership

Details follow in a moment . . .

P201   ORACLE 201   Wed29   Jun   ITN   1026:50

ITN HEADLINES

SURGERY: SECOND MAN HAS ARM SEWN ON	204
CHEQUE-BOOK JOURNALISM: CURBS URGED	206
MIDDLE EAST: PLO 'PURGE' CONTINUES	205
ROYAL TOUR: STORM OVER SPY CAMERA	208
REAGAN DENIES SEEING CARTER PAPERS	207
ROW OVER DISSOLUTION HONOURS LIST	214
RAIL CHIEF TO FACE CRITICS	213
RUGBY: LIONS MAKE FIVE TEST CHANGES	248

Newsround 299   Sport 202   City Ch4   603

P198   CEEFAX 185   Wed 29   Jun   05:57/46

BBC   NEWS

Surgeons in Salisbury have carried out
micro-surgery to replace a man's
severed arm.

The operation on factory worker David
Ruffell came just 24 hours after
doctors at Stoke Mandeville performed
similar surgery on farmhand Roy Tapping.

Mr Ruffell, who worked at a wooden door
factory in Farnham, Surrey, had his
left arm torn off at the elbow as he
tried to clean a wood-planing machine.

A report on his condition will not be
given until later today.

More from CEEFAX AM in a moment . . .

P204   ORACLE
204   Wed29   Jun   ITN   1027:47

ITN ARM SEWN BACK ON

A second man has had a severed left arm sewn
back on by surgeons.

Mr David Ruffell's arm was cut off as he cleaned a
machine at a factory in Farnham, Surrey, yesterday
afternoon.

The accident came less than 24 hours after farmer
Roy Tapping had his severed arm sewn back on.

Mr Ruffell's arm was torn off at the elbow and it
took doctors many hours to sew it back on at a
Salisbury hospital.

Mr Tapping meanwhile is recovering at Stoke
Mandeville Hospital near Aylesbury and has been
able to speak to relatives.

P198   CEEFAX 132   Wed 29   Jun   05:59/35

IN THE PAPERS . . .

The overwhelming courage of the
farmhand who walked half-a-mile for
help carrying his severed arm is the
prominent feature in many of today's
newspapers.

'What a guy,' says The Sun. 'The bravest
man in Britain,' concludes the Daily
Mail. And the Daily Express tells of
'the incredible courage of farm hero
Roy'.

Many of the papers report that cricket-
mad Roy Tapping joked 'Do you know any
one-arm bowlers?' as his arm was placed
in ice and he was rushed to hospital.

P198   CEEFAX 185   Wed 29   Jun   06:00/04

IN THE PAPERS . . .

The Guardian takes a more cautious
line as surgeons wait to see whether an
operation to replace the severed limb
is a long-term success.

The Daily Telegraph gives details of
the micro-surgery techniques used to
sew back the arm in a 10-hour operation.

The Daily Mirror relegates this amazing
human-interest story to page seven, but
leads instead on an equally heart-
warming tale.

It tells of the smiles and the anguish
at the dedication of a memorial to
victims of the IRA bombing in Hyde Park.

The Parkhurst Talkabout

Good evening and welcome again to the *Michael Parkhurst Talkabout*. It is now some years since the government introduced the Sex Discrimination Act, which was intended to ensure equality of opportunity for men and women. We wondered whether the Act had been successful, and our four guests tonight are discussing the general question of equality of opportunity.

Bernard Blackburn, journalist and broadcaster

In my opinion we shall never create real equality of opportunity by making laws about newspaper advertisements. You know, you have to advertise for a 'salesperson' nowadays rather than a salesman or saleswoman ... I'm not saying that these things are unimportant, but basically ... by the time children get to four or five they have already been conditioned into their social roles. It starts in the cradle – girls in pink, boys in blue. I heard about an experiment a few years ago where they took a small baby and dressed it in blue. Then they asked several mothers to play with it. They bounced it up and down, and tickled it, and said things like 'You're a rascal ... a real little devil!', and 'Ooh, what a big strong boy you are!' And they laughed when it yelled and shouted. Well, then they dressed the same baby in pink and got another group to play with it. They cuddled it and said, 'Aren't you pretty? What a lovely little girl!' As soon as it got noisy they tried to hush it and calm it down. Now, that's where sexism begins. And that's long before we give the girls dolls and toy saucepans to play with, and give the boys cars and guns.

Helen Grant, university lecturer

I feel there's a long way to go before we can talk about equality of opportunity. Men still expect their jobs to take priority. Even where both partners work, too many men still expect the woman to cook meals and do housework. I mean, go into a supermarket at lunch time. It's full of working women giving up their lunch hour to do the family shopping. How many men would expect to do the same? They're probably spending the lunch hour laughing and joking ... about women. The same old, tired jokes go on forever ... women drivers, mothers-in-law and sexy secretaries. Secretaries! That's another absurdity. Imagine an office where a man and a woman are doing similar jobs. She's called a secretary, he's called a trainee manager. Of course this is how so many firms avoid obeying the law on equal pay ... by altering the job description. The media, as always, I'm afraid, is so much to blame. Magazines, TV, film and advertising portray women as sex objects, not people. Women are blackmailed into buying useless products because they might fear they are unattractive without them. Too many of us accept the stereotype, and waste our time worrying and dieting to fit some imaginary male ideal.

Dr Alice Lee, a general practitioner

Equality. Yes, well ... I'm a doctor, so I suppose you could say that I have an interesting, rewarding and important job. However, I have experienced tremendous prejudice from male colleagues, and after all, while there are plenty of women doctors, most of the surgeons and top consultants are men. The argument's always the same, in all spheres of activity, that women will leave the job to have babies. Of course not all women want to have babies, so this is tremendously unjust. Personally I did want children ... I've got two ... and I stopped work to have them. Children are always forgotten in the argument. I've always felt that it is a very narrow view of life to value a person purely in terms of job status. I believe we should remove the barriers against women at work, but I also do not see myself only as a working person, 'Dr Lee'. Being a mother is a very important social role, and we need to re-assess our view of motherhood and to regard it as equally valid as any job. It is absurd to think a woman is 'more successful' as a Prime Minister, than as a mother. Of course this is equally true for men. Couples who have swopped roles, where the mother has gone out to work, and the father has

stayed at home, will tell you that both jobs are equally important; and even that being at home is more demanding, emotionally and physically.

Rosemary Valentine, romantic novelist
Perhaps I come from a different generation. When I was a girl things were quite different. I enjoy having doors opened for me. I like it when men stand up as I enter a room, make sure that I am seated before them. I feel that the romance has gone out of life today. I used to love getting dressed up for a party, having my hair done and so on. I never felt inferior – just different. I wouldn't want my husband to help me in the house, and I'd feel strange if he did. I also can't worry about all this fuss about words. We are supposed to say 'chairperson' rather than 'chairman'. I don't dislike it, but I don't see it as terribly important. I think my husband is a typical example of a male chauvinist pig, but I like him that way.

Exercise 1
Take part in the programme. Ask each speaker three questions. Act this out in pairs.

Exercise 2
In groups, choose an entry. Do the figures surprise you? Discuss your views with other groups.

Men and Women: various comparisons — 1981, Great Britain		
	Men	Women
Life expectancy (years)	69.4	75.6
Average weekly earnings	£124.50	£78.80
Average weekly hours	42.7	37.5
Percentages of all		
Employed work force	58	42
Unemployed	64.5	35.5
Trade unionists	71	29
Members of Parliament	97	3
Members of the House of Lords	96	4
Civil servants	60	40
Drug addicts	66	34
Prison population	97	3
Bank managers	99	1
Directors	97	3
Solicitors	93	7
University graduates 1980	63	37
University students	65	35
Credit card holders	80	20

Source: *The Guinness Pocket Book of Facts*, 1982

Sexism in words

'Sexist'	Neutral
chairman/woman	chairperson
salesman/woman	salesperson
air hostess	flight attendant
housewife	homemaker
actor/actress	actor
Mrs/Miss	Ms
he . . .	he or she/they

Exercise 3
Make a table with columns labelled 'male', 'female' or 'neutral'. Put these words into the columns depending on whether you think they apply to one more than another. Discuss your choice with a partner.

aggressive	ambitious	sympathetic
shy	confident	quiet
beautiful	handsome	strong
competitive	caring	gentle
kind	rude	polite
nagging	gossip	discussion
chat	talk	complaining
efficient	argue	row
cry	weep	brave
brutal		

RIGHT, WHO'S GOING TO BE MOTHER AND POUR THE TEA?

CHAIRPERSON

Rules and regulations

Voluntary censorship

In the early 1920s, Hollywood was rocked by a series of scandals involving major stars and directors. The film production companies were afraid that government censorship of films would be introduced, and to avoid this they set up a system of voluntary censorship. Will H. Hays, the US Postmaster-General, was invited to supervise this system in December 1921, and took up his new job as president of the Motion Pictures Producers and Distributors of America (MPPDA) in 1922. After eight years of work, he produced a document which became known as 'The Hays Office Code' in 1930. The code was in operation until 1966, and as a result, American films were never classified (for adults, adults with children, or for children) in the way they were in other countries. All films were supposed to be suitable for everyone. The code began with three general principles:

1 No picture shall be produced which will lower the moral standards of those who see it, hence the sympathy of the audience shall never be thrown to the side of crime, wrong-doing, evil, or sin.
2 Correct standards of life, subject only to the requirements of drama and entertainment, shall be presented.
3 Law, natural or human, shall not be ridiculed, nor shall sympathy be created for its violation.

This was followed by very detailed sections on 'Particular Applications', which included: (1) crimes against the law; (2) sex; (3) vulgarity; (4) obscenity; (5) profanity; (6) costume; (7) dances; (8) religion; (9) location; (10) national feelings; (11) titles; and (12) repellent subjects; together with three sets of extra 'Special Regulations' on (1) crimes in motion pictures, (2) costumes, and (3) cruelty to animals.

The Hays Code was often the subject of jokes, very often because it was so specific. For example, the 'Profanity' section listed 28 forbidden words, and in one case a Shakespearean story had to have its text altered because it used one of them. The 'Vulgarity' section explicitly forbade jokes about 'travelling salesmen and farmers' daughters'. However, since the code disappeared, many people have been worried about the effects of violence, sex, and bad language in the cinema, and there have been calls for a new 'Hays Code'. In Britain, the British Board of Film Censors still exists, but its job is not so much to ban films as to grade them ('U': unrestricted, 'PG': parental guidance, '18': over 18, and '15': over 15). Recent publicity has been directed not so much at the cinema as at video 'nasties', and violence has been more worrying than sex on video. And after all, anyone with £1.00 in cash can rent a video film.

Exercise 1
Listen to Charles Orson, the Hollywood director, talking about the Hays Office Code.

1 What did they have to do before they started filming?
2 Why does he say it was a good thing?
3 What did the Hays Office say he would have to do to his script in 1948 or 1949?
4 What were two things you weren't allowed to show?
5 Why would directors have to use an image?
6 What did he feel about censorship?
7 How does he feel now?

Exercise 2
Look back at the reading passage. What do you imagine it might have said in the twelve 'Particular Applications' in the Hays Code? What about the 'Special Regulations'?
Make sentences with: *weren't allowed to/couldn't/had to/were forbidden to/weren't supposed to*. Work in pairs. Draw up a list.

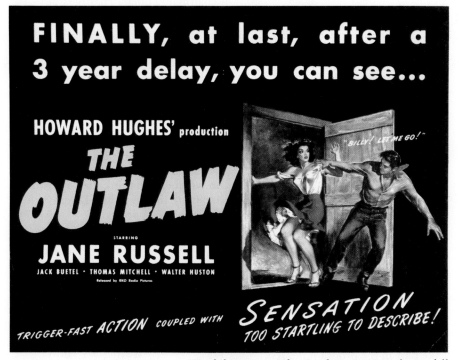

Work began on *The Outlaw* in 1940, but it fell foul of the Hays Code in 1943 and was not released until 1946. Howard Hughes made the most of this notoriety in the film's promotion.

Regulations

BOURNE HALL
UNIVERSITY OF WESSEX
Regulations for Residents

1　All residents are obliged to produce a medical certificate, which shall include the results of a recent chest X-ray.

2　All bills are to be settled within 15 days of presentation.

3　No guests are allowed in students' rooms after 11 p.m.

4　Radios, cassette players, etc. are not to be played between 11 p.m. and 8 a.m. At all other times, the volume must be kept low so as not to disturb other residents.

5　Pictures, posters, etc. are not to be attached to the walls. They may be displayed only on the notice board provided.

6　Residents are not permitted to interfere with the heating controls. Any difficulties must be referred to the resident caretaker.

7　Cars may be parked only in the designated spaces.

8　Tampering with fire extinguishers or the fire alarm system is strictly forbidden. Any breach of this regulation will be referred to the Dean of Students, and may result in expulsion.

9　Smoking is prohibited in all hallways and passages.

UW/BH/REG 14

TADWORTH CITY TRANSPORT
Buses: Regulations

1　Do not stand in such a way as to obstruct the driver's vision.

2　Passengers must not talk to, or otherwise distract the driver whilst the bus is in motion.

3　Smoking is prohibited on the lower floor.

4　Standing is not permitted on the upper floor.

5　Dogs not allowed (unless carried by passenger).

By Order

Transport Manager

Borough of Sandpool
Parks and Beaches Department
Regulations

1　No ball games on the promenade.

2　Camping is strictly forbidden on the beach. The overnight parking of caravans is prohibited on the promenade.

3　Dogs are permitted only in the specified 'Dogs Allowed' sections of the beach.

4　You must not swim when the red flags are flying.

By Order

Town Clerk

Exercise 3

Listen to these three conversations. Then role-play conversations about each of the other rules and regulations.

Exercise 4

Orson says that 'you have to draw the line somewhere'. Do you think that film/video censorship is necessary?

You are going to draw up a code for one of the following: television, cinema, video tapes.

Work in pairs and draw up a list of positive and negative rules. Decide with your partner whether you want the code to be compulsory or voluntary.

Write out the rules and regulations using the language on this page to help you.

Discuss your rules and regulations with another pair.

Would you 'classify' films, TV programmes, and videos for people's guidance? How would you classify them?

Alas!

The most popular programme of the year must be 'Alas!', the exciting and turbulent serial about the Bartholomew family, produced by Midland TV. If you haven't been following it, here's a quick guide to the characters and story.

Timothy Bartholomew 71 year-old chocolate millionaire. Self-made man. Began with a sweet-shop in Salford. Blunt, ruthless. Rules his three sons with a rod of iron.

Edna Bartholomew 59, his wife. Ex-model. Married Timothy at 18. Alcoholic. She has a separate bedroom. Hates Timothy. Lives for her sons. Tries to keep the peace between them.

'TL' Bartholomew Oldest son. Sales director of company. Devious, scheming, and dishonest. Has lied to father about several business deals, which lost two million pounds.

Robbie Bartholomew Second son. 6ft tall, played rugby for England. Tough, honest and uncompromising. Happily married. Marketing manager of company.'

Adrian Bartholomew Youngest son. Spent five years in a commune. Hates his father and won't take his money. Lives with his girlfriend, Sharon.

Helen Bartholomew Married TL ten years ago. No children. Very ambitious. From aristocratic family. Looks down on the others.

Melanie Bartholomew Married Robbie last year. Wants to have children. Beautiful and intelligent. Her father killed himself after Timothy took over his company, Chilton's Chocs.

Sharon Carter College lecturer. Has known Adrian for years. Wrote a book – *Dangers of Advertising* – which criticized Bartholomew's for advertising to children.

The story so far TL wants to get Robbie out of the business, and wants to break up his marriage before he has any children. Has discovered that Melanie was married and divorced before Robbie met her. Wants to blackmail her, but is terrified that Edna might find out. Edna's doctor is Sharon's father. Sharon and Adrian are visiting the family because they have heard that Edna will not live long. Sharon is part of a government enquiry team investigating bribes by Bartholomew's Chocolate to TV companies. Helen hates Adrian and Sharon, but doesn't know that secretly TL is desperately in love with Sharon, who can't bear him.

Listening

Listen to the beginning of Episode 17 of *Alas!*

Who's in the swimming pool?
To find the answer, you have used a process of deduction, i.e.
It can't be him, because …
It can't be her, because …
So, it must be …
(*or* It can't have been her, because …, so it must have been …)

How did you know who was in the pool? Listen again.
So: Voice 1 was _____
    Voice 2 was _____
    Voice 3 was _____
    Voice 4 was _____
    Voice 5 was _____
    Voice 6 was _____
    Voice 7 was _____
    Voice 8 was _____

Language study (1)

It	isn't is		(him). (her).
	can't must could(n't) may might	be	

It	wasn't was		(him). (her).
	can't must could(n't) may might	have been	

Exercise 1
How might she have died?
Who might she have spoken to?
Why might she have died?
Who might have been responsible?
Give reasons for your deductions.

Exercise 2
When you have completed Exercise 1, write out the story of what happened. Write it as 'The story so far' before the next episode in the series.

Language study (2)

What do you mean (by that)?
I don't see your point.
What are you trying to say?
What are you getting at?
What point are you trying to make?

Note: exactly/precisely can be added to any of the patterns.

What	exactly precisely	do you mean?
What do you mean		exactly? precisely?

What's wrong?
What's the matter?
What's the trouble?
What's the problem?
What's happened?
What's going on?
What's all the fuss about?

Tell me		what	*is* wrong.
I don't	see understand know		you *are* getting at. the matter *is*. the fuss *is* about.

Exercise 3

Make sentences like the ones in the examples for each of the patterns in Language study (2).

What are you getting at?
Tell me what you are getting at.

Exercise 4

Complete this conversation. Some of the phrases are in Language study (2).

Robbie Darling! What's _____ ?
Melanie It's nothing. Just something in my eye.
Robbie You're crying. Come on, tell me _____ .
Melanie It isn't _____ . Really.
Robbie It must be _____ . Why won't you _____ ?
Melanie It's just TL. Something he _____ .
Robbie What _____ say?
Melanie Oh, Robbie, if there was a secret, something I'd never told you, could you forgive me?
Robbie What _____ ?
Melanie You really don't know what _____ ?
Robbie No.
Melanie Then ask your brother. He'll tell you soon enough, anyway!

Hairdresser!

Reading

Read the following story from Dr
Robert Clifford's book *Doctor, Dear
Doctor*.

Philomena Fraser visited Tadchester Hospital every week on early closing day to do the hair of the old ladies in the geriatric ward. All she charged was the cost of the materials; her own time and skills she gave for nothing.

Even though in many cases the hair was down to a few white and wispy strands, the fact that it was still worth the attention of a hairdresser raised the morale and self-respect of the old dears no end.

Phil's hairdressing sessions were the social highspot of the week. The old ladies gathered in the little room used as the salon, and sat around as if they were at Vidal Sassoon's. They read magazines as they waited, and chatted away to each other as if they had met for the first time that week.

The sessions were always full of laughter. Phil called all the 'customers' by their first names, and joked incessantly with them.

'Come on, Edie, love,' she'd say as an old dear tottered slowly to the chair. 'The rollers will be cold by the time you get here.' And, 'What do you fancy this time, darling? Something a bit more sexy? Be careful, though: you don't want to get that young doctor going, do you? You know what he's like when he sees you . . . especially with your teeth in.'

The good humour of the afternoon lasted all evening, long after Phil had packed her gear and gone home. The old ladies would be admiring each other's coiffure , recalling all the jokes and laughing at the sauciness until well after lights out.

The sessions were threatened though, after the matron dropped in on one of them. She stood in the doorway of the room, coldly observed the scene, listened to the banter for a few minutes, then left.

As Phil walked down the corridor after the session, lugging the drier and a suitcase full of equipment, she was hailed from the matron's office: 'I say, Hairdressah!'

'Yes, matron?' said Phil cheerily, dropping her gear and poking her head round the office door.

'Come in and close the door behind you, Hairdressah,' said matron. 'There's something I have to say.'

'What's up?' asked Phil, her smile fading at the look on matron's face.

'You must remember that this is a hospital, Hairdressah, not a social club or a beauty parlour. We expect certain standards of behaviour and have certain rules for the benefit of all which must be observed. I'm sure you understand.'

'No, I don't,' said Phil. 'Not a word. What are you on about?'

'Your conduct of the hairdressing sessions,' said matron. 'It puts the wrong ideas into the patients' heads. They are old ladies, not silly bits of girls. Your visits leave them chattering and giggling like flibbertigibbets and totally unamenable to discipline.

'Furthermore, I notice that you are in the habit of addressing them by their first names. This must cease. It has always been a firm rule that patients are to be addressed by their correct titles: Miss or Mrs. followed by their surnames. Is that clear, Hairdressah?'

Phil stood there for a second, shocked and disbelieving, then came suddenly to the boil.

'It's perfectly clear, matron. Now I'd like to make a few things clear to you. Firstly, my name is not Hairdressah. It is Mrs. Philomena Fraser. Everybody calls me Phil, but to you, it's Mrs. Fraser.

'Secondly, I am perfectly aware that they are old ladies. And so are they; only too aware. The one thing they crave is to be young and attractive again. I can't give them back their youth and I can't make them pretty. But I can make them feel good, if it's only for one afternoon a week. You look after their bodies. The consultant geriatrician looks after their poor old minds. But I make them feel *feminine*. And at eighty-odd that must be a good thing for a woman to feel.'

'Now look here!' snapped matron.

I've not finished yet,' said Phil. 'Thirdly, they like being called by their first names: even by the nicknames they had when they were young. Miss Victoria Patience Bassington loves nothing more than to be called Buster, the name she had when she was captain of her school hockey team all those years ago. Mrs. Sarah Elizabeth Holmes was Sally as a girl; inside that old body she's still Sally.'

I shall report your conduct and your attitude to the proper authorities,' said matron.

'Report away,' said Phil. 'Fourthly, the old loves I have sitting around the hairdressing sessions are completely different from the apathetic souls who sit around the ward all week. They relate to each other, they come alive, they're having an adventure. Above all, they're having some laughs. That may be against the rules, but in my book it's the finest tonic in the world.'

From "*Doctor, Dear Doctor*" by Robert Clifford, published by Pelham Books.

Exercise 1

Find words which mean the following:
1. cylindrical object used for waving hair
2. thread of hair
3. the name of a world-famous hairdresser
4. desire, want strongly
5. a specialist doctor for old people
6. also, in addition
7. rudeness or naughtiness
8. equipment
9. a name used instead of the real name
10. joking talk
11. hair style or hair-do
12. continually
13. showing interest in nothing
14. said sharply
15. called out to
16. walked with weak unsteady legs
17. frivolous girls, fond of gossip
18. not willing to be controlled
19. behaviour
20. over 80 but under 90
21. carrying something (with great effort)
22. talking in a friendly way about unimportant things
23. laughing in a silly way
24. talking about things which happened in the past.

Exercise 2

Choose the correct answer (**a, b, c** or **d**) to show what each of the following means in the passage you have just read.

1. 'They relate to each other' means:
a. They're all from the same family.
b. They tell each other stories.
c. They sympathize with each other and get on well together.
d. They tell each other jokes.

2. '... raised their morale and self-respect' means:
a. excited the old ladies
b. gave them confidence
c. improved their behaviour
d. made them vain

3. 'In my book it's the finest tonic in the world' means:
a. I think it's the best thing for them.
b. I've read that it's the best thing for them.
c. I've read about a very good medicine which will help them.
d. Books will make them feel better.

Formal forms of address

1. **Sir/Madam** – usually used by shop assistants to customers. In England it is *not* used when simply addressing a stranger politely. (Although it may be used in this way in the United States.) It is used in letters. (Dear Sir, Dear Madam.)

2. **Ladies/Gentlemen** – used in speeches to an audience, as well as on toilet doors! *Gentlemen* replaces *Dear Sirs*, in American business letters.

3. **My Lord** – used when speaking to a peer (Lord), a bishop or a judge.

4. **Your Honor** – used for American judges.

5. **Your Excellency** – used for ambassadors and sometimes for high government officials.

6. **Mr President** – for Presidents, obviously.

7. **Your Majesty** – the Queen. **Your Highness** – Royal princes and princesses.

8. **Prime Minister, Senator, Congressman, Minister** – are used for the appropriate politicians.

9. **Father** – Catholic priests. **Vicar** – Anglican priests. **Minister** – other Protestant ministers.

10. **Doctor, Nurse, Sister, Matron, Operator, Officer, Constable** are job-titles which can be used as forms of address. **Waiter** and **Driver** are also possible, but might be thought rude if said wrongly. Other job titles are not used as forms of address.

11. **Captain, Major,** and other military ranks can be used. **Captain** would often be used for pilots on civilian planes, and ship captains too.

Informal forms of address

Many of these informal forms can be used in a friendly way to strangers. Shopkeepers might call customers of the opposite sex (or children) *love (luv), dear, darlin', sweetheart, my love, dearie.* Women might also use these to women. Men might use *chum, mate, friend, pal,* in the same way. As in most languages, all of these can be offensive if used at the wrong time, with the wrong tone of voice. None of these expressions would be considered polite.

Old man, old chap, old fellow, will sometimes be found in literary texts. Note that they are old-fashioned, and suggest an English public (i.e. private) school background.

Will that be all, me old mate, me old pal, me old chum, me old beauty......

Yes, thank you very much old chap, old man, old fellow, old bean....

Relay

Events There are four Olympic relay events: men's and women's 4 × 100m, and men's and women's 4 × 400m.

Procedure Each of the four team members runs one stage of the race.

A baton is carried in the hand, and transferred in the take-over zone from one runner to the next. If dropped, the baton must be picked up by the competitor who dropped it.

Composition of teams may be changed after a heat only in the case of injury or illness certified by the official medical officer.

A team may change its running order.

No competitor may run more than one stage in a race.

The relay baton is a smooth, hollow tube made of rigid material in one piece. It must weigh not less than 50g (1¾oz).

Lanes 4 × 100m relay races are run entirely in lanes. 4 × 400m relay races are run in lanes as far as the exit from the first bend of the second lap.

Take-overs The baton must be handed over within the marked take-over zone. Runners about to take over must not start running more than 10m before the take-over zone.

In the stages of the 4 × 400m not run in lanes, competitors must return to their own lanes for the take-over unless they can use the inside position without causing an obstruction.

After handing over the baton, competitors should remain in their lanes or zones until the course is clear.

Teams will be disqualified for deliberately causing an obstruction or for pushing or giving any other assistance at a take-over.

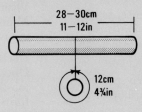

28 – 30cm
11 – 12in

12cm
4¾in

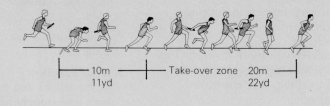

10m
11yd

Take-over zone

20m
22yd

a Staggered start
b First take-over zone
c Second take-over zone
d Third take-over zone
e Finish

The competitors

These are the teams for the Men's 4 × 100 metres relay event in the British Inter-city Athletics championship.

Which one would you predict as the favourite? Why?

LIVERPOOL

Red vests, red shorts
R Sharp/J McCartney/
P Harrison/G Lenton

Winners – last year
Lenton won 100m,
Sharp second.

MANCHESTER

Red vests, white shorts
W J Kramer/G Nash/
T Holly/E O'Neill

Holly won 200m
O'Neill injured foot.

GLASGOW

Green & white vests,
white shorts
R Bruce/K Macbeth/
J Campbell/E McLeish

Youngest team.
Bruce last year's
schools champion,
100m.

OXFORD

Dark blue vests &
shorts
F Hornby/M Hartley/
J Thompson/B Cole

Winners university
championship.

LEEDS

Yellow vests, yellow
shorts
B Lomas/A Henry/
G Exley/R Bremner

Disqualified last year.
Oldest, but most
experienced team.
Won 3 years ago.

BRISTOL

Red vests, blue shorts
A Tankard/J Player/
T Hardy/H Nelson

Player second in
200m.

SOUTH LONDON

White vests, black
shorts
D Waters/G Singh/
W Marley/K Minder

Won 2 years ago.
Second favourites.

CAMBRIDGE

Light blue vests &
shorts
L Jones/N Swan/
K Rose/R Kneebone

Won 4 × 400m relay.

BIRMINGHAM

Purple vests, light
blue shorts
V Aston/C Jasper/
R Bull/N Lloyd

Little-known team.

SWANSEA

Green vests, red
shorts
P Llewelyn/B Jones/
C J Jones/D F Jones

Welsh champions.

DOVER

Yellow vests, blac.
shorts
D Castle/J D Kent/
W Walters/S Ferry

Little-known team.

NEWCASTLE

Black & white vests,
black shorts
M Terry/K Charlton/
N East/T North

North has foot injury.

EXETER

Orange vests, orange
shorts
R West/D Creme/
D Moor/F Penbern

West of England
champions. Moor and
West both Olympic
medallists.

YORK

White vests, white
shorts
J Gates/P Minster/
N Riding/A Rowntree

Unplaced in any
events so far.

BRIGHTON

Light blue vests, red
shorts
B Bell/T Lane/
S Pears/S Gull

Southern champions
unplaced so far.

NOTTINGHAM

White vests, red
shorts
B Clough/N Forrest/
D Lawrence/L Chatterly

Second last year.
Lawrence won 400m.
Second in 4 × 400m.

The draw

There are going to be four heats, with four teams in each. The winner and runner-up of each heat will go on to the semi-finals. The winner and runner-up of each semi-final will go into the finals. Listen to the draw, and write the names of the teams in each heat in the appropriate boxes. (You should use abbreviations, e.g. 'Liv' or 'L'pool' for Liverpool.)

The races

You are going to hear commentaries on all the races. Before you listen, look at the draw for the heats. Decide which team you think is most likely to win each heat. Read the details of each team carefully. Why have you chosen a particular team?

Listen to each race, and put the winners and runners-up in the semi-final boxes.

Now who do you think is most likely to win each semi-final?

Would you be able to predict the final winner? Again enter the names of the winner and runner-up of each semi-final in the final box.

Try to guess the winner now. Listen to the final, and complete the last box.

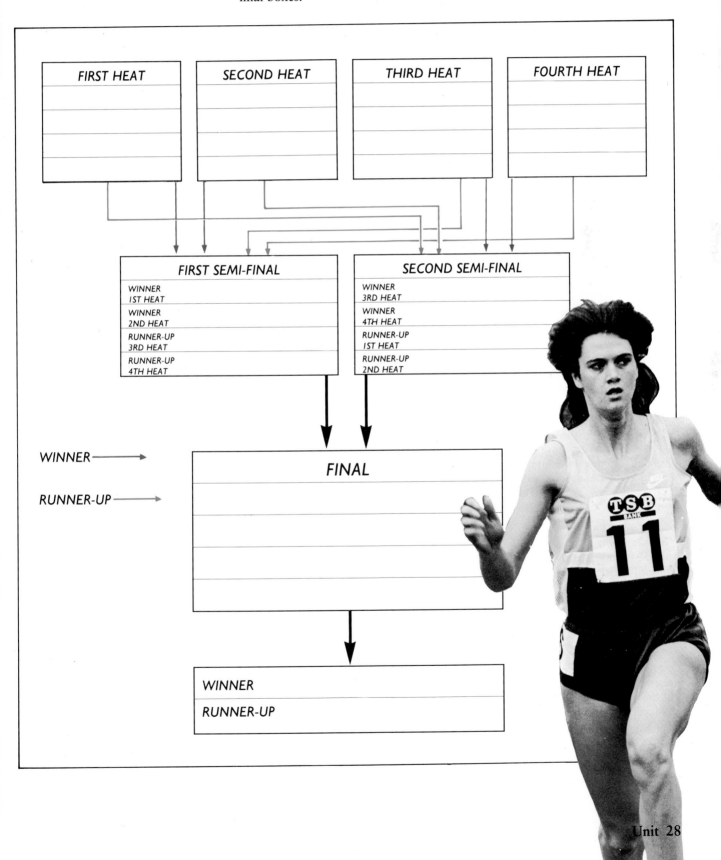

FIRST HEAT

SECOND HEAT

THIRD HEAT

FOURTH HEAT

FIRST SEMI-FINAL

WINNER 1ST HEAT	
RUNNER-UP 3RD HEAT	
WINNER 2ND HEAT	
RUNNER-UP 4TH HEAT	

SECOND SEMI-FINAL

WINNER 3RD HEAT	
WINNER 4TH HEAT	
RUNNER-UP 1ST HEAT	
RUNNER-UP 2ND HEAT	

WINNER ⟶

RUNNER-UP ⟶

FINAL

| WINNER |
| RUNNER-UP |

Design

Raymond Loewy

You've probably never heard of Raymond Loewy, but if you drive a car, buy a can of soup, smoke a cigarette, follow picture-only road signs or look at advertisements, then Loewy has influenced you. What we expect from the outside of a car, the inside of a plane or ship, the colour of a trademark or the general style and feel of most things in shops can be traced back to the ideas of this Frenchman, who was born in 1893.

Loewy designed the classic Coca-Cola bottle, the supermarket trolley, the Shell and BP symbols and the inside of the Apollo spacecraft. He has designed everything from the Kennedy memorial stamp to the interior of Concorde. When he arrived in New York to make his fortune in 1919 he had a business card with this slogan:

'Between two products equal in prices, function and quality, the better looking will outsell the other.'

One of his early designs was a refrigerator which looked so attractive yet functional that eye-appeal became its prime selling point — a factor which has never left the domestic product field. His 1920s' drawings of cars predicted the shapes of the 1980s, and when he sold a collection of his design studies in 1981 he claimed that they were the most remarkable collection of a single person's work since Leonardo da Vinci.

Victor Papanek

Victor Papanek is a designer and author of *Design For The Real World*. He believes that ideas are cheap and plentiful, and he gives away many of his designs to UNESCO. This is an extract from his book:

There are professions more harmful than industrial design, but only a very few of them. And possibly only one profession is phonier. Advertising design, in persuading people to buy things they don't need, with money they don't have, in order to impress others who don't care, is probably the phoniest field in existence today. Industrial design, by concocting the tawdry idiocies hawked by advertisers, comes a close second. Never before in history have grown men sat down and seriously designed electric hairbrushes, rhinestone-covered file boxes, and mink carpeting for bathrooms, and then drawn up elaborate plans to make and sell these gadgets to millions of people. Before (in the 'good old days'), if a person liked killing people, he had to become a general, purchase a coal-mine, or else study nuclear physics. Today, industrial design has put murder on a mass-production basis. By designing criminally unsafe automobiles that kill or maim nearly one million people around the world each year, by creating whole new species of permanent garbage to clutter up the landscape, and by choosing materials and processes that pollute the air we breathe, designers have become a dangerous breed. And the skills needed in these activities are taught carefully to young people.

USE: 'Does it work?' A vitamin bottle should dispense pills singly. An ink bottle should not tip over. A plastic-film package covering sliced pastrami should withstand boiling water. As in any reasonably conducted home, alarm-clocks seldom travel through the air at speeds approaching five hundred miles per hour, 'streamlining' clocks is out of place. Will a cigarette lighter designed like the tailfin of an automobile (the design of that automobile was copied from a pursuit plane of the Korean War) give more efficient service?

Radio receiver designed for the Third World

Designed by Victor Papanek and George Seeger at North Carolina State College, the radio receiver is made of a used juice can, and uses paraffin wax and a wick as power source. The rising heat is converted into enough energy to power this non-selective receiver. Once the wax is gone, it can be replaced by more wax, paper, dried cow dung, or anything else that will burn. Manufacturing costs, on a cottage industry basis: 9 cents.

The radio receives only one channel, but this is all that is broadcast in remote areas. When Papanek was told that it was ugly, he replied: 'Of course, the radio *is* ugly. But there is a reason for this ugliness. It would have been simple to paint it. But painting it would have been wrong. For one thing, it would have raised the price of each unit by maybe one-twentieth of a penny each which is a great deal of money when millions of radios are built. Secondly, and much more importantly, I feel that I have no right to make aesthetic or 'good taste' decisions that will affect millions of people who are members of a different culture.'

So what does Papanek think is good design?

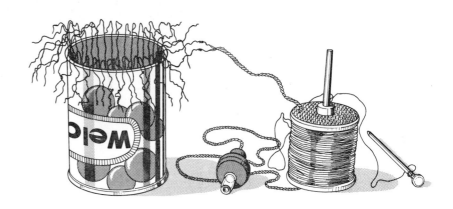

Since the early 1920s we have become used to changing styles in domestic products. After the First World War the American economy boomed as people rushed to buy their first cars, refrigerators, radios, vacuum cleaners and washing machines. However, many of these products were built 'too well'. They didn't wear out quickly enough, and manufacturers discovered that a change in appearance would make people want the latest style, even if the function of the machine had not changed at all. Some designs, though, have changed little over the years. Here are some examples:

The safety bicycle – 1905, Raleigh, England

The bicycle is an outstanding example of a machine which reached a form of mechanical perfection at an early date, and has remained essentially unchanged since.

The standard GPO telephone, 1931, Jean Helberg, Norway

There is no reason why a telephone has to look like this but, with very slight variations, this style dominated for 50 years.

The Anglepoise light, 1934, G. Cawardine, England

The light was based on the human arm, and has only altered in small details since.

The Zippo lighter, 1929 Austria, 1932 USA

This was based on an Austrian design. Perhaps the company's promise to replace parts and repair it for life was important in its success.

The Volkswagen 'Beetle' 1939, Germany

This was designed with economy, cheapness and comfort in mind. A VW advert a few years ago simply showed a 1949 'Beetle' with a collection of American cars of the same year.

The Electrolux Model 5 Vacuum cleaner, Sweden 1918

Because it was portable and had a range of attachments for specific cleaning operations it became enormously popular.

Gadgets

CARAVEL MAIL ORDER LTD

For Him

1 It's battery driven. Novelty pencil-sharpener plus extra blade. Uses three SP11 type batteries (not supplied). Height 13cm (5").
6201 Battery pencil-sharpener £3.15

2 Don't be locked out in the cold. Simply slide the rod into iced-up locks and press for a few moments for the rod to become hot. Comes with a mini-torch built-in and uses HP7 type batteries (not supplied)
143901 Hot Rod De-Icer £2.25

3 Now you have no excuse for not having a clock in the car! A digital clock with a stop watch and a soft back light is incorporated into this real leather gear knob. The clock displays hours, minutes and seconds plus the day and date. Fits most manual gear sticks.
6203 Gear Knob Clock £12.95

4 No more scraping away at frosty wind-screens. Our simple and effective frost shield not only has two suction caps to hold it in place, but tucks **inside** your car door for extra security.
126578 Frost Shield £1.85

5 International Travel Adaptor. Plug your hairdryer, curlers, shaver, tape recorder, radio, etc. into one end of the adaptor and then select the right plug connector at the opposite end. American or European plugs can be fitted. Enables you to use your appliances all over the world.
6205 Travel adaptor £3.99

6 Clears Frosted Screen A 12-volt de-froster gun which plugs into a cigar lighter socket, emitting warm air. For light frost only. Flex length 2.7m (9ft.)
6206 Defroster Gun £3.50

The new Zedex Quartz Electronic watch

This remarkable new watch has no face, no hands, no display. The neatest watch of all time—available in matt black, gold or stain-less steel finish, with matching adjustable strap. When you need to know the time simply press the button—a small strip of paper will emerge showing time, day and date. You can detach it for later reference. Why should complete strangers be able to read the time from YOUR watch? They won't with ZEDEX.
9901 ZEDEX WATCH £15.49

For The Kitchen

AVEL MAIL ORDER LTD

1 Moulinex 343· Electric can opener/knife sharpener. Can opener has magnetic lid lifter. Sharpener attachment will shar-pen most domestic knives. Free standing or wall fixed.
3301 Can Opener £11.99

2 Within minutes up to 7 eggs can be boiled as you wish, soft, medium or hard. Buzzer sounds and automatically switches off when boiled.
3302 Automatic egg boiler £11.49

3 This metal potato chipper makes chipping potatoes fast and easy. Detachable blades for cleaning and shaped easy-grip handle. Length 23cm (9").
3303 Potato chipper £3.99

4 This mini-boiler is a boon when making yourself that favourite hot drink. Whether tea, coffee or soup it can be made in an instant. Ideal for home or office or when holidaying. Length of flex 74cm.
3304 Mini-boiler £4.99

5 Salton CK1 Electric Carving Knife. Twin serrated stain-less steel blades. Knife can be wall hung and cord wrapped around base.
3305 Electric Knife £9.99

6 Cuts tomatoes, hard-boiled eggs, beetroot and new pota-toes into perfect floral shapes. Simple to use. Diameter 14cm (5½")
3306 Tomat'o'matic £2.65

7 For the housewife—this multi-purpose opener. Suit-able for various sizes of screw top jars. Can also be used as a bottle opener. Made of metal construc-tion with plastic handles. 3307 Multi-purpose Jar Opener £1.99

8 Bel de Luxe Electric Yoghurt maker. Makes plain or flav-oured yoghurt. Capacity 6×5 fl.oz. 3308 Yoghurt Maker £6.99

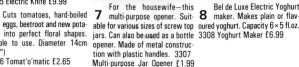

---

gadget /'gædʒɪt/ *n* (colloq) small (usu mechanical) contrivance or device: *a new ~ for opening tin cans.* ~ **ry** *n*[U] ~ s collectively.

Exercise 1

Look at the gadgets in the mail-order catalogue. Ask and answer:

What does it do?
Have you got one?/seen one?
/used one?
Is it useful?
Do you want one?
Do you need one?

If you didn't have one, how would you do the same job?
Which do you think would be quicker? Why?
Did you consider the time it might take to set up, clean and put away the gadget?
Would you buy any of the gadgets for yourself/as a present?

Language study

What	is it for?
	does it do?
	do you do with it?
	can you do with it?
	's the purpose of it?
How does it work?	

It's for (doing this).		
It's used for (doing this).		
You use it (to do this).		

You use it	so	you can	(do
	so that		this).
	in order to		

CARAVEL MAIL ORDER LTD

Health and Beauty

1 Facial sauna by Pifco breathes a warm invigorating mist deep into the pores to promote a healthier, fresher, brighter complexion. Also relieves the discomforts of nasal congestion, catarrh, colds and sinusitis. 240 volts AC only.
5701 Facial Sauna £16.95

2 New — pumice stone and nail brush combined. Handy to use at a basin or in a bath/shower, this is ideal for any home beauty treatment.
5702 Pumice stone nail brush £2.25

3 Keep your soap dry and help stop wastage with this chrome effect plastic soap holder complete with magnetic disc. Length 7.5cm (3")
5703 Soap holder 99p

4 New — the Foot Care System which soothes and relieves tired aching feet. Enjoy an invigorating massage either with or without warm water. The inbuilt thermostatically controlled system automatically maintains the water temperature.
5704 Foot Spa £34.99

5 The Philips Air Purifier contains a powerful motor and the special design 'Scrub-Air' filter. This extracts unpleasant tobacco smoke, pollen, dust and odours giving out cleaner, fresher air with a pleasant citrus scent. Filter has approximate life of 3 months continuous use.
5705 Air Purifier £14.99

6 Battery operated automatic toothbrush by Braun. Complete with four detachable brush heads. Uses one HP2 type battery (not supplied). An aid to better dental health for all your family.
5706 Electric toothbrush £9.75

CARAVEL
SUMMER·SELECTION

E. Perring
55 Norman Row
Leeds LS4 3BZ

CUSTOMER No.
7038174

Please ensure that you have entered your
Order Detail correctly before posting.

84 ROEBUCK STREET, SEARS PARK, TADWORTH TW4 7AG

Office Use Only	Catalogue Number	Size or Width	Price Each £ p	Quantity Required	Yards Metres Pack Set etc.	Colour	Description of Goods

METHOD OF PAYMENT: (please tick) ☐ Cheque ☐ Postal order ☐ Access ☐ Visa

CREDIT CARD No. ☐☐☐☐☐☐☐☐☐☐☐☐☐☐

Signature ....

Exercise 2

Look at this list of gadgets. In pairs, check the meanings, using a dictionary when necessary.

Electric toaster
Electric waffle-maker
Electric kettle
Air pressure bottle-opener
Shoe tree
Trouser press
Slow cooker
Deep-fat fryer
Humidifier
Sun-ray lamp
Infra-red lamp

Electric blanket
Food processor
Knitting machine
Eyelash curler
Potato peeler
Wristwatch/calculator
Car vacuum-cleaner
Hostess trolley
Car can-holder
Deep heat massager
Electric pizza baker
Electric food slicer
Electric hair curlers
Electric hair-styling brush
Telephone amplifier
Telephone answering machine

Ghost plane crash

DAILY EXPRESS Thursday May 19 1983 By PETER MASON

Incredible 1,600-mile flight of the Mary Celeste jet

A Lear jet..."no sign of life"

BRITISH jet fighters flew to investigate a runaway plane last night and started an amazing Mary Celeste mystery of the air.

For when they caught up with the civilian jet that had been flying for 1,600 miles, they reported: "There's no one on board."

As the plane flew on at between 44,000 and 46,000ft., RAF controllers ordered a search-and-rescue Nimrod into the air to keep track of it.

The Learjet 25—codenamed "Snoopy" with a call sign Tango Julia 184—entered British airspace shortly after 5pm.

Earlier, it had taken off from Vienna, bound for Hamburg. But it failed to land there.

West German air traffic controllers followed the plane's path to Holland—then told Dutch authorities it was heading over the North Sea towards Scotland.

A Dutch jet fighter was sent to intercept the runaway plane. The pilot buzzed it for five minutes before reporting: "It's empty."

AUTOMATIC

Then the RAF Rescue Co-ordination Centre at the Pitreavie Castle, Fife, picked up the Learjet as it crossed the coast. They sent two Phantoms after it.

Bill Harold, a spokesman for the Centre, said: "They flew very close to the aircraft and there just didn't appear to be anyone on board.

"The cockpit was apparently empty and there was no sign of life inside the cabin."

As the plane flew on towards Greenland—its course maintained by automatic pilot—aviation experts tried to solve the mystery of what happened to three people reportedly on the plane.

It is likely that the jet ran into a violent storm between Vienna and Hamburg and was hit by lightning. Either could have knocked out its electrical systems.

This, say the experts, could have caused sudden decompression inside the plane, leading to the crew losing consciousness from the effects of hypoxia—oxygen starvation.

Late last night the RAF confirmed the jet had crashed in the sea about 250 miles north-west of Stornoway in the outer Outer Hebrides.

THE SUN, Thursday, May 19 1983

RAF in a grim chase

By NIGEL FREEDMAN

A GHOST jet with no one at the controls flew hundreds of miles over Britain last night on a trip of horror.

It later plunged into the sea. But the three people on board were believed to be already dead.

They are thought to have perished hours before when pressure in the cabin of the Learjet executive plane dropped suddenly at 41,000 feet.

The jet flew on because it was on automatic pilot.

RAF Phantom fighters were scrambled to shadow it as it entered British airspace.

The ghost plane had taken off from Vienna on a short training flight to Hamburg, Germany, yesterday afternoon.

Air traffic controllers hit the panic button when it kept going and headed for Holland.

Then the ghost plane entered British airspace off Scotland and the Phantom fighters roared into the sky from Leuchars, Fife.

But they failed to make contact with the pilot and his two crewmen.

The RAF last saw the jet heading over the North Atlantic.

Stunned pilots reported: "There's nobody flying it. The pilot is slumped over the controls."

It plunged into the sea 200 miles off Iceland.

Plane disappears over Atlantic

Oxygen clue to crash of jet

By John Witherow

The West German authorities yesterday started investigating the disappearance of a private jet over the North Atlantic amid speculation that the crew of the aircraft fell unconscious during an accidental decompression.

Three pilots were on board the Learjet, one of the most widely used and reliable private aircraft in the world, when the plane changed direction on its route from Vienna to Hamburg and headed north west over Scotland towards Iceland. Dutch and RAF fighters intercepted the jet but saw no one at the controls or in the cabin.

The Federal Office of Aviation, in Brunswick, began an inquiry to determine the fate of the aircraft, which was believed to have crashed into the ocean when fuel ran out more than 300 miles north-west of Scotland.

A search on Wednesday night by an RAF Nimrod and a US Navy Orion based in Iceland over an area of 50,000 square miles found no wreckage. It was thought that the plane may have plunged into the sea and quickly sunk. The search was abandoned yesterday when it was decided there could be no survivors.

The Dusseldorf air taxi firm owning the Lear, Air Traffic GMBH, said the plane had taken a passenger to Vienna on Wednesday and the three pilots, two of them experienced captains, had decided to fly to Hamburg to carry out routine tests and add to their flying hours.

The company denied reports that the crew might have simulated a decompression for training purposes only to find that it had gone wrong. A similar incident occurred two years ago during a training flight over England. A Beechcraft Super King Air 200 crashed after the plane's captain released the cabin pressure at 30,000 ft. to demonstrate an emergency descent.

The two pilots put on masks which were not connected to the oxygen supply and were overcome by hypoxia, a state of apparent well being which quickly leads to unconsciousness. The autopilot continued to fly the aircraft and it crashed in a French vineyard seven hours after taking off.

The company's denial widened speculation that the Learjet's crew was victim of an accidental decompression and that for unknown reasons they were unable to use the emergency oxygen masks.

Captain Ian Cooper, one of the few experienced Learjet pilots in Britain, said yesterday: "It is my theory that there had been a decompression that was not apparent to the crew and that they were overcome by lack of oxygen".

He speculated that the man in the cabin would have been alerted to the fall in pressure by the appearance of the automatic oxygen masks, but that the two in the cockpit would have had to reach for them.

It was possible, he said, that the man in the cabin might have tried to drag the two men into the cabin towards the oxygen, before he too was overcome.

That could explain why two RAF Phantom jets from Leuchars, Fife, which intercepted the Learjet, could see no one at the controls. Flying Officer Mark Hanna, aged 23, piloted his Phantom to within 30 ft. of the jet nine miles above Scotland as it flew at 450 mph.

"We could see seats inside the front cockpit and the white headrests. There was certainly no one in there," he said.

The flight from Vienna, which took off at 2.53 pm, was normal until 3.49 pm, when radio contact was lost as the jet flew about 60 miles north-east of Frankfurt. The plane, which had been switched to autopilot soon after takeoff, setting a course and altitude, continued north-west as air traffic controllers alerted Nato air forces.

An aviation expert argued that the plane might have suffered a failure in the machinery which compresses the air from the twin engines and then cools it to cabin temperature.

Dr John Lemon, of the Civil Aviation Authority, said that could lead to a rapid decline in performance through hypoxia.

Exercise 1

Read the three reports. Which report:

a was the most informative
b had the most facts
c was the most sensational
d had the best headline
e was the most speculative
f was the 'best'?

Which would you prefer to read in your morning newspaper? Why?

Exercise 2

All the newspapers assume that the plane 'depressurized'. Which paper suggests each of the following reasons:

Violent storm/lightning strike
A deliberate 'practice' decompression for training
A failure in the decompression machinery
An 'accidental' decompression?

Find these 'facts' in the stories:

The plane was flying at 41,000 ft.
The plane was flying between 44,000 and 46,000 ft.
The plane flew hundreds of miles over Britain (actual figure: 180 miles).
A Dutch jet intercepted the plane first.
There was nobody in the cockpit, certainly.
There was nobody in the cockpit, apparently.
The pilot was slumped over the controls.

Listening

Independent Television News (ITN) interviewed the crew of one of the Phantom jets for *News at Ten* on May 19th 1983.
Listen to the pilot and navigator of the jet and answer the following questions:
What did they imagine might have happened initially?
What did they see in the cockpit the first time?
Were they sure?
What did they see the second time?
Which newspaper reported them least accurately?
Why do you think the navigator was relieved that there was nobody in view?

The language of newspapers

Keith Waterhouse has been a journalist for thirty years. He is also well known as a novelist, dramatist and a screen and TV writer. He writes a twice-weekly column for *The Daily Mirror*, and has written a guide book for journalists called *Daily Mirror Style* (1981). In the book he gives this example of good, popular newspaper reporting.

Bachelor Stephen Howe really has his hands full running his own home.

He even turned down a free trip to the Continent because it would interfere with his housework.

The refusal angered his bosses, who had asked him to represent them at a scientific conference in Brussels.

Stephen, 29, said: 'Spending time away from home creates a backlog of housework, gardening and laundry.'

His bosses at Stone Platt Fluid Fire, Dudley, West Midlands, were amazed.

Company chairman Nathan Myers pointed out that Stephen was the only man capable of telling the conference about research he had been doing.

And Mr. Myers went out of his way to eliminate any fears Stephen might have about the trip.

Frightened of flying? he asked Stephen.

No problem. We'll send you by sea.

Reluctant to spend two days away from home?

No problem. We'll make it a one-day trip.

But Stephen was adamant, and came up with a string of other reasons for not going. Such as . . .

- I don't possess a decent suit.
- Foreign food upsets me.
- I haven't got a passport.
- I would have to buy a suitcase.

Eventually Mr. Myers got tough. Either you go to Brussels, he said—or you're fired.

Stephen, who owns a terraced house on a luxury estate in Wolverhampton, stuck to his guns.

He took Mr. Myers to a Birmingham industrial tribunal alleging wrongful dismissal.

And the judgment went against Stephen—the houseproud bachelor who polished off his job.

False titles

Newspapers often use false titles, 'Top footballer Bryan Robson'. You only find false titles in newspapers. There are two false titles in this story. What are they?
Here are some other examples from newspapers:

DISGRACED AMERICAN PRESIDENT RICHARD NIXON...

Teenage motorcyclist Kevin Hamble...

Attractive mother-of-three June Adams...

Missing murder suspect Lord Lucan...

WHOOPING-COUGH VACCINE VICTIM JULIA BROWN...

These kind of titles are never used outside newspapers. Try and find some for students in your class, e.g. Bicycle-riding 18-year-old John Smith... Blonde genius Mary Brown ...

Exercise 1
You are a journalist. You have to report Stephen Howe's story, but you have only half the amount of space. Decide which points are most important.
Summarize the story in 120 words.

Expressions

There are several expressions used in the story. Many of these appear in newspapers regularly. Try and match the expressions in column A with the explanations in column B

Column A	Column B
He turned down a . . .	He decided to act more strongly . . .
He stuck to his guns . . .	He tried very hard (harder than he needed to)
It creates a backlog . . .	it means that work builds up . . .
He went out of his way to . . .	He refused to change his mind . . .
He got tough . . .	He's completely occupied
He has his hands full . . .	He refused an offer of . . .

Waterhouse supplied these rules for journalists:

Use specific words (*red* and *blue*) not general ones (*brightly coloured*).

Use concrete words (*rain, fog*) rather than abstract ones (*bad weather*).

Use plain words (*began, said, end*) not college-educated ones (*commenced, stated, termination*).

Use positive words (*he was poor*) not negative ones (*he was not rich* — the reader at once wants to know, how not rich was he?*).

Use the active voice (*Police took no action*) not the passive voice (*No action was taken*).

Don't overstate (*fell* is starker than *plunged*).

Don't lard the story with emotive or "dramatic" words (*astonishing, staggering, sensational, shock*).

Avoid non-working words that cluster together like derelicts (*but for the fact that, the question as to whether, there is no doubt that*).

Don't use words thoughtlessly. (*Waiting ambulances don't rush victims to hospital. Waiting ambulances wait. Meteors fall, so there can be no meteoric rise.*)

Don't use auxiliaries or conditionals (*was, might, would, should, may* etc) unless you have to. (*Mrs Thatcher is a political Florence Nightingale*, not *Mrs Thatcher might be termed a political Florence Nightingale.*)

Don't use unknown quantities (*very, really, truly, quite.* How much is *very*?).

Never qualify absolutes. (A thing cannot be *quite impossible, glaringly obvious* or *most essential*, any more than it can be *absolutely absolute.*)

Don't use wrong prepositions. Check them for sense (*we may agree on this point; you may agree with this opinion; he may agree to this proposal.*)

Don't use jargon, clichés, puns, elegant or inelegant variations, or inexact synonyms (*BRAVE WIFE DIED SAVING HER SON* is wrong: *wife* is not a synonym for *mother*).

Use short sentences, but not all of the same length. A succession of one-clause sentences is monotonous and wearying.

Avoid elaborate construction. Take the sentence to pieces and recast it — probably as two sentences.

If a sentence reads as if it has something wrong with it, it has something wrong with it. (*Whether you are motoring to see Mum, play trains in a railway museum or in a stately home, this long Spring weekend can bring agony and death* is technically correct, but ugly.)

Don't vary your rhythms for the sake of it. (*He was not ill, and neither was he poor* is unnecessary variation. But there is a dramatic unity in *He was not ill. He was not poor.*)

Even in a chronological narrative, the story should not start before it begins. (*John Smith was really looking forward to his dinner* starts too early; the reader wants the dinner. Compare this with the opening of a short story by O Henry: *So I went to the doctor.* A whole paragraph has happened offstage, and the reader is plunged straight into the action.)

Words are facts. Check them (spelling and meaning) as you would any other.

Exercise 2

Imagine the stories that might go with these headlines:

Oldest sailor goes round the world
Miracle cure for car crash victim
From a million pounds to nothing – in 6 months!
Influenza epidemics caused by UFOs?
Rock star arrested at airport
Record robbery rocks Rochester
Whatever happened to the summer?

Write the stories out as very brief reports. For example:

Oldest sailor goes round the world
Jack Daniels, an 80-year-old yachting enthusiast, today left Portsmouth. He plans to sail around the world. He set off towards Canada, and expects to arrive in mid-March. Full story p.15.

Exercise 3

Work in groups to assemble a class newspaper.

	Name of newspaper	Date of first publication	Circulation (June 1982)	Political viewpoint
'Quality' or 'serious' papers (Broadsheet size)	THE TIMES	1785	300,700	Independent
	THE GUARDIAN	1821	420,271	Left of centre (Liberal/SDP)
	THE DAILY TELEGRAPH	1855	1,305,575	Conservative
	THE FINANCIAL TIMES	1888	202,545	Conservative
'Popular papers' (Tabloid size)	THE MORNING STAR	1966	30,345	Communist
	THE DAILY EXPRESS	1900	2,034,096	Conservative
	THE DAILY MAIL	1896	1,894,460	Conservative
	THE DAILY MIRROR	1903	3,355,688	Labour
	THE DAILY STAR	1978	1,390,628	Right of centre
	THE SUN	1969	4,077,891	Right of centre

Belief, doubt and certainty

Roy Clark is an investigator for an insurance company. He's investigating a fire at a small warehouse. The contents were insured for half a million pounds. He's talking to Dave Grimes, the owner.

Dave Look, I can't see what you're here for. I've filled out all the forms, right? When do I get my money?

Roy It's not quite that simple, Mr Grimes. We have to be absolutely sure of every detail before we pay you.

Dave It's all on the form, isn't it?

Roy Yes ... well. Where did the fire start?

Dave How should I know? It was three o'clock in the morning.

Roy On the form you've put 'the reception area' down.

Dave That's what the fire brigade thought. I've got no idea.

Roy But you put it on the form.

Dave They said it must have started there – Look, it destroyed half a million quid's worth of stuff!

Roy There's some dispute about that figure. I'll have to see invoices and delivery notes for it, I'm afraid.

Dave Are you calling me a liar?

Roy No, no. I don't doubt your word for a moment, Mr Grimes.

Dave Oh, all right, then.

Roy I'm sorry, but I'm bound to ask you the next question, and please believe me that I'm not disputing your statement ... but is it true that business has been very bad recently?

Dave Who said that? That's nonsense.

Roy As a matter of fact there was a newspaper report a few weeks ago. It said that there would be 20 redundancies here.

Dave Oh, yeah. Well, we're reorganizing.

Roy I see. No doubt the newspaper was exaggerating.

Dave That's right.

Roy It's just that my manager has raised some questions about your business. You must understand that it's hard for us to see ... to see how you could possibly sell half a million pounds worth of electric coffee stirrers. We just can't believe that anybody would buy them ...

Dave Are you accusing me of arson ... saying I set light to the place myself ...

Roy I didn't say that ... it's just, er, slightly suspicious that ...

Language study

Certainty/Belief

I'm sure .../certain .../convinced ...

It's obvious .../certain ...

I know .../don't doubt/have no doubt ...

There's no doubt .../question .../dispute ...

It's bound (to happen)/sure/certain

It must .../must be .../must have been .../can't .../can't be .../can't have been ...

Without doubt .../No doubt .../Doubtless .../I believe .../It's my belief ...

Doubt/Uncertainty

I don't know ...

I'm not sure .../certain .../convinced ...

I doubt if .../whether ...

I have doubts about ...

I doubt .../suspect .../mistrust .../question .../dispute ...

There are some doubts .../is some doubt ...

I'm unsure .../uncertain ...

Truth

... to tell the truth .../... in fact .../... in truth .../... in reality .../as a matter of fact .../in actual fact .../in point of fact ...

Exercise
Say what you think about:

life on other planets
life after death
ghosts
magic
the abominable snowman
planes and ships lost in the Bermuda Triangle
astrology
extra-sensory perception (ESP)

Do you believe the following?

margarine tastes the same as butter
vitamin C cures colds
walking under ladders is unlucky
the number 13 is unlucky
oranges are good for you
too much fatty food is bad for you
cigarettes cause cancer

Do you believe everything you hear?

Game

In groups of three or four compile a list of facts about one member of the group. These should be facts that the rest of the class do not know. Each member should note the facts. They should then each present the facts as true about *themselves* to another group. The second group asks questions. They guess which member of the first group is telling the truth.

HUGGINS Dr Michael on 23rd June at Maltchester General Hospital. Funeral 29 June, Maltchester Crematorium. No flowers. Donations to Cancer Research.

My eyes caught the obituary. Dr Huggins. Well, at last he would find out about the afterlife for certain. For certain ... but he had never doubted it anyway. I suppose it was ten years ago that we met. I was living in the small town where he bred pedigree spaniels, rode an ancient bicycle, and practised medicine. Over a three-year period, I saw rather a lot of him. After all, I had four children of school age. I remember long hours waiting in his tiny surgery. Dr Huggins never hurried anybody, so the queues became rather long. At last the bell would ring, and you would enter his office, which was as scruffy, warm and comfortable as its occupant. Then you would be confronted by his unending enthusiasm, his enthusiasm for anything and everything mysterious and strange. Dr Huggins believed in UFOs, astrology, the lost Atlantis, the extra-terrestrial origin of both the banana

and the common cold, lucky numbers and unlucky cats. He wasn't simply gullible. As he always said, he took a scientific interest in the unexplained. A visit might begin with a detailed discussion of your child's adenoids and end with a short lecture on ... on anything. The shroud of Turin, extra-sensory perception or Vitamin C. Susan and I would often laugh about poor Dr Huggins and his beliefs. We were cynical, and we both felt that cynicism was a healthy thing. But now, when I look back on his plump, red face glowing with excitement as he explained his latest theory, I think that perhaps I envied him. For him, life was always full of a sense of wonder, each day brought a new puzzle, a new theory, a new explanation.

Harry

In tonight's edition of *Reflections* we are going to look at the problems of long-term prisoners. We took our cameras into several prisons, and our first interview is with a man we shall call 'Harry', although that is not his real name. He spoke to Chloe West about his career in crime.

Chloe Harry, you're serving a five-year sentence for robbery with violence.

Harry That's right.

Chloe Perhaps you could begin by telling us about your early life.

Harry Yeah. Well, I grew up in South London. I was on my own a lot; see, my mother used to work down the fish market, and my dad – well, he ran off when I was just a nipper.

Chloe Did you have any friends?

Harry Oh, yeah. All the kids from our street used to meet up at the coffee bar. There was one at the end of the road. We didn't have much money, so we used to hang round there all day. We never used to go to the cinema, or dancing, or anything like that. We couldn't afford it.

Chloe What did you use to do there?

Harry Oh, we just sat around listening to the juke box. Nothing special.

Chloe When did you start getting into trouble?

Harry I suppose I was fourteen, something like that. My friends used to go shoplifting at Woolies ... Woolworths, and one day we were caught. I ended up in Borstal.

Chloe You mean, they sent you to Borstal for ... for shoplifting?

Harry Well, yeah. After the fourth time ... and for beating-up old ladies.

Chloe You used to beat-up old ladies?

Harry Well, only when I was trying to rob them.

Chloe You beat them up and then robbed them?

Harry Yeah. I used to do that.

Chloe Perhaps you'd tell me about your life in prison.

Harry I suppose the worst thing is being shut up all the time. Yeah, and I can't stand getting up at 5.30, either. I just can't get used to that, even though I've been here more than three years. You see, before I came here I liked staying in bed all morning. I was on night work, you see.

Chloe Night work?

Harry Mmm. Burglary, mostly. Hah-ha. I caught you there. I can't get used to going to bed at eight, either.

Chloe Harry, if you don't mind me saying so, a lot of viewers will think of you as an enemy of society.

Harry Well, that's fair enough. But I've admitted doing a lot of things. I've spent a lot of time thinking. I could keep on stealing things, but I'd end up spending half my life behind bars. I'm going straight this time, don't you worry.

Chloe What do you intend doing when you get out?

Harry I'm very fond of working on motor-bikes. I've been studying while I've been inside, and I'm hoping to qualify as a mechanic.

Chloe Do you think you'll be able to get a job?

Harry That's a bit of a problem. People are scared of employing someone with a record like mine, you know, in case they begin stealing again.

Chloe How will you get round that?

Harry I'm planning on working for my brother. He's got a motor-bike shop.

Chloe So, you plan to work for your brother?

Harry That's right. I tell you, I won't be back. I'm not going to risk wasting another five years.

Chloe Well, I wish you luck, Harry.

Harry Thanks.

| She *used* to work in the market. |
| We *never used* / *didn't use* to go out much. |
| What did you *use* to do? |

Exercise 1

Ask and answer in pairs.
Think back to your childhood.
Where did your father use to work?
Did your mother use to work?
What did you use to like doing?
What did you use to dislike doing?
What subjects did you use to study at school then?
Which ones did you use to enjoy/dislike doing?

Exercise 2

We didn't have much money *so* we used to hang round there all day.
or
They used to hang round there *because* they didn't have much money.

Make two sentences with *used to* for each of the following:
1 not much money/not go dancing
2 not much time/not study
3 not many friends/not go to parties
4 not much interest in politics/not read newspapers
5 not much money/not go to pubs
6 not much time/not go to night school

Exercise 3

Harry's parents were poor. List ten things they couldn't afford to do.
List ten things you can't afford to do.
Write sentences beginning:
Even if I could afford it, I wouldn't ...

Exercise 4

Listen to Chloe saying:

You used to beat up old ladies?
... they sent you to Borstal for shoplifting?
You beat them up and then robbed them?

Practise expressing surprise to these statements about Harry:

1 He used to steal cars.
2 He often got into fights.
3 He robbed a bank.
4 He once beat up a policeman.
5 He ran off with his own mother's handbag.
6 He worked for a famous gang.

Exercise 5

The worst thing for Harry is getting up early.
He can't get used to getting up early.

Make sentences about other prisoners, using the following prompts:

1 George/peel potatoes
2 Jack/eat prison food
3 Mike/be locked up
4 Nobby/make mail bags
5 Chris/break rocks
6 Ernie/take orders

Exercise 6

If you were in prison, what wouldn't you be able to get used to? Write four sentences.

Exercise 7

Listen to the conversation again, and mark any verbs which are mentioned in the Language study.

Language study

Some verbs which take the *-ing* form

Liking and disliking	Stopping, starting and continuing	Fear, etc.	Feelings, attitudes with *to be*	Other important examples	
like*	stop*	*to be* afraid of	*to be* tired of	remember*	can't help
love*	start*	scared of	interested in	recollect	resent
enjoy	begin*	frightened of	bored with	recall	risk
dislike	finish	terrified of	excited about	try*	miss
hate	cease		fond of	admit	omit*
loathe	continue*		keen on	deny	recommend*
fancy	give up		worried about	suggest	advise*
can't stand	carry on		annoyed about	propose*	spend time
can't bear	delay		fed up with	intend*	to be used for
can't face	keep (on)			imagine	to get used to
	leave off*			mind	plan on
	end up				think of
	burst out				
	commence				

*Verbs which can also take an infinitive.

Exercise 8

Practise with a partner.

Imagine you are going to be together for a long time (in a prison cell, on a desert island, on a spaceship). List your likes and dislikes, feelings, attitudes and fears. Compare them. See how easily (or not!) you will get on together.

Video games

Read the text quickly. Then read it again and note down the dates mentioned and what happened then.

It all began at the University of Utah. Nolan Bushnell was an undergraduate who used to play space games on the computer in the engineering laboratory. He invented *Pong*, a television table tennis game. Electronic bats pushed a ball back and forth across a black and white TV screen. You could play another person, or more importantly play against the computer. The game went on the market in 1973, and by the end of the year pubs, bars and cafés around the world resounded with the irritating 'blip-blip' of the game. Bushnell sold the idea for 13 million dollars, and went on to found Atari, the leading video-game manufacturer. Today the descendants of *Pong* earn more than 13 million dollars a day.

The idea was developed in Japan, and the video games explosion came in 1978 when Taito inc. launched *Space Invaders*. It was quickly followed by a host of spin-offs, *Defender, Asteroids, Galaxian,* *Centipede, Pac-Man* and *Donkey-Kong*. By 1981 the video games industry was earning twice as much money worldwide as the entire movie industry. There were reports of coin shortages in several countries because the machines had swallowed all the loose change. Then came the reports of video game-related crime, as teenagers stole to support an addiction to the games that could cost £20 a day. The games were banned in the Philippines. West Germany restricted them to the over-18s, France to the over 16s. A move to ban them in Britain was defeated in Parliament. Several American towns restricted the number of machines. In one city, truancy became such a problem that kids were required to show a perfect school attendance record before being admitted to video arcades.

But video games have a natural tendency to become obsolete. It costs a lot of money to master a game, and takes several weeks of determined effort. However, once a game has been mastered you can play all day for 20p, because you will be able to gain free games every time you play. Then, of course, the game becomes boring, and you have to abandon *Space Invaders*, or *Missile Command*, and move on to *Asteroids*, or *Pac-Man*. Then the whole cycle begins again. By 1983 there were too many machines in too many places, and Arcade owners found that a new game would take huge sums of money for a few weeks. At the end of that time, the regular customers would have mastered it, and it would be abandoned to gather dust in the corner. It was said that the 5-year-old boom was over. The home versions of the games had become more sophisticated, and the arcades began to close. While the manufacturers are still spending millions of pounds on research – and one game can cost one million pounds to develop – the boom could begin all over again when a new, more exciting, more complex game arrives on the scene.

Space Invaders – what is it?

So, how do you play *Space Invaders*? You control a 'tank', which you can move from left to right. Rows of bomb-dropping 'aliens' move back and forth across the screen, gradually getting nearer. There are four shields to protect you from the bombs, but these get smaller and smaller as the bomb blasts remove sections of them. Your aim is to emerge from beneath your shield and fire at the aliens, destroying them one at a time. When (or rather *if*) you destroy one complete wave of aliens, another one appears lower down the screen and moving faster. It will probably take 100 attempts to learn to destroy the first wave, at 20p an attempt. There are nine waves.

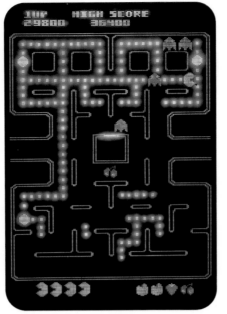

Pac-Man

By 1982 the USA had 60,000 *Space Invaders* machines – but 96,000 *Pac-Man* games. It has been claimed that the Space games, with their war themes, appealed mainly to men. *Pac-Man*, it was said, appealed equally to both sexes. Like many of the modern games *Pac-Man* attempts to instil some humour into the contest. You are a lemon that races around a maze 'eating' electronic dots. You are pursued by Pac-Men. You can reverse the process and chase and eat the Pac-Men. It may sound pretty silly, but it is the most popular game of all.

Martin Amis is a novelist, and the author of *Invasion of the Space Invaders*. This is how he describes his first encounter with a *Space Invader* game.

Exercise 1

Write a paragraph on the history of videogames. Use your notes to help you.

Exercise 2

Invent a videogame of your own or think of one you know. Draw a screen for it and write instructions to go on the machine. Tell another student how to use it.

SUDDENLY ONE SUMMER

It happened in 1979. I was in the South of France—that summer, when the Invasion began.

I was sitting in a bar near the railway station in Toulon. I was drinking coffee and writing letters and generally minding my own business. The bar had a pinball machine, a creaking old hulk with a card-game motif. There were only a few locals in there at the time. Suddenly there was commotion, and the fat, aproned maitre began to supervise a delivery at the door. Grunting heavies were wrestling with what looked like a sheeted refrigerator. They installed it in the corner, plugged it in , and drew back the veil. The Invasion of the Space Invaders had begun.

Now I had played quite a few bar machines in my time. I had driven toy cars, toy aeroplanes, toy submarines, I had shot toy cowboys, toy tanks, toy sharks. But I knew instantly that this was something different, something special. Cinematic melodrama blazing on the screen, infinite firing capacity, the beautiful responsiveness of the defending turret, the sting and pow of the missiles, the background pulse of the quickening heartbeat, the inexorable descent of the bomb-dumping monsters: my awesome task, to save Earth from destruction!

The bar closed at eleven o'clock that night. I was the last to leave, tired but content. The owner's wife smiled at me understandingly as I stumbled out. At first I thought it was just a holiday romance. But deep down I knew all along that this was the real thing. I had been ravished, transfigured, swept away. I had been Invaded.

Now, after nearly three years, the passion has not cooled. I don't see much of Space Invaders any more, it's true—though we're still good friends. These days I fool around with a whole harem of newer, brasher machines. When I get bored with one of them, a younger replacement is always available. (I still spend the odd night with Space Invaders, my first love—just for old times' sake.) The only trouble is, they take up all my time and all my money. And I can't seem to find any girlfriends.

Medical advice

Listening

Before you listen, discuss what advice you would give to someone who was starting a common cold. Make a list of things they could do.

Listen to the recording. Are any of your ideas mentioned? Which ones? Does Dr Lines agree with them?

Answer these questions:

1 How do you get a cold?
2 How much vitamin C seems to help?
3 What's Dr Lines' final advice?
4 What do you think 'an old wives' tale' is?
5 Do you know any other old wives' tales?

Letters

Dear Doctor,
Every time we go out in the car, our little boy gets very sick. Our other two children have no problems. Is there anything we can do? (Mrs. Thomas, Norwich)

Many people experience severe sickness when travelling by road, sea or air. It is usually caused by the unusual motion which upsets the balance mechanism of the ear. Most children grow out of car sickness. It is important to distract the child sufferer. You should try not to mention the possibility of being sick. It's a good idea to take lots of games, toys and puzzles on the journey. Make sure the children can see out of the window and remember to keep the window open slightly. Fresh air helps. Stop the car frequently and let the children walk about. There are several anti-sickness medicines but I wouldn't advise you to use them without consulting your doctor.

Dear Doctor,
When I was in the navy some years ago I had a tattoo on my forearm. It was the name of my girlfriend at that time. I am now engaged to another girl and we are going to get married next year. The tattoo is very embarrassing. Can I have it removed? (Mark Kane, Liverpool)

This problem is a very common one. Whatever you do, don't try to remove it yourself. You may cause a permanently disfiguring scar. A tattoo can be removed by abrasion, either by hand or by using a high speed rotary drill. This always involves a local anaesthetic. If it is available, laser treatment can give very good results. In some cases, plastic surgery may be necessary. Your family doctor will advise you. I suppose there is a moral here. Young people should always think twice before having anything as permanent as a tattoo. They often regret it later.

Dear Doctor,
I have just been told that my daughter is colour blind. Can anything be done about it and how will it affect her future? (Mrs. Wade, Chorley)

Colour blindness affects almost five per cent of the population and far more men than women. Difficulty in distinguishing between colours, particularly red and green, is an inherited defect. It rarely causes serious problems. A child soon learns that grass is green and blood is red or that the top light is red and the bottom light is green on a column of traffic lights. For most people there is no problem living with colour blindness. It does not prevent a person becoming a lorry driver or a bus driver. Some colour blind people even become painters or fashion designers. There are a few jobs where perfect colour vision is essential, such as an airline pilot or electrician.

NOSE-BLEED

A common complaint, affecting mainly the young or middle-aged.
Symptoms
Bleeding from one or both nostrils.
Duration
Most nose-bleeds stop within an hour.
Causes
Often none, but common colds, picking, vigorous blowing or sneezing, nose or head injury, pressure changes. HYPERTENSION and SINUSITIS can all cause bleeding. Occasionally BLOOD disorders may be responsible.
Complications
None likely.
Treatment in the home
Sit upright in a chair with the head slightly forward and firmly pinch the soft part of the nose for at least 15 minutes. Swallow or spit out any blood going down the back of the nose. Breathe through the mouth. After 15 minutes release the nostrils and sit quietly. If bleeding restarts, squeeze the nostrils for a further 15 minutes.
When bleeding stops, sit quietly or lie down for a while. Do not blow the nose for at least three hours.
When to consult the doctor
If a nose-bleed cannot be stopped by the above measures (particularly in an elderly person), or if so much blood is lost that the patient becomes pale or dizzy.
If nose-bleeds recur.
What the doctor may do
Numb the nose with a local anaesthetic and then pack it with gauze or an inflatable balloon.
Severe cases will be sent to hospital.
Check the blood pressure for hypertension and provide treatment if necessary.
CAUTERISE blood vessels that are prone to bleed.
Prevention
Do not pick the nose or insert foreign objects into it.

DANDRUFF

Scales of dead skin from the scalp. It is most common in early adulthood, but may occur at other ages.
Symptoms
Dry scales showering on to clothing and surrounds.
Less commonly the scales are greasy and stuck to the head and scalp. These cause severe irritation. If removed by scratching, the skin may bleed.
Duration
This depends on how the condition is managed.
Causes
The cause is not known. The tendency is inherited and the greasier the skin the worse the dandruff.
Treatment in the home
Twice weekly use of detergent shampoo helps: for example, one containing 1 per cent of cetrimide.
In the more severe forms, proprietary preparations containing salicylic acid, tar or selenium should be tried.
When to consult the doctor
If the scalp becomes infected after scratching the head.
If the scales persist or get worse after several weeks of home treatment.
If the scales appear to be thick.
What the doctor may do
Check that the scales are not caused by an infection.
Give further advice on how to treat the dandruff.
Prevention
No specific steps are available. See SEBORRHOEA.
Outlook
Dandruff can be controlled even if not cured.

HICCUPS

Repeated and involuntary spasms of the diaphragm.
Duration
An attack is usually over in ten to twenty minutes, though prolonged bouts may occur. Persistent hiccups suggest there are underlying abnormalities.
Causes
Irritation of the diaphragm by overfilling the stomach after swallowing an excess of food or drink—especially hot fluids.
Some bouts seem to have no cause.
Rarely, kidney, liver, lung and abdominal disorders.
Treatment in the home
Carbon dioxide inhibits hiccups, and simply holding the breath several times will allow carbon dioxide to build up in the body.
Breathing in and out of a paper bag works the same way. *Do not* use a plastic bag as this may fatally obstruct respiration. Most other successful home remedies act by making the patient hold his breath.
Sucking ice, drinking water slowly, inducing vomiting, and pulling on the tongue are ways of trying to stop hiccups.
When to consult the doctor
If you have persistent or recurrent bouts of hiccups that last more than a day.
What the doctor may do
Prescribe a sedative by mouth or injection. *See* MEDICINES, 17.
Arrange a supply of 5 per cent carbon dioxide for you to inhale.

Exercise 1
Study the ailments above and write brief replies to the following letters.

Dear Doctor,
My children often suffer from nose bleeds. Can you advise me?
(Mrs Travis, Swindon)

Dear Doctor,
I can't seem to get rid of my dandruff. I have tried shampoos but they don't seem to work. Is there anything I can do?
(Ms Davis, Leeds)

Dear Doctor,
I frequently get hiccups. What is the cause of them and what can I do about them?
(Mr Young, Oxford)

Exercise 2
Discuss with a friend what you would do about the following ailments:
a headache
a cold
sunburn
a twisted ankle
indigestion
spots on the face
baldness
cold sores
chapped lips
a cut finger

Close encounters

Is there something dangerous in encouraging us to hate and fear possible visitors from outer space? Steven Spielberg thinks so, and Spielberg's phenomenal popular success with *Close Encounters of the Third Kind* and *E.T.* may be helping to change the attitudes of a generation. Spielberg's aliens are gentle, even vulnerable. Their aims are unfrightening; to communicate with us in *Close Encounters*, or to collect flowers and plants in *E.T.*. In both films, when frightening creatures appear in spacesuits, they are investigators from Earth governments.

Spielberg is an important director, if only for his ability to relate to the emotions of large numbers of people. His 1975 film *Jaws* (one of the two Top-Ten films not on a sci-fi theme) emptied beaches all over the world. He is proud of the fact that *Close Encounters* inspired interest instead of fear, and that '*E.T.* inspired affection in place of terror'. We can only hope that should an alien spaceship ever land on Earth, then the reception party will have been influenced by Spielberg's vision, not that of his contemporary directors.

Close Encounters of the Third Kind (Special edition)

Roy Neary is a repair man for an electricity company. He sees UFOs near his home. His home is in Indiana. Jillian Guiler sees them. She is with her son, Barry. Both of them become obsessed by a vision of a mountain. Roy makes models of the mountain with several different things, e.g. shaving foam, mashed potato, clay. His wife thinks he is crazy, not really influenced by a UFO. Jillian and Barry also try to recreate the mountain, e.g. by drawings, children's models. All over the world people are affected by the vision, and by a strange tune they remember, e.g. we see a crowd chanting the tune in India. The investigation is led by a Frenchman, his name is Claude Lacombe. He is played by the French director Francois Truffaut. We see the investigators in various places, e.g. Mongolia. Roy and Jillian meet again. Many people are watching for UFOs. They see a light. It is a helicopter, not a UFO. Roy's wife and children leave him. He makes a huge model of the mountain. Jillian and Barry live alone. One night they see lights, and hear a UFO. Jillian locks all the doors. Electric appliances switch themselves on and off. She is afraid. Barry is interested, not afraid. He wants to go out. There is a 'cat door' in the front door. The cat can use it to go in and out when the door is locked. Barry is pulled through the door. A strange light seems to pull him. She had locked all the doors but not the cat door. Barry disappears with the UFO.

The investigators are picking up radio signals from space. They discover the signals are numbers. They discover the numbers are a map reference. They look it up. It is a mountain in Wyoming. It is called 'Devil's Tower'. It's the mountain in Roy and Jillian's vision. The investigators are expecting a UFO landing. They close the area to the public. They give false reports on TV of a train crash. They say the train was carrying nerve gas. The area is evacuated. Roy and Jillian see the mountain on TV. They rush to the area. Everybody is wearing gas masks, but not Roy and Jillian. Finally they put on gasmasks. They are 'arrested'. The soldiers arrest them. They are wearing space suits. There are 10 or 12 people like them. They all had a vision and rushed to the area. They are put in a helicopter. The investigators want to send them away. Roy, Jillian and another man escape. The helicopter takes away the people who had had the vision, but not Roy, Jillian and the other man. They climb the mountain. Helicopters drop sleeping gas on the mountain. The third man falls asleep, but not Roy and Jillian. They see the UFO land. It communicates with the musical notes. The notes all of them imagined. A door opens. A lot of humans come out. They had all disappeared since 1947 or 1948. Barry comes out. He runs to Jillian. A group of earthmen prepare to go onto the spaceship. Roy wants to go. he dresses in uniform. They go onto the spaceship. We see an alien. He has a large head and thin, spidery limbs. The film ends.

Exercise 1

The notes on Spielberg's *Close Encounters of the Third Kind* are written in short sentences, with a lot of repetition. Write them out again, using the Language study section to give variety. Try and connect the sentences with relative pronouns, *and, but, because* or *so*. For example: 'Roy Neary is an electricity repair man *who* sees UFO's near his home in Indiana'.

Exercise 2

Read this brief biography of Steven Spielberg, and write it out as a connected paragraph.

Steven Spielberg – born Cincinnati, Ohio, 1946. Raised Phoenix, Arizona. Started making 8mm and 16mm films at High School. Majored in English at California State, but main interest experimental movies. 1st 35mm film was *Amblin'*, which Spielberg wrote, directed and edited. Signed to Universal as a TV Director. Made *Duel* for TV, but such a success that it was released for the cinema.

1975 film *Jaws* made him famous. Other films *Close Encounters of the Third Kind, Poltergeist, 1941, Sugar Land Express, Twilight Zone, E.T.* and *Gremlins*. He also made *Raiders of the Lost Ark* and *Indiana Jones* with George Lucas. They have collaborated for years, and together absolutely dominate the cinema of the last decade. Keeps himself to himself. Makes lots of movies and lots of money, but avoids the 'Rolls-Royce' Hollywood image.

Exercise 3

Describe the plot of a favourite film (or book, or TV programme) to a partner. Listen to his/her description of a favourite film. Ask each other questions about the story.

Write out the plot of your favourite film/book/programme for homework.

Language study

Give examples	Make exceptions	Replacement and contrast
For example	... except (Spielberg)	... interest not fear
For instance	... but not (Spielberg)	rather than
	... with the exception of (Spielberg)	instead of
The best-known example ...	... excepting (Spielberg)	in place of
A well-known example ...		
One example is ...		
... such as ...		

Chinese horoscopes

Most people are aware of their astrological signs, and know the characteristics associated with the twelve signs of the zodiac. Astrology is based upon your month of birth. Traditional Chinese astrology is different. It's based on your year of birth. There are twelve signs, too, but they are named after animals. The Chinese New Year falls on a different date each year, but it begins somewhere between mid-January and mid-February. You will have to use the chart below to find out your Chinese sign. The twelve-year cycle begins with the year of the Rat, which this century first fell in 1900, so it is easy to calculate Chinese years. The legend is that the order was decided thousands of years ago by Buddha, who called all the animals to a New Year meeting. Only twelve came, and the years were named after the twelve animals in the order in which they arrived. First was the aggressive Rat, second was the hard-working Ox. Then came the smiling Tiger, followed by the cautious Rabbit. The showy Dragon came next, then the wise Snake. The gifted Horse was next, followed by the gentle Goat, then the merry Monkey and the proud Rooster. Last were the faithful Dog and the honest Pig.

People born in specific years are supposed to have characteristics of the year's animal. This should not be taken too seriously. The animals are symbols, and the Chinese idea of each animal's character is often different from a traditional Western view. The interesting thing about the cycle of Chinese years is that they relate to the cycles of change in the Sun, which is known to affect the Earth's weather, and may also relate to earthquakes and electrical changes in the atmosphere.

It's up to you how seriously you take them. Anyway, it makes a change when someone comes up to you and says, 'I can always tell people's birth signs – you're a Virgo'. You can always reply by saying, 'And I can always tell people's Chinese signs. You're a Pig!'

Calculate your sign

Key: 18.2.12–6.2.13 = 18th February 1912 – 6th February 1913

The Rat	The Ox	The Tiger	The Rabbit	The Dragon	The Snake
31.1.00–19.2.01	20.2.01–8.2.02	9.2.02–29.1.03	30.1.03–16.2.04	17.2.04–4.2.05	5.2.05–25.1.06
19.2.12–6.2.13	7.2.13–26.1.14	27.1.14–14.2.15	15.2.15–3.2.16	4.2.16–23.1.17	24.1.17–11.2.18
6.2.24–25.1.25	26.1.25–13.2.26	14.2.26–2.2.27	3.2.27–23.1.28	24.1.28–10.2.29	11.2.29–30.1.30
25.1.36–11.2.37	12.2.37–31.1.38	1.2.39–19.2.39	20.2.39–8.2.40	9.2.40–27.1.41	28.1.41–15.2.42
11.2.48–29.1.49	30.1.49–17.2.50	18.2.50–6.2.51	7.2.51–27.1.52	28.1.52–14.2.53	15.2.53–3.2.54
29.1.60–15.2.61	16.2.61–5.2.62	6.2.62–25.1.63	26.1.63–13.2.64	14.2.64–2.2.65	3.2.65–21.1.66
15.2.72–2.2.73	3.2.73–22.1.74	23.1.74–10.2.75	11.2.75–30.1.76	31.1.76–17.2.77	18.2.77–6.2.78
2.2.84–19.2.85	20.2.85–8.2.86	9.2.86–28.1.87	29.1.87–16.2.88	17.2.88–5.2.89	6.2.89–26.1.90
19.2.96–6.2.97	7.2.97–27.1.98	28.1.98–15.2.99	16.2.99–4.2.2000		

The Horse	The Goat	The Monkey	The Rooster	The Dog	The Pig
26.1.06–13.2.07	14.2.07–2.2.08	3.2.08–22.1.09	23.1.09–10.2.10	11.2.10–30.1.11	31.1.11–18.2.12
12.2.18–1.2.19	2.2.19–20.2.20	21.2.20–8.2.21	9.2.21–28.1.22	29.1.22–16.2.23	17.2.23–5.2.24
31.1.30–17.2.31	18.2.31–6.2.32	7.2.32–26.1.33	27.1.33–14.2.34	15.2.34–4.2.35	5.2.35–24.1.36
16.2.42–5.2.43	6.2.43–25.1.44	26.1.44–13.2.45	14.2.45–2.2.46	3.2.46–22.1.47	23.1.47–10.2.48
4.2.54–24.1.55	25.1.55–12.2.56	13.2.56–31.1.57	1.2.57–16.2.58	17.2.58–8.2.59	9.2.59–28.1.60
22.1.66–9.2.67	10.2.67–29.1.68	30.1.68–16.2.69	17.2.69–5.2.70	6.2.70–26.1.71	27.1.71–14.2.72
7.2.78–27.1.79	28.1.79–15.2.80	16.2.80–4.2.81	5.2.81–24.1.82	25.1.82–12.2.83	13.2.82–1.2.84
27.1.90–14.2.91	15.2.91–3.2.92	4.2.92–22.1.93	23.1.93–9.2.94	10.2.94–30.1.95	31.1.95–18.2.96

Exercise 1
Look at the chart of characteristics for each sign. Work out your sign, and the signs of three people you know very well. Go through the list, putting a tick (√) by characteristics you think are right, a cross (x) against ones you think are wrong, or a zero (0) if you don't know. Be honest – especially the Monkeys – and open-minded – especially the Oxen!

Exercise 2
Compare your results with a partner's. Try and assess each other. Do the same in a group. How well do you think the signs work?

Exercise 3
Look at the famous names given for each sign. How many of their characteristics match the ones you have heard of?

Exercise 4
Draw up a table on a separate sheet of paper. Divide it into columns, labelled as follows:
___ ic/ ___ ous/ ___ able/ ___ ive/ ___ al/ ___ ish/ ___ ful/ ___ less/ ___ ent/ ___ y/ ___ ed/
Put the words from the chart in the columns. Try to add five words to each of the columns.

Exercise 5
'Rats are small-minded.'
How many compounds like 'small-minded' can you find? Add any other words you know of the same type to a list.

Exercise 6
a Rats are *not only* charming, *but also* generous.
b *Although* Rats are generous, they can *also* be greedy.
c Rats can be energetic. *In addition,* they can be persistent.
d Rats can be energetic. *Also,* they can be persistent.
e Rats can be energetic. *Furthermore,* they can be persistent.
Use the five patterns (a–e) above, and make five sentences for each of the other signs.

Exercise 7
Read through the lists of qualities again, and mark all the words beginning with: un ___ / dis ___ / mis ___ / non ___ Try to think of more words of each type.

Exercise 8
Write a paragraph about yourself. The title is: 'Why I am/am not a typical ___ '.

The Rat	The Ox	The Tiger	The Rabbit	The Dragon	The Snake
aggressive	hard-working	smiling	cautious	showy	wise
energetic	lonely	magnetic	clever	artistic	sympathetic
jolly	leaders	lucky	hospitable	enthusiastic	lucky
charming	strong	strong	sociable	lucky	sophisticated
sociable	proud	honourable	friendly	healthy	calm
humorous	reserved	leaders	sensitive	generous	decisive
generous	methodical	liberal-minded	ambitious	sentimental	attractive
intellectual	original	courageous	careful	successful	philosophical
sentimental	eloquent	generous		independent	elegant
honest	patient	passionate			compassionate
persistent	silent				
greedy	rigid	vain	private	demanding	lazy
small-minded	bad losers	rash	timid	irritable	possessive
power-hungry	authoritarian	disobedient	thin-skinned	loud-mouthed	tight-fisted
destructive	conventional	undisciplined	old-fashioned	stubborn	bad losers
suspicious	jealous	argumentative	hypochondriac	discontented	changeable
tiresome	stubborn	rebellious	squeamish	wilful	vengeful
gamblers	slow				extravagant
Nixon	Chaplin	Elizabeth II	Einstein	John Lennon	J.F. Kennedy
Brando	Hitler	De Gaulle	Bob Hope	Ringo Starr	Jackie Kennedy
Shakespeare	Napoleon	Ayatollah Khomeini	Confucius	Al Pacino	Howard Hughes
Mozart	Walt Disney	Beethoven	Sinatra	Abraham Lincoln	Bob Dylan
Tolstoy	Mrs Thatcher	Marilyn Monroe		Freud	Mao Tse Tung
	Nehru			Charles Darwin	Gandhi

The Horse	The Goat	The Monkey	The Rooster	The Dog	The Pig
gifted	gentle	merry	proud	faithful	scrupulous
athletic	artistic	enthusiastic	enthusiastic	loyal	loyal
charming	peace-loving	witty	stylish	noble	sincere
quick-witted	sweet-natured	good in business	popular	modest	honest
hard-working	lovable	clever	lively	devoted	loving
entertaining	creative	fascinating	amusing	prosperous	sociable
powerful	inventive	passionate	generous	courageous	sensitive
skilful	amorous	youthful	adventurous	respectable	sensual
cheerful	tasteful	very intelligent	industrious	selfless	truthful
eloquent	intelligent	inventive	conservative	dutiful	peaceful
independent			courageous	intelligent	intelligent
weak	insecure	vain	pompous	introverted	naive
unfeeling	pessimistic	adolescent	pedantic	cynical	epicurean
hot-headed	unpunctual	long-winded	short-sighted	critical	insecure
selfish	undisciplined	unfaithful	boastful	moralizing	gullible
ruthless	dissatisfied	untruthful	mistrustful	stubborn	defenceless
tactless	irresponsible	untrustworthy	extravagant	defensive	non-competitive
impatient					earthy
rebellious					
Buzz Aldrin	Mick Jagger	Yul Brynner	Katharine Hepburn	Winston Churchill	Al Capone
Neil Armstrong	Joni Mitchell	many comedians	many military officers	Elvis Presley	Lucille Ball
Paul Simon				Sophia Loren	Elton John
Paul McCartney				Brigitte Bardot	Humphrey Bogart
Jimi Hendrix					Alfred Hitchcock

Artificial intelligence

Computers have become part of everyday life. Today's schoolchildren carry around calculating power which would have filled a large room forty years ago. Computer scientists are now working on the next generation of computers; ones which will have true intelligence. The first step on the way is the development of 'expert systems'. An expert system is partially intelligent.

At Stanford University a computer has been developed for medical diagnosis. It stores 125 facts about each of 600 diseases. It can tell doctors which questions to ask, and which measurements to take. It can then analyse the result and make an accurate diagnosis.

At the University of California they have been working on computers which can write stories, while IBM has developed the *Epistle* program for business letters which can correct spelling, improve grammar and style and even check for mistakes by giving a list of words with similar sounds. One of the most interesting programs has been developed at Massachusetts Institute of Technology (MIT), and it is a kind of computer psychiatrist.

The program, which was developed by Professor Joseph Weizenbaum, is called *Eliza*. It uses a technique known as 'reflective listening'. The computer seems to understand, and

to make sympathetic responses. In fact it does not understand a word that is being typed into it. Nevertheless, Weizenbaum's secretary fell under the spell of the machine. Weizenbaum says:

'Well, I asked her to my office and sat her down at the keyboard, and she began to type and of course I

looked at her to make sure everything was operating properly. After two or three interchanges with the machine she turned to me and she said, "Would you mind leaving the room please?" '

Here is an example of Eliza in operation:

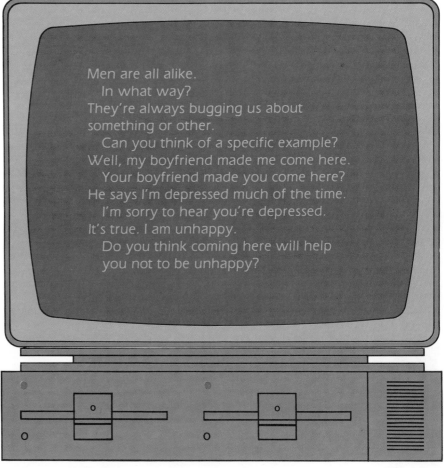

Men are all alike.
   In what way?
They're always bugging us about something or other.
   Can you think of a specific example?
Well, my boyfriend made me come here.
   Your boyfriend made you come here?
He says I'm depressed much of the time.
   I'm sorry to hear you're depressed.
It's true. I am unhappy.
   Do you think coming here will help you not to be unhappy?

You will notice that Eliza responds sympathetically to what is typed in, but that it never adds new information, or gives an opinion. Ordinary psychiatrists use this 'reflective listening' technique, too. Opposite is another example.

Psychiatrists (and teachers!) say that this technique helps people to talk about themselves, and that talking about themselves helps them.

Input	Eliza
It's my girlfriend.	So, you're worried about your girlfriend.
I'm a bit upset.	Why do you say you're upset? / feel upset?
She doesn't understand me.	She doesn't understand you?
She argues with everything I say.	Why do you think she argues with you?
She's afraid of me.	Does it please you to think she's afraid of you?
No, but ... she goes crazy.	What exactly do you mean by crazy?
She makes me miserable.	I'm sorry to hear you're miserable.

Exercise 1

Try this technique with some fellow students. A is consulting B. B does not give any opinion, but simply listens sympathetically.
Make a list of 'problems' for A to speak about. It's a good way of keeping a conversation going.

Eliza simply operates a clever program and cannot be described as artificial intelligence. The program can be fooled:

However it may not be very long before truly intelligent computers are created. What will happen? Two eminent scientists at MIT have expressed views on this:

Professor Edward Fredken (MIT)

Professor Fredken thinks that the artificial intelligences of the future will be concerned with 'weighty' problems that humans cannot understand. He thinks that they may condescend to talk to us occasionally, to amuse us and to play games that we enjoy. In some sense they might, he suggests, keep us as pets.

Professor Joseph Weizenbaum (MIT)

Professor Weizenbaum expanded on the idea of computers keeping us as pets and quoted Arthur C. Clarke (the author of *2001*) as saying it would serve 'us' right. Weizenbaum queries the use of the word 'us'. He points out that the thousand or so people working on the high-level computers are doing so without having asked the rest of 'us' our opinion/permission. We will all be affected, however, if they produce the monstrosities that are being forecast. He concludes that this situation says a great deal about the issue of responsibility in science.

Exercise 2

Say what you think about the future role of the computer.

```
             ELIZA                      I see
Hi!  I'm Eliza.  What's your problem?   Where are your eyes?
Computers                               why are you interested in whether or
What is it about machines that          not I am r eyes
worries you?                            That is rubbish
They are stupid                         I'm not sure I understand you fully
I'm not sure I understand you fully     I cannot help that
You cannot think                        Come, come elucidate your thoughts
Oh, I cannot think                      You are repeating yourself
That is correct                         Does it please you to believe I
Come, come elucidate your thoughts      am repeating myself?
why                                     No
What else comes to mind when you ask    Why not?
that?                                   Please leave the room
Bananas                                 Can you elaborate on that?
Can you elaborate on that?              Go
What does that suggest to you?          Say, do you have any psychological
Me                                      problems?
```

Reading

This is an extract from a novel, *Satan* by Jeremy Leven, in which Lupa meets a truly intelligent computer.

Lupa laughed. She liked the voice that had been selected for the computer. It wasn't the typical low mechanical voice that sounded like a record being played at too slow a speed. It sounded natural. It had charm to it.

"Do you have a name?" Lupa asked.

"Not yet," the computer answered.

"They're running a contest. The kids are supposed to name me. I'm dreading the whole thing, believe me."

Now Lupa thought this was clever, the way they had programmed the computer. She wondered if there was some way to screw up the program. She had once heard that even a sophisticated analog computer couldn't pick up certain subtleties in the English language, no matter how good the programming, so she decided to give it a try.

"My paws give me pause," she said.

The computer was silent.

"My paws give me pause," Lupa repeated. "It's a clause without claws."

Lupa waited in silence for a response.

"You know something," the computer said. "I thought you'd be different. Just once today I was hoping I'd get someone who wouldn't try to beat the program."

Lupa smiled. This was marvelous, she thought to herself. They'd thought of everything.

"Mi dispiace."

"Sorry," she said. "Mi dispiace."

"Ah, you speak Italian," the computer said with some sarcasm.

"Oui, d'accord," Lupa answered.

"C'est vrai."

"And French, too. Your French is better than your Italian. Though neither one is great. Now, if you'll excuse me, I have to shut down. It's closing time."

Lupa stood up and walked around the room. It was evident to her that somewhere in the building, listening through an intercom, was someone with a microphone. She thought about how to test for this.

"You wouldn't happen to know what day of the week September the fourteenth, 1321, fell on, would you?" Lupa asked.

"It was a Sunday," the computer answered, "but how do you know whether I'm right? Thank you for visiting the computer exhibit."

Exercise 3

Design a computer for your home. Write a description of it and its functions.

Youth culture

These extracts come from a lecture on *Youth Culture*. Listen and read.

1 Introduction

In this series of lectures we shall be examining British society since 1945. Our first topic is youth culture. Now, what exactly do we mean by 'youth culture'? In 1950, a teenager was simply someone aged between 13 and 19. By 1980 the word 'teenager' had developed a much wider and more complex meaning. This was probably because of a whole series of industries which grew up during the 1950s which were specifically directed at the teenage market. Why should this have happened? The main reason was that teenagers were a section of the community with surplus money — spending money. At that time people left school at 15 or 16, but didn't usually marry until their early twenties. More often than not they lived at home in the meantime. Their parents had little spare money. Almost every penny was accounted for, since they were buying a house, bringing up a family, and perhaps saving for a first car, or even a first holiday abroad. Because few parents asked their children for realistic sums of money for food and lodging, the kids had money to spend. Consequently, industry wasted no time in finding them something to spend it on. We shall go on to look at some of the resulting changes in existing industries, and also at some of the new industries which sprang up.

2 Cinema

Listen, then look at the notes and listen again.

One of the first changes was in the cinema. During the 1930s the average person saw two films a week. By 1960 this had been reduced to 12 films a year, and the current figure is less than half of that. The cause of the cinema's decline is obvious. Audiences fell as a result of the increase in television ownership.

In fact a similar increase was happening in other countries for 2 reasons. First, the general world economic recovery from the war. The second reason was that technology was making mass production possible, and therefore sets were becoming cheaper. The effect of this was that the cinema lost its family audience. Because families were smaller, and because they often lived in different areas from grandparents, the cinema had become an expensive night out. There were no 'free' babysitters, i.e. grandparents. Of course many cinemas closed, and the ones which survived were the ones in the town centres. Therefore cinemas became more expensive to get to, and in consequence audience numbers declined even more. The end result was a cinema aimed at the youth market, 16–25. This meant different kinds of films, and in the end an even greater loss of the family audience.

3 Fashion

Look at the notes, not at the text. Listen. Then read the text.

Another area of change was fashion. Styles have always changed, but the change has usually been slow. A man's suit of 1925 would not have looked out of place in 1950 ... or in 1985. Because they were made of natural materials, such as wool, silk or leather, clothes had been an expensive item for the family of the 1920s or 1930s, and 'high fashion' was positively undesirable. Due mainly to changes in technology, clothes today are much cheaper. That is they cost a much smaller percentage of our income. Man-made fibres and mass production are the basic causes of these reductions in real price. The first consequence was that people could afford to buy more clothes more often, because they didn't have to wait until clothes were almost worn out before replacing them. Man-made fibres are hard-wearing and long-lasting, as well as cheap. The clothing industry did not want to lose sales so the idea of fashion was promoted more heavily, especially to the youth market. One result of a national TV network was that new fashions in clothes, dance or music spread rapidly throughout the country, and this led to even more rapid changes in fashions and styles. In contrast to the man's suit of 1925, which would look normal today, look at the fashions of 1956.

4 Pop music

In this section we only have the lecture notes made by a student. Listen carefully to the lecture while looking at the notes, then try to write a paragraph based on the notes.

5 Other entertainments

Listen to this section of the lecture once. Listen again and make notes. After the lesson, write a paragraph based on your notes.

Cinema

1930's — 2 films/wk
1960's — 12 " p.a.
Now — ½ that (6 p.a.)
Why? — TV
Other countries too —
1. World economy ↑
2. tech — mass prod / cheaper
So — cin. lost family audience
Small families — no babysitters
(9/ parents.)
Many closed. Only left town centres
More expensive, so aud ↓
∴ cinema for 16 – 25
Diff. films. fam. aud ↓ again.

Fashion

Change — slow
Man suit '25 = '50 = '85
Nat. mats. — expens — 20's /
30's / not want 'fash'.
Now cheaper (techn).
Smaller % income (man made
f's + mass prod)
1. more cl. more oft.
2. m.m.f's cheap, hard-w.,
long last
So, fashion pushed heavily —
esp. to youth.
Nat. T.V. — fash. spread —
changes faster
Man Suit '25, OK today.
1956 clothes — strange.

Pop Music

classic e.g. Y.C. — pop.
Always 'music / popular'
Up to c. 1950 — music wkg
class.
c. 1955 — pop music — classless
modern pop — US R&B +
US C&W ?
We / interest / Effects.
w / wide popularity Due To
techn. → inv. of transistor
trans. — teens — own source
music.
freed family radio.
Demand teen music. Ind respond
Also 45 record → + Sales.

Language study

It happened	*because* it was hot.	
	because of *on account of* *as a result of* *as a consequence of* *due to*	the heat.

It was hot,	*that's why* *so* *therefore* *consequently*	it happened.

As/Since/Because he was tired, he went to bed.

Because of his tiredness, he went to bed.

The *result/effect/consequence* was that she failed.

She failed	*because* of it. *because* she hadn't studied.

The heat	*caused* it to happen. *made* it happen. *led to* it happening.

He did it *so (that)* it would happen.

Exercise 1
Write a paragraph entitled 'Summing up', based on your notes.

Exercise 2
Go back to the text, and mark all the words or expressions showing reason, result or cause.

Unit 40

Animal rights and wrongs

DAILY STAR 6 January 1983

4 DIE BECAUSE OF A PET DOG

THIS was Blackpool's gale-lashed promenade where four people died yesterday—for a dog.

In a chain of tragedy:—

● The dog, named Henry, plunged into the sea to retrieve a rubber ball.

● The owner, Alistair Anthony, tall, powerful, and a strong swimmer, went in after his pet.

● Mr Anthony's father stopped a police car and gave the alarm.

● Four policemen and young WPC Angela Bradley started a rescue attempt which swiftly turned into disaster.

FULL STORY: Pages 2,3

Alistair Anthony died with his dog in the raging seas. So did Angela Bradley and Constables Colin Morrison and Gordon Connolly. The two other policemen were brought ashore and taken to hospital.

A senior officer said of his colleagues: "They never gave a thought for their safety. They died doing their duty."

NEWS OF THE WORLD 31 July 1983

Animal lib squad raid circus ring

ANIMAL rights demonstrators were thrown out of a circus after leaping into the ring and chaining themselves to lion cages.

Burly show-hands freed the protesters with wire-cutters and bundled them past astonished spectators.

The Animal Liberation Front squad had smuggled chains into the Bournemouth Ice Rink where Sally Chipperfield's Circus is held. Demonstrators jumped into the ring while cages were being put up for the "big cats" act.

Two women and two men fastened their chains in protest at the way they claim circus animals are treated.

Outraged citizens save pups of war

From Christopher Thomas Washington

Rarely does all the ominous talk of war in Central America or elsewhere cause the Pentagon switchboard to be inundated by fearful and outraged citizens.

Yesterday it happened, but not because of war. It was because the *Washington Post* revealed that the Department of Defence was going to shoot dogs with high-powered weapons so that scientists could study their wounds. Many of the callers were children.

Such was the wrath of the nation that Mr Caspar Weinberger, Secretary of Defence, quickly issued a succinct instruction that "no dogs will be shot for medical experimentation or training".

The plan was to shoot scores of dogs and other animals at a newly built $70,000 (£46,000) establishment in Washington named ominously and officially the Wound Laboratory.

The Wound Laboratory said it wanted to shoot dogs in order to train aspiring doctors for battlefield medicine and to research better ways of treating wounds in battles.

THE TIMES 27 July 1983

Dear Sir,

When is something going to be done to protect the children of this town from the so-called 'dog lovers'? The streets are filthy, and so are the beaches. What annoys me most though, are the owners who allow their dogs to foul children's playgrounds and playing fields. Dogs are carriers of several serious diseases which can affect children for life. In theory you can be fined for allowing your dog to foul pavements or playgrounds. In practice, nothing is ever done to prevent it happening. I've heard enough about 'animal rights'. What about childrens' rights?

P. Stephens.

Mrs P Stephens

Sandbourne, Dorset

(Sandbourne Echo, 15 May 1983)

In 1981 there were a total of 4,344,843 experiments on animals in Britain. They include everything from trials of new pet foods involving no suffering whatsoever, to experiments in which dogs and monkeys are forced to smoke continuously, or are deliberately injured to evaluate the effects of pain-killing drugs.

Which animals are used

Mice	60%	Birds	5%
Cats & Dogs	0.5%	Guinea Pigs & Rabbits	8%
Rats	21%	Others	5.5%

What the experiments are for

Development of medical and veterinary products	55%
Developing and testing pesticides, herbicides, food additives, etc	5%
Study of normal and abnormal body structure and function.	26%
Testing cosmetics, etc.	0.6%
Other	13.4%

There have been protests from animal rights groups about experiments on animals (vivisection) for many years. In the last few years extreme groups have raided laboratories and released animals, and some scientists have had their homes daubed with slogans and have even received letter bombs. Attitudes to animals vary greatly between two extremes. Some of us regard animals as simply lumps of walking meat, others see them as almost human. How should we react to animals? How do you feel about these situations?

● Dolphins and whales have larger brains than us. There is considerable evidence that they are able to communicate with each other. Scientists who have worked with dolphins consider them to be truly intelligent. Some believe that they might even be more intelligent than us. Because their environment provides all their needs they have developed in a different non-material way. They are still being hunted and killed.

● Calves and other animals are 'factory farmed'. In the case of calves, they are kept in the dark, unable to move for their entire short lives, so as to produce white tender meat (veal). Most eggs are produced by battery hens kept in similar conditions, although many consumers are prepared to pay more for 'free-range eggs'.

● In southern England one particularly popular picnic area has a fairly large population of adders, which are poisonous and fairly common, and smooth snakes which are not poisonous and fairly rare. The local council decided to try and kill all the snakes in the area. Environmental groups protested, and nothing has yet been done.

● In the United States there are animal cemeteries, and it's possible to buy 'biodegradable' (i.e. cardboard) caskets so that your pet hamster or gerbil can be buried in style.

● An Englishman was very angry because cats were fouling his lawn and digging up his flowers. He put down poisoned meat, and warned the owners not to let their cats out of their houses. The owners prosecuted him and he was fined.

● A road-safety advert in Britain shows a car swerving to avoid a dog, and hitting a lamp post, severely injuring the driver. A few years ago a car swerved so as not to hit a dog and killed four people in a bus queue.

● Fox-hunting and other blood sports are under discussion in Britain. Those who want to ban fox-hunting say it is both cruel to the fox, and de-humanizing for the hunter. Supporters say that farmers would soon make foxes extinct by using traps and guns, and that guns might injure without killing.

● A rich Londoner discovered that her poodle was diabetic. She paid for daily injections for 16 years in order to keep it alive and when it died, had a memorial erected to it at London's Battersea Dogs' Home.

Exercise 1
What is your reaction to each of the situations?
What would you have done in each situation?
How would you assess your attitude to animals?
Have you ever kept a pet? (When? What? Why?)
Have you ever worked with animals?
Do animals matter? Should we worry about what happens to them?

Exercise 2
Read through all the texts and answer the following questions.

1 Why did the dog in Blackpool plunge into the sea?
2 Why did four people chain themselves to a circus cage?
3 Why did the Department of Defence want to shoot dogs?
4 What was the plan?
5 What *two* reasons did the Wound Laboratory give for wanting to shoot dogs?
6 What's done in Sandbourne to prevent dogs from fouling the pavement?
7 Why do you think dogs are forced to smoke?
8 Why are some laboratory animals deliberately injured?
9 Why did extreme groups raid laboratories?
10 Why are calves factory-farmed?
11 Why did the council want to kill snakes, do you think?
12 Why do people buy cardboard caskets for hamsters?
13 What did the Englishman want to prevent the cats doing?
14 Why had the car swerved before hitting a bus queue?
15 Why would farmers kill foxes?
16 Why did the Londoner pay for daily injections?

Strong language

A Oi! You! I was waiting to back into that space.
B Were you? Bad luck, mate.
A But I was indicating ... I've been here for ages ...
B Well, you were too slow, weren't you?
A Look, I'm not letting you get away with this. You'd better move or else.
B Or else what?
A Or else I'll ...
B Clear off, chum. I haven't got time.
A Here, you'd better watch it.
B Leave it, mate. Don't be so stupid.
A Just watch it ... or I'll ...
B Will you? You, and whose army?
A Right, come on, then. I'll give you one.
B Is that a threat or a promise, darling? Look I'm off, I haven't got all day.
A Come back here! I'll ... I'll ...

C Excuse me, Miss ... over here. Miss!
D Yeah?
C I wonder if you'd be kind enough to get me a size 18 in this ... if it's not too much trouble, that is.
D 18? We don't do extra-large, luv. Sorry. You want the outsize department.
C Well, what have you got in size 18?

D Eh? I thought I'd told you. We don't do extra-large in anything.
C All right, but there's no need to be so unpleasant, you know. I say ... I'm talking to you. I said ...
D Oh? I *am* sorry, madam. I didn't want to upset madam, did I, madam. I was listening to madam, madam ...

E ... and another thing. I'm going to ring your mother and tell her to stop interfering.
F Look, she's only trying to be helpful.
E Helpful? She phones every day to see if you've had enough to eat! I mean, for goodness' sake! We *have* been married three years. Anyway, I'll tell her, next time.
F Don't you dare ring her.
E Look, Martin. I'll do what the hell I like, OK?
F I'll never forgive you if you upset her. She worries, that's all.
E Upset *her*? What about me? I'm just going to tell her ... very politely ... to mind her own business.
F You ... you dare!
E You'd better not try and stop me, either. I've had enough.
F I warn you ... you phone her, and that's it!
E That's it ... that's it. What the hell do you mean 'that's it'?

F I tell you ... I'll leave if you do.
E Leave? Run home to Mummy? Don't threaten me, Martin. I couldn't care less what you do.
F You ...

G Hello, hello. Where's the fire?
H Sorry, I don't understand.
G You seem to be in a bit of a hurry, sir. I wondered if there was an emergency of some kind?
H No, no. No emergency.
G In that case I'd better see your licence. You have got a licence, I suppose?
H Yes, what do you mean?
G Oh, it's just the way you were driving. I wondered if you'd passed your test, that's all.
H Very funny. Here it is.
G Right. David Humphreys. What's your date of birth, David?
H 9/7/57.
G That's right. OK Dave, get out of the car.
H What?
G C'mon, Davey. I think we'll just take a breath test, eh?
H Look here, officer. I have not been drinking.
G I'm sure you haven't, Dave. But the test will settle that, won't it?
H I don't like your attitude, constable. I mean all I was doing ...

Language study

There are plenty of ways of being rude in English. Here are some of them.

1 **Tone of voice** It doesn't matter what you say, it's how you say it. Even the most polite phrases can sound rude if said in a certain way.

2 **Threats and warnings** for example:
I'll (tell him) if you do that.
Do that and I'll …
Stop doing that or I'll …
Stop doing that or else!
Don't you dare do it!
You dare!
I warn you (not to do it).
You'd better do it./You'd better not do it.

3 **Friendly/familiar terms used to strangers** boy/son/mate/old chap/old boy/old fellow/my lad/chum/friend/luv.

4 **Sarcasm** Polite formulas and ways of addressing people can be used sarcastically, sometimes by being *too* polite or *too* formal. Words like Miss/Sir/Madam can be used in this way.

5 **Aggressive expressions**
Hey you!
Look here …
Watch it!
Mind your own business!
Watch out!
Just watch yourself/your step.
Don't be stupid!
Go to hell!

6 **Use of taboo words** 'Taboo' words are words which are deliberately designed to shock and outrage people. (See the note below.)

7 **Use of social role** In a conflict situation people try and establish some kind of superiority by making it clear what their social role is. A middle-class motorist might become very condescending in an argument, while a working-class motorist might play up his role as an honest but tough working man.

Exercise 1
Go through the four conversations and discuss *how* people are trying to insult each other.
Which of the seven categories of abuse are they using, and why?
Are there any other ways in which they are trying to be rude?

Exercise 2
There are four situations. Go through and role-play the characters.
a Try and be ruder.
b Try and conduct the same dialogues *without* being so rude.
Try to use other expressions in both cases.

Exercise 3
Role-play the arguments which might arise in these situations:
1 A boss accuses an employee of constant lateness. The employee denies it.
2 A married couple are at home. One accuses the other of not taking a fair share of household duties. (Remember family rows usually sound the worst.)
3 A customer accuses a shop assistant of giving short change.
4 Someone in a pub accuses another person of taking his drink/chair.
5 You ask a friend for money (a small sum). The friend refuses.
6 A young engaged couple accuse each other of seeing other boyfriends/girlfriends.

Reading

A final word of warning! Read this extract from *Practical English Usage* by Michael Swan (OUP).

Many languages have words which are considered dangerous, holy, magic or shocking, and which are only used in certain situations, or by certain people. For instance, in some African tribes the names of dead chiefs must not be said; in many cultures, words associated with religious beliefs are used only on religious occasions, or by priests. Words of this kind can be called 'taboo words'.

Linguistic taboos are less strong than they used to be. However, students should be very careful about using taboo words and swearwords. There are two reasons for this. First of all, it is not easy to know the exact strength of these expressions in a foreign language, or to know what kind of people are shocked by them, and in what circumstances. One may easily say something that is meant as a joke, but which seriously upsets the people one is talking to. And secondly, swearing generally indicates membership of a group: one most often swears in front of people one knows well, who belong to one's own 'social circle', age group, etc. (Children usually avoid swearing in front of adults, so as not to annoy or shock them, and adults avoid swearing in front of children for similar reasons.) So if a foreigner uses swearwords, he may give the impression that he is claiming membership of a group that he does not belong to.

Typewriter types

What can you say about a valuable, desperately needed skill that:
- takes twice as long as it should to learn;
- takes twice as long as it should to use;
- makes you work perhaps 20 times harder than necessary;
- uses equipment that forces you to make errors;
- uses equipment that has persisted out of sheer inertia since 1872;
- is still being taught to millions of unsuspecting people?

Well, you can't say much!

The skill in question is typing, typing on 'qwerty'. Qwerty is the name for the standard typewriter keyboard. Q,W,E,R,T and Y are the first six keys in the upper row of letters. Together they make up the traditional name for the keyboard.

The first practical typewriter was put together in Milwaukee between 1867 and 1872. The letters were arranged alphabetically at first, but this proved useless. Because of the mechanics of the machine the letters jammed together when you typed fast. The inventors asked a schoolteacher which letters were used most in English, and then designed a keyboard where the most-used letters were as far apart as possible – qwerty. Since then typewriters have changed completely, but, despite all the changes, the keyboard has remained the same. Even though they operate in quite a different way, computer keyboards have followed the typewriter, so that we have qwerty computers, too.

It seems as if qwerty might last forever, in spite of the fact that a logical alternative has been available since 1932. After 20 years of study August Dvorak invented a new keyboard (The Dvorak Simplified Keyboard, or DSK). The middle row of letters on a typewriter is called 'the home row', because it's the starting point for the typist's fingers. On a qwerty machine you can type only about 50 words using the home row by itself, compared with around 3000 on the home row of a DSK. On a DSK all of the vowels are on the home row, under the left hand.

The most frequent consonants, H, T, N and S come under the right hand with D just to the left of the right index finger. 70% of the work is done in the home row, 22% on the top row, and only 8% in the bottom row. Dvorak also considered the work load of each hand and each individual finger.

He had studied thousands of words to discover the frequency of letter combinations, studied slow-motion films of typists' fingers, and tested 250 possible arrangements. He decided that any random arrangement was probably better than qwerty, which by separating frequent letters, deliberately made typing more difficult.

Since Dvorak there have been other designs, including the modern 'microwriter' which has 5 keys, is held in one hand and types letters by combination of keys. DSK, however, is believed to be the best conventional arrangement. Most manufacturers can supply a DSK typewriter at a small extra charge, but they say that there is little demand. Typists, industry and schools are committed to the system they already know.

What are the advantages of DSK?

a Tests by the US Navy showed that typists produced 74% more work, which was 68% more accurate.

b A typist's fingers move between 12 and 20 miles on QWERTY, in contrast a DSK typist's fingers move about 1 mile a day.

c Many DSK typists double their speeds, and often break the '100 wpm' barrier. World champion typist Lenore MacClain, who previously averaged 70 wpm, managed 182 wpm on DSK

d Anyone, even children, begins to master DSK in two weeks.

e Speeds at 40–50 wpm can be achieved in 2–3 months.

f Speeds of 100 wpm are possible for many within a year.

g Present classes fail to bring 70% of students up to 40 wpm. DSK classes bring nearly 100% up to 60 wpm.

What are the disadvantages?

a Conversion of old machines is expensive, although it is true that few commercial typewriters are used for more than 8 years. Most firms trade-in after 5 years. However, expensive electric models could be changed cheaply.

b Firms would have to retrain operators, although much of the expense might be paid back by greater productivity.

c It takes about 6 weeks to retrain, but you should probably take a short 'rest' from QWERTY before starting on DSK.

d Once you have retrained, you would need to stay with DSK machines. Tests showed that typists could not become 'bi-digital' i.e. you would then have to retrain for QWERTY, if you changed your job.

e Big companies who have studied DSK are reluctant to change, even though they believe it's better. They say that if it was going to become popular, it would already have done so.

Language study

Although/Though/Even though DSK machines are more logical, they haven't become more popular.

In spite of/Despite illogical keyboards, QWERTY machines have never been replaced.

A typist's fingers move 12 miles a day on QWERTY.
In contrast/In comparison, a DSK typist moves the fingers only a mile a day.

If DSK machines are *contrasted to/compared with* QWERTY machines, they come out better.

Many companies have tested DSK, but *nevertheless* continue to use QWERTY.

A	is	more less	efficient	than	B.
		faster			
		as	fast	as	B.

A	is	the	most least	efficient	machine you can buy.
			fastest		

Exercise 1
Compare DSK and QWERTY, making as many sentences as you can with the above patterns.

Exercise 2
Complete the spaces with *although* or *in spite of*.

_____ few people have heard of him, Bert Marshall was one of the greatest engineers of the century. He owned a small garage in Norfolk in the 1920s. He always worked alone _____ job offers from car manufacturers. At last Bert completed his task, the invention of a perfect steam engine. _____ he spent years trying to sell it, nobody was interested. Finally, in 1934 Bert was invited to meet the owner of one of the great car manufacturers. After signing a legal document, Bert was given a cheque for £200,000. Then, _____ his protests, the engine was never manufactured. Bert went to live in Monte Carlo. He was sure that he was being watched, _____ he could never prove it. He died two years later, an unhappy man _____ his money. _____ his engine could cover 250 miles on a gallon of petrol, it was suppressed.

Exercise 3
Have you heard any similar stories? Do you believe this one? Why/why not? Why hasn't his engine been manufactured? What do you think the legal document said?

Exercise 4
difficult/difficulties   happy/happiness
angry/anger   young/youth
annoyed/annoyance   old/age

It was difficult. He did it.
Though/although it was difficult, he did it.
Despite/in spite of the difficulties, he did it.

Make two sentences for each of these, one with *although* or *though*, one with *despite* or *in spite of*.

1 He was angry. He kept smiling.
2 She was annoyed. She didn't show it.
3 They were happy. They didn't laugh or smile.
4 He was young. He had a very important job.
5 She was old. She was still fit and energetic.

Exercise 5
very late/she/not sleep
Although it was very late, she couldn't sleep/she wasn't sleeping.

Try and write out the story below.

1 very late/she/not sleep
2 lay awake/hours
3 heard something
4 very frightened/not make a noise
5 terrified/but went to window
6 looked out/lots of rain
7 someone in garden/but pouring
8 a man/on hands and knees near bushes
9 open window/call out
10 rain/but wearing just a shirt and trousers
11 man apologized
12 looking for dog/lost

New hospital

It is not often that modern architects have the chance to build a major new hospital on a 'green fields site' in Britain. However, that's just what's happened in the East Dorset area of southern England. The area has a population of around 400,000, spread over the four main towns (Bournemouth, Poole, Christchurch and Wimborne) and their surrounding suburbs. However, four of the existing hospitals were in Victorian buildings, and the main hospital, Poole General, was in the town centre, with difficult access for traffic. Most post-war hospitals have been squeezed into city centres with the result that they are difficult to distinguish from office blocks. On a larger site architects have a chance to think what a hospital really should be like.

---

28 July 1983

Ministry go-ahead for £37m hospital

FEARS of delays in starting Bournemouth's urgently needed new £37 million general hospital were allayed this week with the announcement of Government approval for the Castle Lane development.

The go-ahead was given by Health Minister, Mr. Kenneth Clarke, following concerned lobbying by one of the two medical staff committees of the East Dorset Health Authority protesting about hold-ups.

The 670 bed hospital will be built in two stages on a 40 acre site – the first section ready in 1987 and the second in 1990.

"Marvellous news" was the reaction of Mr. Douglas Smith, East Dorset Health Authority chairman, to the announcement. "We are now definitely on the way to providing much needed new accommodation for local people and I know the whole of Bournemouth will be delighted."

A spokesman for the Wessex Regional Health Authority said the announcement was "great news" and confirmed that tenders for work on the first phase would be invited immediately. Work on this stage will begin in January 1984 and the cost will be £20½ million including fees and equipment.

The second phase will follow, costing a further £17 million.

Phase one will include 224 general acute beds, 49 geriatric assessment beds, eight intensive therapy and coronary care beds, operating theatres, X-ray and rehabilitation facilities, a pharmacy, education centre and residential accommodation.

Some of these services will be expanded in the second phase which will provide 389 beds and new out-patient and accident emergency departments.

The end of the first phase will herald the closure of the Royal National, and the Royal Victoria Hospital, Boscombe, will close on the completion of the second phase.

The need for a new hospital has been recognised for years and agreement to buy the Castle Lane site was made as far back as 1966. Originally a 900 bed hospital was planned with building due to start in 1976-79. But nothing happened and in 1980 the Department of Health reduced the number of beds to about 600 – the figure has since been fixed at 670 – despite fears expressed by doctors that this would be insufficient for local needs.

At the same time a start date for building was fixed for June 1982. Since then it has been twice deferred.

---

4 August 1983

How new hospital will be planned

A MODEL of the £37 million district general hospital which will be built north of Castle Lane East and east of the Ringwood Spur Road is now on view. As we reported last week, go-ahead has been given by the Minister of Health for the 670-bed hospital.

The first phase – providing 281 beds – will be started in January and is due to be completed in 1987. The second phase is scheduled for completion in 1990.

The new hospital will serve the whole East Dorset area and not simply Bournemouth. Some patients who are now taken to Poole and Christchurch hospitals will go to the new hospital according to the particular specialist treatment required. It will also include a major accident unit to relieve the pressure on the sole existing department at Poole.

As can be seen, the hospital itself will be L-shaped. The main section on the left will not be built until the second phase. In the right hand corner of the foreground is the car park and behind it the main entrance.

Tucked into the inside angle of the "L" is a lake covering about one acre of the 40-acre site. Besides being ornamental it will have a functional purpose in absorbing the large volume of rainwater expected to pour off the many roofs of the complex.

The existing surface water drainage system was not thought to be adequate to cope with the extra water so the alternative would have been to build an expensive new pipe system.

Beyond the lake are staff residential quarters and an off-duty community centre together with an education centre and the building with the tall chimney which will supply the hospital's energy.

The whole site will be heavily planted and screened with shrubs and trees – not surprising in view of the architects' notes on their sketch plans.

They aren't exactly complimentary about the outlook. The prospect to the west, on the other side of the Ringwood Spur Road, is referred to as "nasty views" and "bleak, brash new council housing".

Other comments on the periphery: "smell from sewage works (probably infrequent)"; "30's nurses' home – a real eyesore" (this is Riverside Avenue to the east of the site).

"This is a flat, featureless site", say the architects, "sparsely vegetated and exposed to both climatic and man-made disturbances, i.e. sea winds, poor views of suburban sprawl and traffic noise and fumes".

But there is a relieving note: "The biotic conditions for establishing new planting were, however, found to be excellent".

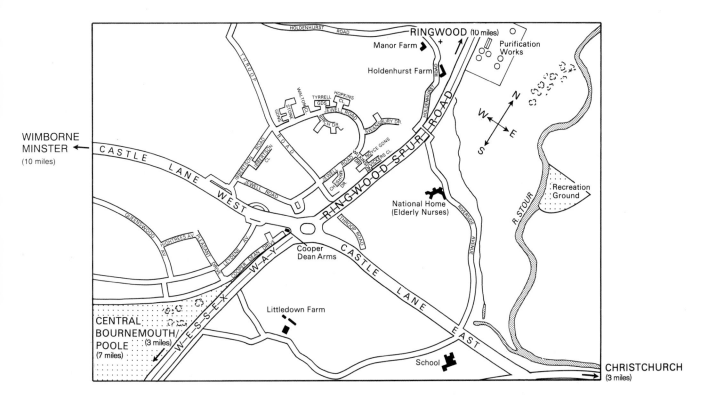

Exercise 1
Read *Ministry go-ahead for £37m hospital* and complete this chart:

Date of newspaper	
Date site bought	
Original starting date	
Date size reduced by 30%	
Date fixed at that time for start	
Work actually to begin	
1st phase open	
2nd phase open	

Number of beds in original plan	
Number of beds planned in 1980	
Number planned in 1983	
Number of general acute beds	
Number of geriatric beds	
Number of intensive care beds	

Cost of hospital	
Cost of phase one	
Cost of phase two	

Exercise 2
Now read *How new hospital will be planned*

Mark the following numbers on the picture:

1 the lake
2 the staff quarters and community centre
3 the building which will supply power
4 the car park
5 the main entrance

Exercise 3
Look at the road map of the area surrounding the hospital. Mark:

1 the site of the new hospital
2 the council housing estate
3 the sewage works
4 the site of the existing 1930s nurses' home

Exercise 4
Answer these questions:
1 In 1983, how many of the hospitals in the area had accident departments?
2 Give two reasons for putting a lake on the site.
3 Why will the site be heavily planted with trees and shrubs?
4 Will patients from Poole use the new hospital?
5 If so, when? If not, why not?
6 What did the architects think about the outlook?

Design a hospital

Listed below are some factors which might be important when planning a new hospital. Try to put them in order of importance. Tick (√) the ones mentioned in either of the articles. Put a cross (X) for any that the new hospital might not be good for. (Remember to compare it with a city centre hospital.)

1 Good access for emergency vehicles from all parts of the area.
2 Quiet, peaceful surroundings.
3 Beautiful views.
4 Good public transport for staff and visitors.
5 Good parking space for staff and visitors.
6 Well-designed attractive buildings.
7 Away from traffic noise and fumes.
8 Easy to get from one section to another under cover.

Discuss reasons for the order of your list.

Note
For a map of Bournemouth and the surrounding area, see Unit 47.

Precautions

Listening

'Sky-diving' must be one of the most exciting sports to watch. A sky-diving team can leave an aeroplane at 1300 metres and free fall to around 300 metres before opening their parachutes, which they can then steer so that they eventually land on a 1 metre × 1 metre cross on the ground. When sky-divers do a display, they rely heavily on the ground crew, who light a smoke flare and help to guide them safely down.

Listen to the conversation between the ground crew and a team of sky-divers.

Exercise 1
Listen again. Pause the tape, and report the instructions.
Why did the ground crew warn them about the telephone lines? What did he advise them to avoid? Why did the pilot 'cut the engine right back' as they jumped? Why did the pilot tell him to be careful of the flare?

Language study

Instruction/Command	Report			
Be careful! Mind out! Watch out! Look out!	He	told warned advised	them to	be careful. mind out. watch out. look out.
Don't jump!	He	told warned advised	them not to jump.	

You must do it carefully	*in case* you burn yourself.[1] *in case of* burns.[2]

You must be careful	*to avoid*	burns. burning yourself.
Firemen wear special clothes *to prevent* them from burning themselves.		

In case is followed by a clause.
Compare this to *because* (Unit 40) and *although*.
   In case of is followed by a noun.
Compare this to *because of* (Unit 40) and *in spite of*.

Exercise 2

I'd put in some sticking plaster in case I cut myself.
I'd take a spare can of petrol in case we ran out.
I'd take a hammer because we'd need to put in tent pegs.

Make lists of:
1 things you might put in a first-aid kit.
2 things you might check on a car before a very long journey.
3 things you might take on a two-week camping holiday.

Compare your lists with other pairs. Say *why* you have included all the items on your list. For example:

Although it might be useful, I wouldn't bother to take a spare can of water.

Now criticize other students' lists.

Decide on a final list of the best items to take.

Exercise 3
Look at the pictures.
Why do you think the advice is given? Think of reasons for each piece of advice and make a list of accidents which might happen as a result of ignoring the advice.

Exercise 4
Use your list, and make conversations like this:
A I fell off the ladder. It slipped sideways.
B You should | have used
               | have been using
   a heavier step-ladder.
A Why?
B A heavier step-ladder wouldn't slip sideways.

Preventing fires

Keep a close eye on oil or fat on the cooker. And don't fill your chip pan too full. Chip pan fires are very common.

Keep curtains well away from fires and cookers. Make sure electric fires are not too close to furniture or drying clothes.

Never smoke in bed. And beware of falling asleep in a chair when you're smoking.

Don't leave burning cigarettes in ashtrays.

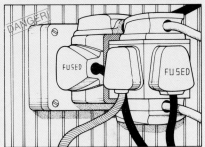

Always unplug the television and other electrical appliances when you're not using them to make absolutely sure they are safe. Otherwise a fault can cause a fire. Remember too that fires can be caused by faulty wiring. Check that your plugs are correctly wired and sockets are not overloaded.

Outdoor fires

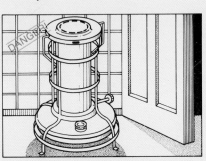

Don't leave paraffin heaters in a draught or where they're in danger of being knocked over. Fasten them to the wall if possible. Be especially careful with the older type of paraffin heater.

Fireworks cause tragedies every year. Teach your children to handle them carefully. And don't let children get too close to bonfires in case they fall onto them.

Use camping stoves with great care. They can be very dangerous, especially with your children around.

Don't let children have matches or candles inside a tent if they're camping.

From "Play if Safe" Health Education Council

The crime of the century?

Read the text. Number the pictures in the right order.

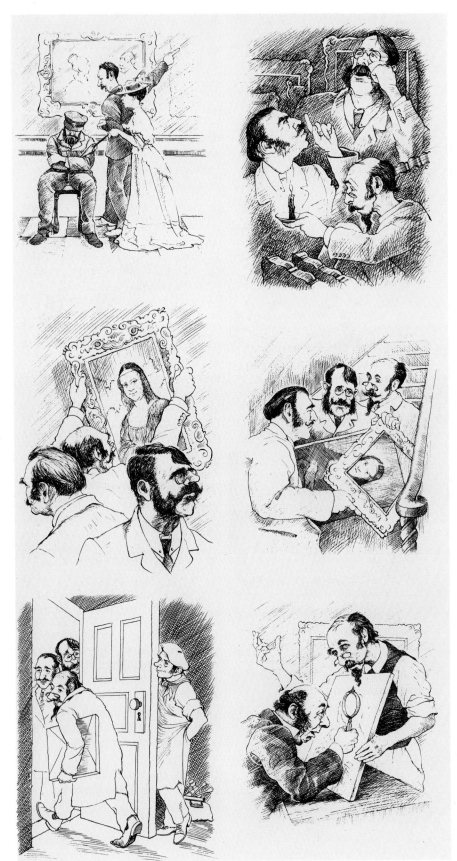

On Tuesday August 11th 1911 a young artist, Louis Beraud, arrived at the Louvre in Paris to complete a painting of the Salon Carré. This was the room where the world's most famous painting, the *Mona Lisa* by Leonardo da Vinci, was on display. To his surprise there was an empty space where the painting should have been. A guard told him it was probably being photographed. An hour later several visitors had complained about the missing picture, and so the guard went to enquire about it. At 11 o'clock the museum authorities realized that the painting had been stolen. The police were called, but it was 3 pm before the exits were locked. The newspapers were told at 4 pm, and the next day headlines all over the world announced the theft.

Actually the Leonardo had been gone for more than twenty-four hours before anyone noticed it was missing. The museum was always closed on Mondays for maintenance. Just before closing time on Sunday 9th three men had entered the museum, where they had hidden themselves in a storeroom. They were Vincenzo Perrugia, an Italian house painter, who had helped cover the picture with glass a few months previously, and two brothers, Vincenzo and Michele Lancelotti. Early on Monday morning they left the store-room, where they had spent the night, and mingled with the cleaners and workmen. They were wearing the official white tunics of the maintenance men. The actual theft was quick and simple. Perrugia removed the painting from the wall while the others kept watch. They took it from its frame on a stairway and headed for a back exit. To their horror the duplicate key which they had made did not fit the lock. Fortunately a passing workman obligingly opened the door for them, and they walked out.

In spite of massive publicity and the offer of a large reward, nothing was seen or heard of the painting for two years, until Perrugia turned up in Florence with it hidden in the false bottom of a trunk. Perrugia tried to sell it to a dealer for half a million lire. The dealer contacted the Uffizi Gallery, where experts examined it. They contacted the police, who arrested Perrugia on December 13th 1913. Perrugia claimed he had stolen it as an act of patriotism, because, he said, the painting had been looted from the Italian nation by Napoleon. Actually it had been bought from Leonardo by King Francis I of France 400 years earlier. The painting was returned to Paris, and Perrugia was imprisoned for 7 months. The court believed he was insane, but genuinely guided by patriotic motives. It seemed that the crime of the century had been solved.

But had it? Perrugia was keen to claim all responsibility for the theft, and it was twenty years before the whole story came out. In fact Perrugia had been working for two master criminals, who went unpunished for their crime. They were Eduardo de Valfierno, a confidence trickster, and Yves Chaudron, a brilliant forger.

Valfierno and Chaudron had made their fortunes in South America through a complicated art fraud. They would offer to steal a famous painting from a gallery for a crooked dealer or an unscrupulous private collector. They would then make a copy of the picture and, with the help of bribed gallery attendants, would then tape the copy to the back of the original painting. The dealer would then be taken to the gallery and would be invited to make a secret mark on the back of the painting. Of course the dealer would actually be marking the copy. Valfierno would later produce forged newspaper cuttings announcing the theft of the original, and then produce the copy, complete with secret marking. If the dealer were to see the painting still in the gallery, he would be persuaded that it was a copy, and that he possessed the genuine one.

They made enough money from this to move to Paris in 1910. Chaudron then painted not one, but six copies of the *Mona Lisa*, using 400-year-old wood panels from antique Italian furniture. The forgeries were carefully aged, so that the varnish was cracked and dirty. Valfierno commissioned Perrugia to steal the original, and told him to hide it until Valfierno contacted him. Perrugia waited in vain in a tiny room in Paris with the painting, but heard nothing from his partners in crime. They had gone to New York, where the six

copies were already in store. They had sent them there before the original was stolen. At that time it was quite common for artists to copy old masters, which would be sold quite honestly as imitations, so there had been no problems with US Customs. Valfierno went on to sell all six copies for $300,000 each. The buyers were committing a serious crime themselves, so could do nothing when the original turned up in 1913. Valfierno told the story to a journalist in 1914, on condition that it would not be published until his death.

Does the story end there? The painting was missing for two years, and collectors (and conmen) have claimed that Perrugia returned a copy. It is also possible that Leonardo may have painted several versions of the Mona Lisa. Certainly there are genuinely old Mona Lisas which are not replicas, because they are significantly different from the one in the Louvre, showing a younger Mona Lisa, or different backgrounds. They might be copies made by Leonardo's pupils, or they might even be by Leonardo himself. A biography of Leonardo written in 1550 says that the painting bought by Francis I was unfinished. Perhaps his definitive version is one of the others. There has been a lot of controversy and argument about a 450-year-old painting, but after all, maybe that's what she's smiling about.

Language study

> They would make a copy of the picture. (*would do*)
> The dealer would actually be marking a copy. (*would be doing*)
> The dealer would be taken to the gallery. (*would be done*)

Exercise 1
You could tell the story of Valfierno's trick in the present tense, as if Valfierno were telling a friend about it now. Explain the trick. Begin: *What we do is this. We offer to steal ...*

Now imagine one of Valfierno's victims telling the story. Explain the trick again. *You see what he did was this. He offered ...*

Exercise 2
It was the room. The Mona Lisa was there.

It was the room | *where / in which* | the Mona Lisa was.

Go through the text and find examples with *where/which/when/who*. Look at the commas and discuss whether they are necessary.

Advice and suggestions

Scene 1

Ralph's house in London

Chuck Yes, boss?
Ralph Have you seen this ... in the morning paper?
Chuck Let me see ... 'semi-literate' ... 'half-wit' ... 'least intelligent' ... I don't think he liked the film, boss.
Ralph It's Anderson, again. I'm going down there to see him.
Chuck Should I come with you, boss?
Ralph What? Yes ... get the car.
Chuck If I were you, I'd punch him on the nose, boss.
Ralph That's what I'm going to do.
Chuck You want to really show him this time.
Ralph Well, let's go then.
Chuck Boss ... don't you think we'd better tell Sam first?
Ralph Huh? Yeah, perhaps we should. Get him on the phone.

Scene 2

Sam is Ralph's manager

Sam Samuel Compton.
Ralph Sam, it's me ... Ralph.
Sam Oh, hi, Ralph. Did you see the paper?
Ralph Yes. I'm going down to see Anderson now.
Sam What? No, you'd better not, Ralph. Leave it.
Ralph Did you see what he called me? 'Semi-literate' ...
Sam He's a critic, Ralph.
Ralph That's not criticism ... it's ... it's libel! He's not going to get away with it.
Sam All right, Ralph. Calm down. Perhaps you ought to talk to a lawyer.
Ralph A lawyer?
Sam Mm. Maybe you could sue him.
Ralph I'll sue him for every penny he's got.
Sam Yes, well ... why don't you just phone a lawyer. Go and have a talk about it ...

29th February   'London Telegram'

FILM REVIEWS
by Laurie Anderson

South-side Mac (Charles Orson, WBC)
I was frankly shocked by this film, which is a version of *Macbeth* set in present-day Chicago. In particular the performance of young British actor Ralph James as Mac Betts (i.e. Macbeth!) was appalling. James is the semi-literate half-wit, whose sudden rise to fame in *Batman III* surprised everybody. He must be the least intelligent millionaire in Hollywood, and as Betts his slow monotonous voice

Scene 3

Mrs Spencer is Ralph's lawyer.

Mrs Spencer Mr James ... do come in. Take a seat.
Ralph Did Sam speak to you?
Mrs Spencer Yes, Mr Compton showed me the review.
Ralph I want to sue.
Mrs Spencer I would strongly advise you to think it over most carefully, Mr James.
Ralph I've thought it over already.
Mrs Spencer The best thing you can do is to forget all about it.
Ralph Look! You're my lawyer, aren't you? Sue him.
Mrs Spencer I don't think we should, Mr James. The review was in one newspaper ... not a popular one, either. Very few people will have read it, probably few of your fans read the more serious papers ... if you don't mind me saying so. If you sue, there'll be a lot of publicity, bad publicity. You know the saying 'mud sticks'.
Ralph But ... it's Anderson again! Do you remember what he wrote about my marriage last year?
Mrs Spencer But you may remember that his report was true, Mr James. Really, I suggest you forget it.
Ralph You mean ... I shouldn't sue.
Mrs Spencer Exactly.
Ralph Well I'll just go down there and have a little talk with him.
Mrs Spencer I would recommend you not to do that, Mr James. Really. My advice is to forget it.

Exercise 1
Go through the three conversations. Note each time that someone gives Ralph advice.

Language study

Giving advice			
You	ought want*	to	do this.
You	should 'd better		do this.
I	'd advise advise strongly advise		you to do this.
If I were you, I'd do this. Why don't you do this?			
The best thing		to do is ... you can do is ...	
I would recommend you to do this.			

* colloquial

Making suggestions		
I suggest we do this.		
Shall Should	we do this?	
Let's (not) do this.		
How What	about (doing) this?	
Why not do this? Why don't you do this?		
We	might could	do this.
We can do this, if you like. Do you fancy doing this? Fancy doing this?*		

Exercise 2

1 Student A is a travel agent. Student B wants a 14-day holiday. The travel agent recommends Bournemouth, and advises on places to go in the area.

2 You are *both* planning a holiday in Bournemouth. Plan 14 days, deciding when to take excursions, and on which days.

Exercise 3

Four of you are on holiday in Bournemouth. One likes sunbathing and shopping, one is very interested in historical buildings and churches, one likes to see countryside and coastal areas, the fourth likes wildlife and is a car enthusiast. Decide how to divide up the 14-day holiday. Decide if it's worth renting a car.

Exercise 4

1 There are four adults on holiday for 14 days in Bournemouth. Decide **a** whether to hire a car **b** how many days to hire it for **c** which kind of car to hire.

2 Student A works in a car hire office. Student B enquires about hire. Make recommendations.

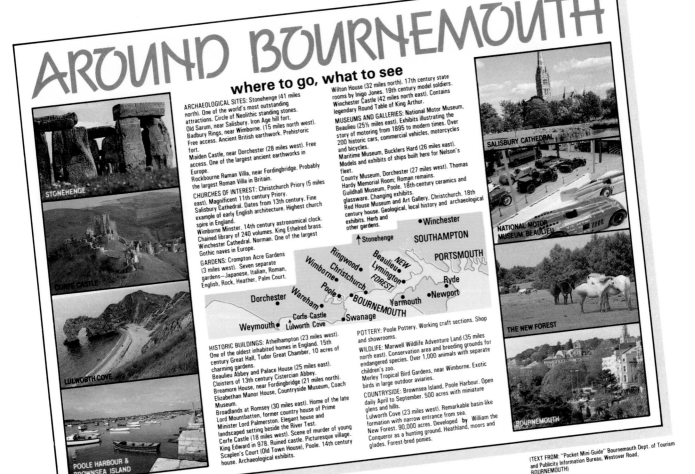

AROUND BOURNEMOUTH

where to go, what to see

ARCHAEOLOGICAL SITES: Stonehenge (41 miles north). One of the world's most outstanding attractions. Circle of Neolithic standing stones. Old Sarum, near Salisbury. Iron Age hill fort. Badbury Rings, near Wimborne. (15 miles north west). Free access. Ancient British earthwork. Prehistoric fort.
Maiden Castle, near Dorchester (28 miles west). Free access. One of the largest ancient earthworks in Europe.
Rockbourne Roman Villa, near Fordingbridge. Probably the largest Roman Villa in Britain.

CHURCHES OF INTEREST: Christchurch Priory (5 miles east). Magnificent 11th century Priory.
Salisbury Cathedral. Dates from 13th century. Fine example of early English architecture. Highest church spire in England.
Wimborne Minster. 14th century astronomical clock. Chained library of 240 volumes. King Ethelred brass. Winchester Cathedral. Norman. One of the largest Gothic naves in Europe.

GARDENS: Crompton Acre Gardens (3 miles west). Seven separate gardens—Japanese, Italian, Roman, English, Rock, Heather, Palm Court.

HISTORIC BUILDINGS: Athelhampton (23 miles west). One of the oldest inhabited homes in England. 15th century Great Hall, Tudor Great Chamber, 10 acres of charming gardens.
Beaulieu Abbey and Palace House (25 miles east). Cloisters of 13th century Cistercian Abbey.
Breamore House, near Fordingbridge (21 miles north). Elizabethan Manor House, Countryside Museum, Coach Museum.
Broadlands at Romsey (30 miles east). Home of the late Lord Mountbatten, former country house of Prime Minister Lord Palmerston. Elegant house and landscaped setting beside the River Test.
Corfe Castle (18 miles west). Scene of murder of young King Edward in 978. Ruined castle. Picturesque village.
Scaplen's Court (Old Town House), Poole. 14th century house. Archaeological exhibits.

Wilton House (32 miles north). 17th century state rooms by Inigo Jones. 19th century model soldiers.
Winchester Castle (42 miles north east). Contains legendary Round Table of King Arthur.

MUSEUMS AND GALLERIES: National Motor Museum, Beaulieu (25½ miles east). Exhibits illustrating the story of motoring from 1895 to modern times. Over 200 historic cars, commercial vehicles, motorcycles and bicycles.
Maritime Museum, Bucklers Hard (26 miles east). Models and exhibits of ships built here for Nelson's fleet.
County Museum, Dorchester (27 miles west). Thomas Hardy Memorial Room; Roman remains.
Guildhall Museum, Poole. 18th-century ceramics and glassware. Changing exhibits.
Red House Museum and Art Gallery, Christchurch. 18th century house. Geological, local history and archaeological exhibits. Herb and other gardens.

POTTERY: Poole Pottery. Working craft sections. Shop and showrooms.

WILDLIFE: Marwell Wildlife Adventure Land (35 miles north east). Conservation area and breeding grounds for endangered species. Over 1,000 animals with separate children's zoo.
Merley Tropical Bird Gardens, near Wimborne. Exotic birds in large outdoor aviaries.

COUNTRYSIDE: Brownsea Island, Poole Harbour. Open daily April to September. 500 acres with miniature glens and hills.
Lulworth Cove (23 miles west). Remarkable basin-like formation with narrow entrance from sea. Developed by William the Conqueror as a hunting ground. Heathland, moors and glades. Forest-bred ponies.
New Forest. 90,000 acres.

STONEHENGE

CORFE CASTLE

LULWORTH COVE

POOLE HARBOUR & BROWNSEA ISLAND

SALISBURY CATHEDRAL

NATIONAL MOTOR MUSEUM, BEAULIEU

THE NEW FOREST

BOURNEMOUTH

Map labels: Winchester, SOUTHAMPTON, Stonehenge, PORTSMOUTH, Ringwood, Beaulieu, NEW, Lymington, FOREST, Wimborne, Christchurch, Ryde, Poole, Newport, Dorchester, Wareham, BOURNEMOUTH, Yarmouth, Weymouth, Corfe Castle, Lulworth Cove, Swanage

(TEXT FROM: "Pocket Mini-Guide" Bournemouth Dept. of Tourism and Publicity Information Bureau, Westover Road, BOURNEMOUTH)

UNITED KINGDOM NATIONAL TARIFF—1983

All Hertz cars are fitted with radios. Specific car models cannot be guaranteed.

GROUP	SEATS	MANUAL TRANSMISSION		TIME & MILEAGE 1 & 2 DAYS ONLY PER DAY	PER MILE	UNLIMITED MILEAGE RATES ON ALL RENTALS 3 DAYS OR MORE 3-6 DAYS PER DAY	7-27 DAYS PER DAY	28 DAYS + PER DAY
A	4	FORD Fiesta / BL Metro	■	£13.50	15p	£27.00	£21.00	£14.00
B	4	FORD Escort / VAUXHALL Astra / BL Maestro	■	£16.00	16p	£31.50	£24.00	£16.25
C	5	FORD Sierra 1.6L / VAUXHALL Cavalier 1.6L	■	£17.00	18p	£35.00	£27.00	£20.50
D	4	BMW 316 or similar	■ ○	£25.00	26p	£47.00	£36.00	£29.50
		AUTOMATIC TRANSMISSION						
E	4	*VAUXHALL Astra 1.3L	■	£17.00	17p	£35.25	£28.00	£20.50
F	5	FORD Sierra 2.0GL / VAUXHALL Carlton / SAAB 900GLS	■ □ ▲ ■ ▲	£26.00	27p	£50.00	£39.00	£31.50
G	5	*FORD Granada / *BMW 520i	■ □ ▲ ■ ▲ ○	£40.00	42p	£79.00	£61.00	£45.00
		ESTATE CARS/STATION WAGONS - MINIBUS						
I	5	FORD Escort 1.6L / VAUXHALL Astra 1.6L	■	£23.00	23p	£46.00	£35.00	£28.00

■ RADIO □ STEREO PLAYER ○ SUNROOF ▲ POWER ASSISTED STEERING

Sleep

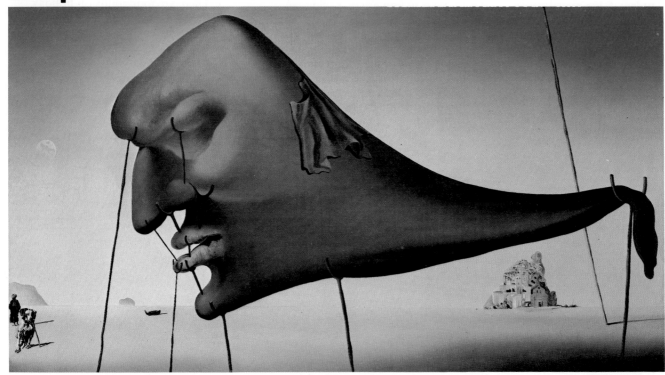

sleep¹/sliip/ *n* 1 (U) condition of the body and mind such as recurs regularly every night, in which the eyes are closed and the muscles, nervous system, etc are relaxed: *How many hours' — do you need? He didn't get much —. Do you ever talk in your —? get to —,* manage to fall asleep, succeed in passing into the condition of —: *I couldn't get to — last night. go to —,* fall asleep. *have one's — out,* continue *—ing* until one wakes up naturally: *Don't wake her up — let her have her — out. put sb to —,* cause him to fall asleep. *put (a pet animal) to —,* (euphem) deliberately kill it (because of illness, etc). 2a —, period of —: *have a short/good/restful, etc. —; a — of three hours.* '*—walker n* person who walks while asleep. *— less adj* without —: *pass a — less night. — lessly. adv—.less.ness n.*
sleep²/sliip/*vi,vt (pp,pt* slept/slept/) 1 (VP2A,B,C) rest in the condition of —, be or fall asleep: *We go to bed to —. He —s well/badly. She slept (for) eight hours. — like a top/log, — very soundly. — round the clock; — the clock round, —* for twelve hours continuously. 2 (VP6A) provide beds for: *This hotel —s 300 guests. —ing n* (in compounds) '*—ing-bag n* warmly lined and waterproof bag in which to — when out of doors (eg on holiday) or in a tent. '*—ing-car n* railway coach fitted with beds or berths. '*—ing-draught/-pill n* one that contains a drug to help sb to —

Nobody knows why we sleep, but we all need to. There are no rules about how much sleep is necessary but the average adult sleeps for 7 hours 20 minutes. About 8% of adults are happy with five hours or less and 4% want ten hours or more. Babies need between fourteen to eighteen hours whereas the elderly need less than they did when young but often take a nap during the day.

Normal sleep is made up of two alternating phases – orthodox sleep and paradoxical sleep. Orthodox sleep, which involves no dreaming, usually takes place in the early part of the night. Paradoxical sleep or (REM) rapid-eye-movement sleep, which is associated with dreaming, occurs mostly in the later part of the night for varying periods of time. If you wake up during an REM phase you will almost certainly remember your dreams.

When we are asleep, the bodily functions slow down. Body temperature falls. This is because your body keeps to a regular 24 hour cycle – the circadian rhythm – during which body temperature rises and falls at fixed times. Normally body temperature is lowest in the middle of the night and highest in the afternoon. People who change time zones interfere with the circadian rhythm and get 'jet lag'. It takes

some time for the circadian rhythm to adjust to the new pattern of day and night.

Everyone at some time has difficulty in sleeping but if you miss a couple of hours of sleep no harm is done. You may feel tired and irritable the next day but the body soon makes up for the loss. If you try to stay awake night after night however, you soon begin to behave strangely. You lose the ability to concentrate and judgement is impaired. You begin to imagine strange things and your behaviour becomes deranged.

A lot of people have serious sleep problems. Some people find that they cannot get to sleep or wake up in the middle of the night or too early in the morning. There are a number of causes. Worry and depression are the most common. All kinds of things in the environment can affect sleep – noise, light, heat, cold or new surroundings. Pain in illness can also keep people awake. Most of us can accept temporary sleeplessness without seeking help but 3½ million people in Britain take drugs to help them sleep. Many people become addicted to their sleeping pills but sleeping pills do not deal with the causes of insomnia and it is better to avoid them if you can. It is much better to identify the problem and remove it.

Exercise 1
Which of the following might help you to sleep and which might prevent you from sleeping? Draw up two lists and discuss with a partner.

a hot bath/soft music/doing a crossword/a cup of coffee/somebody snoring/a cold room/the sound of rain/an aspirin/vigorous exercise/ counting sheep/deep breathing/birds singing/an eye shade/a cold shower/a closed window/a cup of tea/a clock ticking/watching a film on TV/ear plugs/an alcoholic drink/closed curtains/silence/an open window/a cheese sandwich/a walk/open curtains/a hard bed/a warm room/ darkness/running water/people talking/a big meal/a cigarette/reading a book/a new bed/traffic noise/a baby crying/a dripping tap/a milky drink/ soft lighting

Exercise 2
Many people follow a routine before they go to sleep. Write down five things you normally do before you go to sleep.

Exercise 3
What percentage of adults like between 5 and 10 hours sleep? What are the two phases of sleep known as? What happens if you wake up during a REM phase? What's the circadian rhythm? What's jet lag? What happens if you miss sleep for a long period? What environmental factors affect sleep? How many British people regularly take sleeping tablets? Write down five things you do after you wake up.

Exercise 4
Which of the following adjectives would you associate with someone having had a good or a bad night's sleep? Make two lists.
alert/drowsy/nervy/bright/irritable/ energetic/active/dozy/sluggish/weary/ relaxed/efficient/tired/exhausted/ fresh/good-tempered

Exercise 5
Describe what happens when we do the following:
a yawn
b snore
c dream
d sleepwalk.
Why do you think we do these things?

Exercise 6
Write a paragraph, describing your bedroom.

dream[1] /driːm/ *n* (C) 1 sth which one seems to see or experience during sleep: *to have a —(about sth); to awake from a—. '—land; '—world,* region outside the laws of nature, as experienced in sleep or in the imagination. 2 state of mind in which things going on around one seem unreal: *to live/go about in a —.* 3 mental picture(s) of the future: *to have —s of wealth and happiness.* 4 (colloq) beautiful or pleasing person, thing, experience, etc: *His holiday by the sea was a —.* —less *adj* without —s. —like/'driːmlark/*adj* like a —.
dream[2] /driːm/ *vi.vt (pt.pp* —ed /driːmd/ or dreamt /dremt/) 1 (VP2A, 3A, 6A, 15B, 9, 8, 10) — *(about/of),* have —s; see experience, in a dream: imagine; suppose: *He often —s. The soldier often —t of/about home. He —t that he was at sea. I certainly didn't promise you £100; you must have —t it. I wouldn't — of doing such a thing,* The idea would never occur to me. *He little —ed that...* did not imagine or suppose that... 2 (VP15B) —*away,* spend idly: *— away one's time/the hours.* 3. (VP15B) — up, *(colloq) imagine, conceive (a plan etc).* — er *n* person who —s; person with impractical ideas, plans, etc.

snore /snoː(r)/ *vi* (VP2A,C) breathe roughly and noisily while sleeping: *Does my snoring bother you?* *n* sound of snoring: *His —s woke me up.* **snorer** *n* person who —s.

yawn /jɔːn/ *vi* (VP2A,C) 1 take (usu involuntarily) a deep breath with the mouth wide open, as when sleepy or bored. 2 be wide open: *a —ing fissure. A gulf —ed at our feet.* *n* (C) act of —ing (1).

The Importance of Being Earnest

Oscar Wilde's comedy, *The Importance of Being Earnest* was first performed in 1895, and since then it has become the most performed play in the English theatre. They say that every Englishman is (or wants to be) an actor, and amateur dramatics are certainly a popular pastime. Local groups from churches, schools and clubs perform plays in small halls all over the country, and this is their favourite play. On any Friday or Saturday night in the winter months it is being performed somewhere in the country.

In this scene, Jack Worthing is being interviewed by his prospective mother-in-law, the formidable Lady Bracknell, for the first time.

Exercise 1
Look through the text. What sentences might make you think that Lady Bracknell is more interested in appearances than facts?

Exercise 2
Read through the text in pairs. What information does Lady Bracknell elicit from Jack?

Lady Bracknell [*sitting down*] You can take a seat, Mr Worthing.

[*Looks in her pocket for note-book and pencil.*]

Jack Thank you, Lady Bracknell, I prefer standing.

Lady Bracknell [*pencil and note-book in hand*] I feel bound to tell you that you are not down on my list of eligible young men, although I have the same list as the dear Duchess of Bolton has. We work together, in fact. However, I am quite ready to enter your name, should your answers be what a really affectionate mother requires. Do you smoke?

Jack Well, yes, I must admit I smoke.

Lady Bracknell I am glad to hear it. A man should always have an occupation of some kind. There are far too many idle men in London as it is. How old are you?

Jack Twenty-nine.

Lady Bracknell A very good age to be married at. I have always been of the opinion that a man who desires to get married should know either everything or nothing. Which do you know?

Jack [*after some hesitation*] I know nothing, Lady Bracknell.

Lady Bracknell I am pleased to hear it. I do not approve of anything that tampers with natural ignorance. Ignorance is like a delicate exotic fruit; touch it and the bloom is gone. The whole theory of modern education is radically unsound. Fortunately in England, at any rate, education produces no effect whatsoever. If it did, it would prove a serious danger to the upper classes, and probably lead to acts of violence in Grosvenor Square. What is your income?

Jack Between seven and eight thousand a year.

Lady Bracknell [*makes a note in her book*] In land, or in investments?

Jack In investments, chiefly.

Lady Bracknell That is satisfactory. What between the duties expected of one during one's lifetime, and the duties exacted from one after one's death, land has ceased to be either a profit or a pleasure. It gives one position, and prevents one from keeping it up. That's all that can be said about land.

Jack I have a country house with some land, of course, attached to it, about fifteen hundred acres, I believe; but I don't depend on that for my real income. In fact, as far as I can make out, the poachers are the only people who make anything out of it.

Lady Bracknell A country house! How many bedrooms? Well, that point can be cleared up afterwards. You have a town house, I hope? A girl with a simple, unspoiled nature, like Gwendolen, could hardly be expected to reside in the country.

Jack Well, I own a house in Belgrave Square, but it is let by the year to Lady Bloxham. Of course, I can get it back whenever I like, at six months' notice.

Lady Bracknell Lady Bloxham? I don't know her.

Jack Oh, she goes about very little. She is a lady considerably advanced in years.

Lady Bracknell Ah, nowadays that is no guarantee of respectability of character. What number in Belgrave Square?

Jack 149.

Lady Bracknell [*shaking her head*] The unfashionable side. I thought there was something. However, that could easily be altered.

Jack Do you mean the fashion, or the side?

Lady Bracknell [*sternly*] Both, if necessary, I presume. What are your politics?

Jack Well, I am afraid I really have none. I am a Liberal Unionist.

Lady Bracknell Oh, they count as Tories. They dine with us. Or come in the evening, at any rate. Now to minor matters. Are your parents living?

Jack I have lost both my parents.

Lady Bracknell To lose one parent, Mr Worthing, may be regarded as a misfortune; to lose both looks like carelessness. Who was your father? He was evidently a man of some wealth. Was he born in what the Radical papers call the purple of commerce, or did he rise from the ranks of the aristocracy?

Jack I am afraid I really don't know. The fact is, Lady Bracknell, I said I had lost my parents. It would be nearer the truth to say that my parents seem to have lost me. . . I don't actually know who I am by birth. I was . . . well, I was found.

Lady Bracknell Found!

Jack The late Mr Thomas Cardew, an old gentleman of a very charitable and kindly disposition, found me, and gave me the name of Worthing, because he happened to have a first-class ticket for Worthing in his pocket at the time. Worthing is a place in Sussex. It is a seaside resort.

Lady Bracknell Where did the charitable gentleman who had a first-class ticket for this seaside resort find you?

Jack [*gravely*] In a hand-bag.

Lady Bracknell A hand-bag?

Jack [*very seriously*] Yes, Lady Bracknell. I was in a hand-bag – a somewhat large, black leather hand-bag, with handles to it – an ordinary hand-bag in fact.

Lady Bracknell In what locality did this Mr James, or Thomas, Cardew come across this ordinary hand-bag?

Jack In the cloak-room at Victoria Station. It was given to him in mistake for his own.

Lady Bracknell The cloak-room at Victoria Station?

Jack Yes. The Brighton line.

Lady Bracknell The line is immaterial. Mr Worthing, I confess I feel somewhat bewildered by what you have just told me. To be born, or at any rate bred, in a hand-bag, whether it had handles or not, seems to me to display a contempt for the ordinary decencies of family life that reminds one of the worst excesses of the French Revolution. And I presume you know what that unfortunate movement led to? As for the particular locality in which the hand-bag was found, a cloak-room at a railway station might serve to conceal a social indiscretion – has probably, indeed, been used for that purpose before now – but it could hardly be regarded as an assured basis for a recognized position in good society.

Jack May I ask you then what you would advise me to do? I need hardly say I would do anything in the world to ensure Gwendolen's happiness.

Lady Bracknell I would strongly advise you, Mr Worthing, to try and acquire some relations as soon as possible, and to make a definite effort to produce at any rate one parent, of either sex, before the season is quite over.

Jack Well, I don't see how I could possibly manage to do that. I can produce the hand-bag at any moment. It is in my dressing-room at home. I really think that should satisfy you, Lady Bracknell.

Lady Bracknell Me, sir! What has it to do with me? You can hardly imagine that I and Lord Bracknell would dream of allowing our only daughter – a girl brought up with the utmost care – to marry into a cloak-room, and form an alliance with a parcel. Good morning, Mr Worthing!

Language study

Find two uses of *presume* and one of *believe* in the text.

We use words like this when we are assuming something . . . about a fact, or someone's knowledge, or that an event will happen or has happened.

There are other words we can use for assumptions:

more formal	neutral	less formal
I presume I assume I believe	I think I suppose I understand	I reckon I guess

Look through the dialogue, find phrases people use when they are appealing to facts, or to their knowledge. Look at the list below. Which ones are used in the dialogue?

Actually . . . As a matter of fact . . . In fact . . . ., in fact The fact is . . . The fact of the matter is . . . On a point of fact . . .	As far as I know . . . As far as I can make out . . . To the best of my knowledge . . . As far as I can tell . . . From what I've been told . . . As far as I've heard . . . I've always understood that . . .

Exercise 3

Imagine a conversation between a parent and someone who wishes to marry their son or daughter. What kind of information will they wish to elicit?

Act out the conversation. Look at the Language study section, on assumptions and facts. Try to elicit information by using assumption words. The replies should use factual phrases.

Parent *I assume you've got a job.*
Young Person *Well . . . as a matter of fact, I haven't. I'm . . . er . . . looking for one.*

Exercise 4

Try it again. This time make the parent very formal and clearly against the young person. The young person should be more informal.

Parent *Weddings are very expensive, you know.*
Young person *Yeah, well, I guess you'll pay for all that.*

Exercise 5

Work in groups of four or five. The group consists of father, mother, son or daughter and their prospective fiancé(e), (and a grandparent). The prospective fiancé(e) is a singer in a rock group. The father and mother should take different attitudes. (The grandparent could be sympathetic, perhaps even a fan of the group.)

Act out a similar situation. The son or daughter has returned, from University. The parents have invited the 'boy/girl next door' for dinner, and the parents very much approve of him/her. However, their child dislikes him/her intensely.

Away from it all?

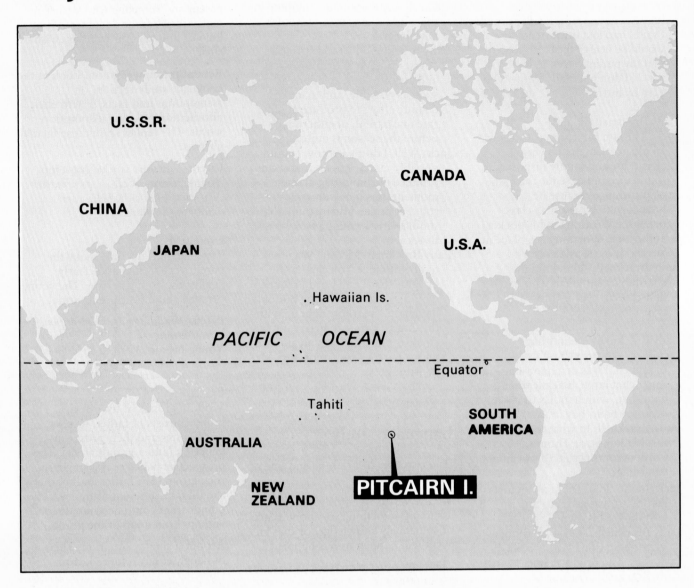

Many of us might sometimes dream of 'getting away from it all', of living on a remote and beautiful desert island like some latter-day Robinson Crusoe. Desert islands are fascinating places, we can imagine escaping from the pressures of modern life to an image of simplicity and tranquillity. There is something appealing in the story of Philip Quarll, an Englishman who was shipwrecked on an island off the Pacific coast of Mexico in 1675. He lived alone for 50 years before a ship arrived. Quarll refused to leave, saying to his would-be savers: 'I was shipwrecked, thanks to my Maker, and was cast away. Were I made Emperor of the Universe, I would not be concerned with the world again, nor would you require me (to be concerned), did you but know the happiness I enjoy out of it.'

There are other desert island stories. A group of English seamen who mutinied against the harsh regime on board HMS Bounty in 1789, escaped with some Tahitian women to Pitcairn Island in the South Pacific, which has been called 'the most remote and inaccessible, inhabited island on Earth'. The descendants of the mutineers still live there, living a simple and peaceful life.

After Marlon Brando had finished working on the film Mutiny on the Bounty he bought an island, Tetiaroa, in the Tahitian group. He said that he wanted it to be 'a laboratory for developing ways for the South Pacific to survive the onslaught of civilization'.

For most of us, however, the dream remains unreal, and we never think

seriously about escaping from civilization. For one man, though, the dream is becoming reality.

His name is Arthur 'Smiley' Ratcliffe. He's a millionaire who owns large areas of Virginia and West Virginia, who has five Rolls-Royces, and who started his career with a loan of $1,500. Ratcliffe spent years exploring the Pacific looking for a place to escape from the modern world. In 1981 he finally discovered Henderson Island, an uninhabited island 110 miles north of Pitcairn Island. He offered to spend one million dollars on Pitcairn (population 44) in return for permission to establish a home on Henderson. Smiley, a 57-year-old, who is a teetotaller, and who works 20 hours a day, 52 weeks a year, was interviewed by Simon Winchester for the *Sunday Times* in May 1983. This is what he said:

'I've thought about it for many, many years. I've wanted to set up my own place where goddam people like Freud aren't worth a hill of beans, where there ain't no rules, and where people don't give a damn about doing an honest day's work. I'll work like hell and build a place for myself and my grand-children, and then I'll die a happy man. That's my dream, and now it looks like it may come true.'

'I had been to Pitcairn first and hell, you couldn't wish for a nicer place. The people are just like Virginians were 50 years ago when I was growing up. They were so happy and kind and pleased to see me, and when I said I was figuring on living near them they just near about flipped, they were so happy. We took off for Henderson – God! was it stormy. All the rest of the fellers on the boat got sick, but not me. I was that screwed up inside with excitement that I didn't feel a thing. It took a couple of days sailing, and then we got there one afternoon.'

'It was just what I wanted. Flat as a pancake. Good beach. Landing place. Jungle thick as hell, mind you, but I figure I can clear that. And the weather's about as perfect as you can get – 70 every day, a little rain once in a while. Just a great place for old Smiley Ratcliffe to come and settle down. So that's what I'm figgerin' to do.'

But Smiley Ratcliffe has no intention of living like Robinson Crusoe. The list of what he intends to take begins like this:

Eight men (all Virginians who work on his farm; strong fellows who can wield axes and drive mechanical diggers, and who have agreed to accompany him.)

A concrete block maker. A well-driver. Six tractors. Two graders. Six bush-hogs (devices for clearing undergrowth). Generators. Four aircraft. Three landing craft. Ten milk cows. Ten beef cows. Cement . . .
The list goes on for pages. He already has a seaplane and a private jet, and is arranging to buy a ship which will make its initial journey from San Diego. 'We'll call in at Pitcairn and pick up some of the fellers who'd like to work. Then we'll tool up to Henderson and start digging and building. If we start next year we should have the main house done in six months and the airstrip finished by '85. Then it's all plain sailing from then on. So long as I can get a cool glass of milk and my chewing tobacco, I'll be happy.'

Smiley told reporters he wanted his grandchildren to grow up in a society free from 'crime and dope and Elvis Presley'. That's one man's paradise.

Exercise 1
Desert Island Discs has been a popular radio programme for about 40 years in England. Famous people are asked to choose eight records, a book (excluding The Bible and Shakespeare) and a luxury that they would take to a desert island. What would you take? Why would you choose that?

Exercise 2
Imagine now that you are Smiley Ratcliffe. What sort of paradise would you try and establish? Think about things like the political system, education, religion and whether you would have television and radio. Draw up a 'master plan' in groups.

Exercise 3
I'm not a millionaire, so I won't buy a desert island.
But if I were a millionaire, I would buy a desert island.
Transform these sentences in the same way:
1 I've got flu, so I won't go to school tomorrow.
2 I'm very busy, so I can't watch TV this evening.
3 I'm tired, so I'll go to bed early.
4 I don't like sunbathing, so I won't choose a beach holiday.
5 I haven't been to London, so I don't know anything about it.

Exercise 4
Check the meanings of the slang expressions in the interview with Smiley.

Unit 50

Dear Sir

The best modern business letters are written simply, clearly and directly. Elaborate formulas and expressions are not necessary, but you will still find examples in some business letters.

Trouble in store for Mr Claus

1 Dear Sir, I regret to inform you that we have not chosen you to fill the position of Santa in our Toy Department Christmas Grotto. With thanks for your interest.

pp *Deirdre Dowdy*, Personnel Assistant
Grimsly and Harbinger Ltd.

2 Dear Mr Pamsbottom, Thank you for your letter of 13th inst. May I assure you that we are as sorry as you are that we are only able to employ one Santa Claus. Thank you for your kind offer to stand in at short notice if our Santa does not come up to standard. We are not expecting such an eventuality, but thank you for your continued interest.

pp *Deirdre Dowdy*, Personnel Assistant,
Grimsly and Harbinger Ltd.

3 Dear Mr Ramsbottom, Thank you for your letter dated the 19th. May I apologize at once for the misspelling of your surname in the letter from my assistant, Miss Dowdy. I can understand how embarrassing the error must have been, especially as your wife's name is Pamela.

Thank you for the comments you made about our selection procedure for our Toy Department casual staff. With respect, there is only room for one Santa and the present incumbent is proving most satisfactory. We took on the man most suited to the job, which is not to say that you would not have filled the bill most admirably. I can understand your disappointment.

With best wishes,

Robert Leech, Personnel Manager,
Grimsly and Harbinger Ltd.

4 Dear Mr Ramsbottom, Thank you for your further letter. May I say right away that I very much resent the implication that we rejected your application to become a member of our casual staff this Christmas because of racial prejudice. I had no knowledge that your mother's uncle was partly Jewish nor would it have made any difference to our decision. Nor was your speech impediment considered to be important. As we did not call you for interview, this would hardly have been apparent.

Yours sincerely,

R. Leech, Personnel Manager,
Grimsly and Harbinger Ltd.

5 Dear Mr Ramsbottom, Thank you for your letter including the many references from former employers, which are returned to you now, with compliments. The tone of their comment must prove some solace that we were not able to find a place for you in the Toy Department. The letter from the President of the West Ham Scottish Dancing Club gave particular enjoyment here. I did not know of your two parking fines and can assure you that these would not taint our judgment either way in recruitment situations. The fact is that we have appointed another person to the job to which you aspired and, as far as this company is concerned, that is an end to the matter.

Yours, *Deirdre Dowdy*

pp R. Leech, Personnel Manager,
Grimsly and Harbinger Ltd.

6 Dear Mr Ramsbottom, I cannot take seriously your complaints made against the member of our staff acting as Santa in our Christmas Grotto. The adjectives "short-tempered", "snappy", "impatient" and "aggressive", which you use, do not accord with our knowledge of the man in question. May I remind you that the Grotto is intended for children only and that your visits to the Toy Department are now becoming an embarrassment here.

Yours,

Robert Leech, Personnel Manager,
Grimsly and Harbinger Ltd.

7 Dear Mr Ramsbottom, Thank you for drawing to my attention the behaviour of the Santa in our Toys Department. If, as you say, the man was drunk, rude and using foul language, there can be no excuse. I shall make immediate enquiries and thank you again for bringing this sorry state of affairs to my notice.

With thanks,

Yours sincerely,

H.J. Barrington-Cox, General Manager,
Grimsly and Harbinger Ltd.

8 Dear Mr.Ramsbottom, The allegations which you made recently to our general manager, Mr Barrington-Cox, have proved to be unfounded. May I say that this came as no surprise to this department. We would be delighted if you would stop your irrational vendetta against this company.

Yours,

R. Leech, Personnel Manager,
Grimsly and Harbinger Ltd.

Language study

Dear Mr Ramsbottom, I am very sorry to hear that you and your wife will no longer be customers at Grimsly and Harbinger. A little bit of me dies when I hear that old customers have been ill-treated. I am most saddened to hear your reasons and I promise you that I will be making every effort to get to the root of your complaint.

Yours, with deepest regret,

T.W.I. Trumpington,
Chairman and Managing Director,
Grimsly and Harbinger Ltd.

9

Dear Sir, I regret to inform you that we have not chosen you to fill the position of Demonstrator in our Do-It-Yourself Department during our Easter Event. With thanks for your interest.

pp *Gladys Snubwinkle,*
Personnel Assistant,
Grimsly and Harbinger Ltd.

10

Reference to a previous business letter

| Thank you for your letter | of October 14th/14th October |
| In our/my letter | of the 14th/ dated the 14th. |

Expressing regret

| I regret | to inform you | that ... |
| I am sorry | to say/hear/read | |

Acknowledging previous letters

| I/We acknowledge receipt of | your letter of ... |
| Thank you for | |

Polite and formal thanks

Thank you for (doing it). (*note the use of the -ing form*)

Apologies

May I apologize	for (not replying sooner)
I must apologize	
I am sorry that	I was unable to reply sooner, but ...

Polite formulas

With respect, (I must point out that you are mistaken)

| I enclose | a catalogue, | with our compliments. |

By Nicholas Wapshott
(*The Times Countdown to Christmas,*
November 22 1980)
© Times Newspaper Ltd.

Exercise 1

1 How is he told he hasn't got the job?
2 Is Mr Ramsbottom prepared to start the job without much warning?
3 How does the secretary show she is signing a letter on her boss's behalf?
4 How do they reject Mr Ramsbottom's application without saying he was unsuitable?
5 Why did Mr Leach not know that Mr Ramsbottom couldn't speak properly?
6 What apart from his own letters did Mr Ramsbottom send to support his application?
7 What does Mr Ramsbottom think of the person who got the job?
8 Who does Mr Ramsbottom write to apart from Mr Leach and why?
9 How true do the allegations made by Mr Ramsbottom prove to be?
10 What does Mr Trumpington promise to do?
11 What job does Mr Ramsbottom apply for next?

Exercise 2

Look at the Language study. Go through the letters and mark examples of each type of formula. Write a formal letter of application for the job advertised. State why you would be good at it and make up a c.v. (curriculum vitae).

Exercise 3

Role-play the manager and the applicant. Conduct an interview for the job.

Exercise 4

Discuss the probable content of the letters to which Grimsly and Harbinger has replied. Make notes. Then write the letters as if from Mr Ramsbottom. Give them a formal layout and make them as short and direct as you can.

You the jury

LADY WYATT ACCUSED OF SHOP-LIFTING

On Wednesday morning I went to Hall's Department Store to do some shopping and to meet a friend for lunch. In the Ladies' Fashion Department I bought a belt and a bag and paid for them. As I was waiting for the lift to go up to the Rooftop Coffee Lounge, I saw a silk scarf that I liked. I tried it on and decided to buy it. I looked around for an assistant to pay but couldn't see anybody. The lift came and as I was late for my appointment, I put the scarf with my other purchases, intending to pay for it later on my way out. Unfortunately, I forgot to pay and was stopped at the door by the store detective who asked me to go to the manager's office where I was accused of having stolen the scarf. It's quite ridiculous. I simply forgot to pay.

I was on duty on the second floor when I observed Lady Wyatt trying on a scarf. She looked at herself in the mirror, looked round several times and then put the scarf in her bag. She then went up in the lift to the top floor café where she met a man. I kept up my observation and when they left together, I followed them to the door. She had made no attempt to pay so I stopped her and asked her to accompany me to the manager's office. She became abusive and refused to go with me until a policeman arrived on the scene.

Exercise 1
A police officer is checking through Lady Wyatt's statement.

Police officer You said that you had gone there to do some shopping. Is that right?
Lady Wyatt Yes, it is.
Police officer You also mentioned that you were going to meet a friend for lunch.
Lady Wyatt That's correct.

Continue the conversation with another student.
Then role-play a police officer and a store detective. Have a similar conversation, checking the information in the statement.

Unit 52

Read the reports on the evidence
given by four people.

DAVID WILTON'S EVIDENCE (REPORT)

David Wilton said that he was an old friend of Lady
Wyatt and that he had been the Wyatt family's accountant
for fourteen years. He had arranged to meet Lady Wyatt
for lunch at 12 o'clock to discuss some family business.
He said that he had not noticed anything unusual about
Lady Wyatt's behaviour except that twice during lunch
she had taken a pill. He added that he did not know what
the pill was for and had not asked. He stated that he
was astonished that anyone could think that Lady Wyatt
might steal as she was a very wealthy woman who could
afford to buy anything she wanted.

THE STORE MANAGER'S EVIDENCE (REPORT)

The store manager said that he did not know Lady Wyatt as
a regular customer because he had only been in his
present job for two weeks. He said that the store lost
hundreds of pounds worth of goods every week which was
why he had appointed a store detective in whom he had
the greatest confidence. He added that it was not only
the poorer members of the community who resorted to
shop-lifting.

THE DOCTOR'S EVIDENCE (REPORT)

Soames, the Wyatt family doctor, stated that he had been
prescribing pills for Lady Wyatt for some time. She had
been suffering from regular bouts of depression. He said
that a side-effect of the pill could cause erratic or
unusual behaviour though he knew of no case where moral
judgement had been affected.

THE SHOP ASSISTANT'S EVIDENCE (REPORT)

The shop assistant said that she had worked at Hall's
for seven years and knew Lady Wyatt as a regular
customer. On Wednesday morning Lady Wyatt had bought
a belt and handbag and had paid by cheque. She said
that Lady Wyatt had behaved quite normally. She said
that she hadn't seen Lady Wyatt trying on the scarf
as the scarf counter was on the opposite side of the
store. She added that there had been two assistants on
duty that morning and that neither of them had left the
department.

Listening

Now listen to Lady Wyatt being
cross-examined, first by the
Prosecution, and then by the
Defence.
Listen again. Answer these questions.

Prosecution's cross-examination
What did she say she had intended to
do?
Why hadn't she done it?
Why didn't she spend more time
looking for an assistant?
Is she usually punctual?
How long had she been taking the
pills?
Had she ever suffered from loss of
memory?
Had she ever stolen anything?

Defence's cross-examination
How wealthy is she?
Does she need to work?
Is she a regular customer?
How much does she spend there a
year?
What would she have done if she
hadn't been caught?

Exercise 2
Listen again to the cross-
examination. Write a report similar
to the four above.

Exercise 3
Read through the four reports again.
Role-play Prosecution, Defence and
Witness. Try to recreate the situation
as each of the four gave evidence and
were cross-examined.

Exercise 4
Form groups. You are the jury.
Appoint a chairman to report back
to the judge. You have to decide
whether she was 'Guilty' or 'Not
Guilty'.
(In British law a person is innocent
until proved guilty. The Prosecution
must prove its case. The Defence
needs only to maintain that it has not
been proved.)

Justice?

'The punishment should fit the crime.'

National and local newspapers regularly print accounts of legal cases, and quite often the stories they choose are ones in which the punishment does not appear to fit the crime. It is easy to read a paragraph about a criminal case and to become outraged at the sentence passed by a judge. We have to remember that the short paragraph sums up a complicated legal case which might have taken hours, days or even weeks of court time, and that the judge knew a lot more about the case than the casual newspaper reader. However, sentences and penalties vary widely from one court to another. As every football fan knows, referees make mistakes, and the referee is much more likely to be mistaken when his decision goes against one's own team.

Here are some examples of crimes, and the penalties chosen by particular judges. Read through them and try to answer these questions.

Was justice done?
If you had been the judge, would you have given a different sentence? Would you have chosen a lighter sentence, or a more severe one? How would you have felt if you had been the victim of the crime? How would you have felt if you had been the defendant? If you had been the judges, what other facts and circumstances would you have wanted to know?

Manslaughter
(the act of killing someone, unlawfully, but not intentionally)

In 1981 Marianne Bachmeir, from Lubeck, West Germany, was in court watching the trial of Klaus Grabowski, who had murdered her 7-year-old daughter. Grabowski had a history of attacking children. During the trial, Frau Bachmeir pulled a Beretta 22 pistol from her handbag and fired eight bullets, six of which hit Grabowski, killing him. The defence said she had bought the pistol with the intention of committing suicide, but when she saw Grabowski in court she drew the pistol and pulled the trigger. She was found not guilty of murder, but was given six years imprisonment for manslaughter. West German newspapers reflected the opinion of millions of Germans that she should have been freed, calling her 'the avenging mother'.

Murder

In 1952 two youths in Mitcham, London decided to rob a dairy. They were Christopher Craig, aged 16 and Derek William Bentley, 19. During the robbery they were disturbed by Sydney Miles, a policeman. Craig produced a gun and killed the policeman. At that time Britain still had the death penalty for certain types of murder, including murder during a robbery. Because Craig was under 18, he was sentenced to life imprisonment. Bentley who had never touched the gun, was over 18. He was hanged in 1953. The case was quoted by opponents of capital punishment, which was abolished in 1965.

Assault

In 1976 a drunk walked into a supermarket. When the manager asked him to leave, the drunk assaulted him, knocking out a tooth. A policeman who arrived and tried to stop the fight had his jaw broken. The drunk was fined £10.

Shop-lifting

In June 1980 Lady Isabel Barnett, a well-known TV personality was convicted of stealing a tin of tuna fish and a carton of cream, total value 87p, from a small shop. The case was given enormous publicity. She was fined £75 and had to pay £200 towards the cost of the case. A few days later she killed herself.

Fraud

This is an example of a civil case rather than a criminal one. A man had taken out an insurance policy of £100,000 on his life. The policy was due to expire at 3 o'clock on a certain day. The man was in serious financial difficulties, and at 2.30 on the expiry day he consulted his solicitor. He then went out and called a taxi. He asked the driver to make a note of the time, 2.50. He then shot himself. Suicide used not to cancel an insurance policy automatically. (It does nowadays.) The company refused to pay the man's wife, and the courts supported them.

Language study

What would you have done?

| If | I | 'd
had
hadn't
had not | done that
been there | I | 'd
would
wouldn't
would not | 've
have | done this.
been there. |

Look at these statements. What do you think about them?

Exercise 1

Look at this list of 'crimes'. Try and rate each crime on a scale from 1–10. (1 is a minor misdemeanour, 10 is a very serious crime). They are in no order.

1 driving in excess of the speed limit
2 common assault (e.g. a fight in a discotheque)
3 drinking and driving
4 malicious wounding (e.g. stabbing someone in a fight)
5 murdering a policeman during a robbery
6 murdering a child
7 causing death by dangerous driving
8 smoking marijuana
9 selling drugs (such as heroin)
10 stealing £1,000 from a bank, by fraud
11 stealing £1,000 worth of goods from someone's home
12 rape
13 grievous bodily harm (almost killing someone)
14 shoplifting
15 stealing £1,000 from a bank, by threatening someone with a gun
16 possession of a gun without a licence

Exercise 2

Compare your list with another student's. Which of you would be the harsher judge? Which would be the kinder?

Penalties – England

In England there are no minimum sentences, except for murder, which carries a penalty of life imprisonment. There are maximum sentences for other crimes. Crimes are first heard by a magistrate who can either pass sentence, or refer the crime to a Crown Court with a judge and jury. Here are maximum sentences for some crimes:

Sentences can be reduced for good behaviour, often by one-third or more. 'Life' sentences are rarely more than 14 years, and it would be possible to release prisoners after 7 years.

Crime	Magistrates Court		Crown Court	
	Fine	Prison	Fine	Prison
Burglary	£1000	6 months	unlimited	14 years
Grievous bodily harm	£1000	6 months	unlimited	5 years
Possession of firearm	£1000	6 months	unlimited	5 years
Possession of cannabis	£500	3 months	unlimited	5 years
Common assault	£200	2 months		
'Going equipped for stealing'	£1000	6 months	unlimited	3 years
Murder			life imprisonment	

Exercise 3

How do you think these compare with sentences in your country? Remember they are maximum, not average!

Where's Mr Greyson?

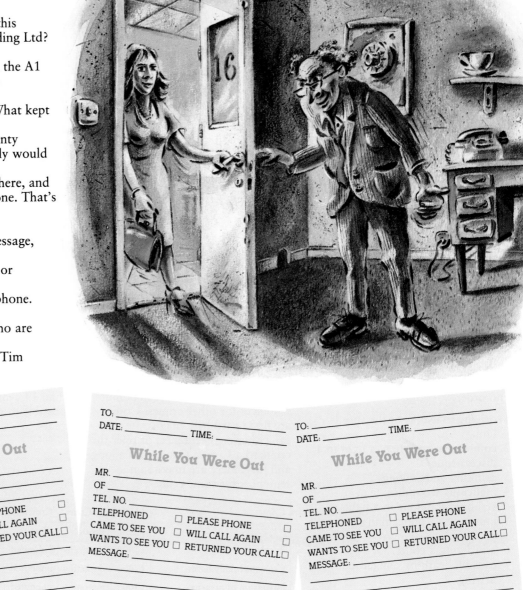

Suzy Oh, excuse me . . . Is this Greyson Worldwide Trading Ltd?

Mr Greyson Who are you?

Suzy I'm Suzy Miller, from the A1 Secretarial Agency, is this Mr Greyson . . . ?

Mr Greyson Yeah, yeah. What kept you? I've been waiting.

Suzy You only phoned twenty minutes ago. What exactly would you like me to do?

Mr Greyson Uh, just wait here, and . . . uh . . . answer the phone. That's all. I'll be back later.

Suzy But what shall I say?

Mr Greyson Just take a message, that's all.

Suzy Shall I . . . tidy up . . . or anything?

Mr Greyson No. Just the phone. OK? See you later.

Suzy Oh . . . hold on . . . who are you?

Mr Greyson I'm Greyson. Tim Greyson. See you.

TO: _____
DATE: _____ TIME: _____

While You Were Out

MR. _____
OF _____
TEL. NO. _____
TELEPHONED   ☐ PLEASE PHONE   ☐
CAME TO SEE YOU   ☐ WILL CALL AGAIN   ☐
WANTS TO SEE YOU ☐ RETURNED YOUR CALL ☐
MESSAGE: _____
_____
_____

TAKEN BY: _____

TO: _____
DATE: _____ TIME: _____

While You Were Out

MR. _____
OF _____
TEL. NO. _____
TELEPHONED   ☐ PLEASE PHONE   ☐
CAME TO SEE YOU   ☐ WILL CALL AGAIN   ☐
WANTS TO SEE YOU ☐ RETURNED YOUR CALL ☐
MESSAGE: _____

TAKEN BY: _____

TO: _____
DATE: _____ TIME: _____

While You Were Out

MR. _____
OF _____
TEL. NO. _____
TELEPHONED   ☐ PLEASE PHONE   ☐
CAME TO SEE YOU   ☐ WILL CALL AGAIN   ☐
WANTS TO SEE YOU ☐ RETURNED YOUR CALL ☐
MESSAGE: _____

TAKEN BY: _____

TO: _____
DATE: _____ TIME: _____

While You Were Out

MR. _____
OF _____
TEL. NO. _____
TELEPHONED   ☐ PLEASE PHONE   ☐
CAME TO SEE YOU   ☐ WILL CALL AGAIN   ☐
WANTS TO SEE YOU ☐ RETURNED YOUR CALL ☐
MESSAGE: _____
_____
_____

TAKEN BY: _____

TO: _____
DATE: _____ TIME: _____

While You Were Out

MR. _____
OF _____
TEL. NO. _____
TELEPHONED   ☐ PLEASE PHONE   ☐
CAME TO SEE YOU   ☐ WILL CALL AGAIN   ☐
WANTS TO SEE YOU ☐ RETURNED YOUR CALL ☐
MESSAGE: _____

TAKEN BY: _____

TO: _____
DATE: _____ TIME: _____

While You Were Out

MR. _____
OF _____
TEL. NO. _____
TELEPHONED   ☐ PLEASE PHONE   ☐
CAME TO SEE YOU   ☐ WILL CALL AGAIN   ☐
WANTS TO SEE YOU ☐ RETURNED YOUR CALL ☐
MESSAGE: _____

TAKEN BY: _____

Exercise 1
Suzy had to take several messages that morning. Use the notepads opposite, and make a note of the messages.

Exercise 2
Look at your notes, and pretend you are Suzy reporting back to Mr Greyson.
Example
A *Mr Jackson called, from Midland Bank.*
B *What did he want?*
A *I don't know. He asked if you could call him.*
B *Anything else?*
A *No. That was all.*

Exercise 3
As you've probably guessed, Suzy never reported back to Mr Greyson. Later the same day a police inspector called at the A1 Agency, and asked Suzy to describe her conversation with Greyson, and the phone calls.

Exercise 4
Use the notes you've made and give a verbal report. For homework, write out your report as a statement to the police.

Language study

'Is he there?'	He asked if he was here.
'When will he be back?'.	He asked when he would be back.
'Is he in London or Birmingham?'	He asked whether he was in London or Birmingham.

am/is	*was*	saw	*had seen*	may	*might*
are	*were*	have seen	*had seen*	had done	
have/has	*had*	was/were	*had been*	would	
do/don't	*did/didn't*	will/won't	*would/wouldn't*	could	*no change*
want	*wanted*	shall/shan't	*should/shouldn't*	should	
didn't do	*hadn't done*	can/can't	*could/couldn't*	ought	
				might	
				must	*had to*

this	*that*	yesterday	*the day before* *the previous day*	last month	*the month before* *the previous month*
these	*those*	tomorrow	*the next day*	next year	*the next year*
here	*there*	this (week)	*that (week)*		
now	*then*				

Exercise 5
Report these questions, which the Inspector asked Suzy.
1 'Did you see Mr Greyson?'
2 'What time did he leave the office?'
3 'Had you ever seen him before?'
4 'Did he pay you by cash or by cheque?'
5 'Would you recognize him again?'
6 'Will you look at these photographs?'
7 'Can you see Greyson in them?'
8 'Which one is he?'
9 'Was he wearing an overcoat?'
10 'Has he got a beard or a moustache now?'
11 'Could you describe the moustache for me?'
12 'Was he wearing glasses or not?'
13 'Do you know what he has been doing?'
14 'Can you guess?'

Exercise 6
Imagine that you are a reporter. Your partner is a famous person. Decide on the famous person for yourselves. Think of five questions you would like to ask. Ask them. The 'famous person' should then write a report about the questions asked. The 'reporter' should write a report of the answers.
Then change roles, and repeat the exercise.

Exercise 7
Listen to the phone calls again. List Suzy's apologies and excuses to the callers.

The language of rock

MODERN pop began with rock 'n' roll in the middle fifties and, basically, it was a mixture of two traditions – Negro rhythm 'n' blues and white romantic crooning, coloured beat and white sentiment.

What was new about it was its aggression, its sexuality, its sheer noise and most of this came from its beat. This was bigger and louder than any beat before it, simply because it was amplified. Mostly, pop boiled down to electric guitars.

ROCK 'n' roll was very simple music. All that mattered was the noise it made, its drive, its aggression, its newness. All that was taboo was boredom.

The lyrics were mostly non-existent, simple slogans one step away from gibberish. This wasn't just stupidity, simple inability to write anything better. It was a kind of teen code, almost a sign language, that would make rock entirely incomprehensible to adults.

For instance, the first record I ever bought was by Little Richard and, at one throw, it taught me everything I ever need to know about pop.

The message went: 'Tutti frutti all rootie, tutti frutti all rootie, tutti frutti all rootie, awopbopaloobop alopbamboom! As a summing up of what rock 'n' roll was really all about, this was nothing but masterly.

Nik Cohn, novelist

Was one to believe, for example, that the technical virtuosity of a guitarist such as Jimi Hendrix and the musical illiteracy of a group like The Love Affair should both be described as 'pop music'? They are totally different not only in degree but in kind. Was one to say that a singer with the spine-chilling anger of Bob Dylan was in the same world, let alone the same league, as a singer with the raucous, tear-jerking tastelessness of Vikki Carr? Yet, for better or worse, all four are categorised as 'pop music'.

Pop is more misunderstood, misquoted, misrepresented and maligned than any other comparable phenomenon today. Its products are often inflated out of existence through self-important and over-zealous praise, or else unnecessarily brought down by the adolescent and gossip-laden gruntings of many of those involved. The result has been that what is known as pop music has become confused and confusing. That some pop music may now have ceased to be popular and become music, is a possibility hardly given its proper chance to be heard.

Tony Palmer, film director

'I like pop as I like Coca-Cola or wrapped bread or fish fingers. They're instant and they give an illusion of nourishment. But I get very frightened when intellectuals start elevating pop to the level of important art. When *they* say such and such a record is great, *I* have to say, well Beethoven's Ninth Symphony is great, Tristan and Isolde is great, Mahler's Song of the Earth is great; do they mean great in the same way? I presume they must. They must be making out that pop contains the same elements of emotional satisfaction and intellectual complexity as Beethoven, Brahms, or Wagner. This doesn't seem to me to be possible.

Anthony Burgess, novelist, composer, critic

Unit 55

Rock composers have always tried to represent the authentic sound of spoken English, and have therefore written what they have heard, rather than used standard spellings. Over 30 years rock has probably spread basically American pronunciation across the world. Look at this lyric and listen to the recording.

Everybody tells me rock 'n' roll is dead.
'Forget it, son – you gotta get a job instead.'
But I'm gonna turn on my radio,
gimmee my rock 'n' roll shoes,
I'm gonna dance all night, and sleep all day, (*Repeat*)
'coz I can't stop the music
that's beatin' inside my head.

My mom 'n' poppa say I can't keep singin' the blues.
My brother says, 'The blues just ain't good news.'
But I'm gonna turn on my radio,
gimmee my rock 'n' roll shoes,
I'm gonna dance all night, and sleep all day, (*Repeat*)
'coz I can't stop the music
and I wanna wear out these shoes.

When the songs come on the radio station
gonna rock 'n' roll with no hesitation,
don't wanna work from nine to five,
the music's playin' and I come alive,
your heart's beatin' rhythm and your soul is on fire,
rock with me, baby, you're my desire.

Oh, everybody tells me that rock 'n' roll is dead.
My sister says, 'I can see you're easily led.'
But I'm gonna turn on my radio,
gimmee my rock 'n' roll shoes,
I'm gonna dance all night, and sleep all day, (*Repeat*)
'coz I can't stop the music
that's beatin' inside my head.
No, I can't stop the music,
that's beatin' inside my head.

Rock 'n' roll is dead
by The Rats
(words and music) © J. Rabid, 1983

Exercise 1
How many 'non-standard' spellings can you find? Can you 'translate' them into standard English?

Exercise 2
What do you think these might mean?

gonna	kinda	'bout	ol'
gotta	sorta	'coz/'cos	lil'
gotcha	gimmee	me	c'mon
dontcha	luv	d'ja	runnin'
ain't	wanna	sez	walkin'
gerroffa	watcha	ev'ry	o'
yeah	innit	'n'	'em
see you	bin	lemme	git
outta	tho'		

Have you heard any songs with them in?

A lot of rock songs use non-standard structures too, for example:
'We don't need no educashion ...'
'I ain't got nobody ...'
'She don't need me no more ...'
'We was drivin' down the highway ...'
'He never had no money ...'

Rock tries to reproduce speech. In the 1980s many people make a distinction between *pop* (songs designed for the Top 50) *rock* (more serious popular music in the rock idiom) and *rock 'n' roll* (songs in the style of the late 1950s). The difference shows in the lyrics. A pop love-song might say:

'I still love you darling, though we're far apart
you needn't ever worry, for you're always in my heart.'

A rock song is more likely to say:
'Oh, babe, you sure have treated me mean,
Oh, baby, you sure have treated me mean,
but if you keep on messin'
then I'm gonna quit the scene.'

They're both English ... or are they?

Unit 55

William Shakespeare (1564-1616)

Read the texts. Take notes. Write a summary of Shakespeare's life and work.

'No household in the English-speaking world is properly furnished unless it contains a copy of the Holy Bible and one of "The Works of William Shakespeare". It is not always thought necessary that these books should be read in maturer years, but they must be present as symbols of Religion and English Culture.

Shakespeare has not always been so symbolic a figure. He was an actor and a playwright, when neither actors nor the stage were regarded as respectable or of any importance. The notion that he was the supreme Genius of the English Race did not begin until he had been dead more than a century; but since then it has become so firmly accepted that no schoolboy can avoid a detailed study of at least one of his plays.'

Introducing Shakespeare
G B Harrison

The facts

26 April 1564
Baptised, Stratford. Son of John Shakespeare and Mary Arden.
27 Nov 1582
Obtained a marriage licence, with Anne Hathaway.
1583
Daughter, Susanna, born.
1585
Twins, Hammet and Judith, born.
1592
First mentioned as an actor and playwright, living in London.
1593/4
Published two narrative poems, *Venus and Adonis* and *Rape of Lucrece.*
1594
A founder member of *The Chamberlain's Men,* a group of actors.
1594/5
Performed in front of Queen Elizabeth I.
1597
Bought a large house in Stratford.
1603
His acting company became *The King's Men,* under the patronage of James I.
1611
Probably retired to Stratford.
23 April 1616
Died, Stratford.
25 April 1616
Buried, Stratford.

Shakespeare wrote at least thirty-seven plays, although few were published in his lifetime and the first eight didn't even carry his name. Eighteen plays were published in his lifetime. The first collection (*The First Folio*) wasn't published until 1623, seven years after his death, and contains thirty-six plays.

He was a working actor, as well as a shareholder in London's most important theatre, The Globe. He usually wrote for a specific group of actors, and as they grew older he wrote plays with older characters to suit them. There were no female actors, and boys took all the female parts in the plays.

1588–93	*A Comedy of Errors*
1592–93	*Richard III*
1594–96	*Romeo and Juliet*
1594–96	*A Midsummer Night's Dream*
1598–99	*Henry V*
1599	*Julius Caesar*
1600–01	*Hamlet*
1603–04	*Othello*
1605–06	*King Lear*
1605–06	*Macbeth*
1606–07	*Anthony and Cleopatra*
1611	*The Tempest*

Elizabethan and Jacobean drama

The first official public theatre, (The Theatre) was built in London in 1576. It looked very much like a modern bullring (and was probably used for animal baiting on days when no plays were being performed). There were also private indoor theatres in the universities and palaces.

Quotations

There are many expressions in modern English which have come from Shakespeare's plays. They have often been changed a little, modernized and used in a different way than Shakespeare intended. Here are some examples.

Exercise 1
Read through the modern sayings and compare them with the originals.

Source	Shakespeare's original	Modern saying	
Henry IV – Part 2	1 He hath eaten me out of house and home.	Love's blind.	☐
Hamlet	2 I must be cruel, only to be kind.	All the world's a stage.	☐
Cymbeline	3 I have not slept one wink.	He's eaten me out of house and home!	☐
Hamlet	4 A countenance more in sorrow than in anger.	That's cold comfort.	☐
As You Like It	5 All the world's a stage. And all the men and women merely players: They have their exits and their entrances.	Discretion is the better part of valour.	☐
All's well that ends well.	6 All's well that ends well.	You've got to be cruel to be kind.	☐
Hamlet	7 Though this be madness, yet there is method in it.	A rose by any other name ... (would smell as sweet)	☐
Romeo and Juliet	8 What's in a name? That which we call a rose. By any other name would smell as sweet.	In my/the mind's eye.	☐
The Merchant of Venice	9 But love is blind, and lovers cannot see.	I haven't slept a wink.	☐
King Lear	10 The wheel is come full circle.	Neither a borrower nor a lender be.	☐
Hamlet	11 The lady doth protest too much, methinks.	Methinks the lady doth protest to much.	☐
King Lear	12 I am a man more sinned against than sinning.	(I did it) more in sorrow than in anger.	☐
Henry IV – Part 1	13 The better part of valour is discretion.	Brevity is the soul of wit.	☐
Hamlet	14 It is a custom more honoured in the breach than the observance.	Tell the truth and shame the devil.	☐
Hamlet	15 Brevity is the soul of wit.	There's method in his madness.	☐
Hamlet	16 Neither a borrower nor a lender be.	A custom more honoured in the breach than the observance	☐
Hamlet	17 In my mind's eye, Horatio.	The wheel has come full circle.	☐
Henry IV – Part 1	18 O! While you live, tell truth, and shame the devil.	All's well that ends well.	☐
King John	19 I beg cold comfort.	(He's) more sinned against than sinning.	☐

The Frankenstein robot

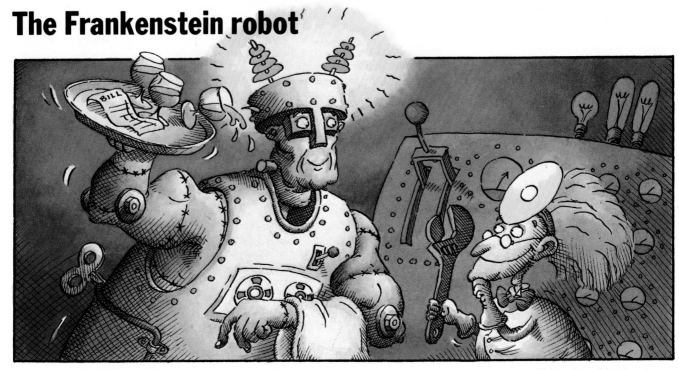

JP This week *Film Horizons* has an action-packed bill for you. We're going to see extracts from Lucas Simon's latest film, *Interplanetary Patrol,* and from the new Clive Westwood production, *Gunfire at Dusk.* Our nostalgia section looks at horror films of the 1930s, but let's waste no time. We're beginning with an interview with Lucas Simon, whose *Interplanetary Patrol* goes on general release this week. I spoke to him earlier today at Heathrow Airport.

JP Here we are at London's Heathrow Airport, where Lucas Simon has just landed from Los Angeles. Excuse me! Mr Simon!

LS Where's that car? I've got to be at a meeting by 4 o'clock.

JP Could you let us have a few words, Mr Simon?

LS Yeah, get the hell out of my way.

JP I'm Jason Philips from the BBC, we're recording for *Film Horizons* and ...

LS Hell! Why didn't you say so before? I'd just like to say I love your cute little country, and I'm very pleased to be here. Isn't that right, Jake?

JP Jason.

LS That's right.

JP Could you tell us about your new film?

LS Sure. It's being produced right here in England, as you know.

JP Is it going to be another space movie?

LS I feel it's time for a new direction. *Interplanetary Patrol* was my last space adventure. The new one will be called *The Frankenstein Robot.*

JP *The Frankenstein Robot?*

LS That's it. It's set in the 26th century, when this scientist who happens to be the great-great-great grandson of Dr Frankenstein, well, he decides that the robots are being sold at too high a price, you see, the whole civilization depends on robots. Anyway, he reckons he can make a robot much cheaper by using bits of dead bodies instead of silicon chips and computers and that kind of thing, right ...

JP I thought you said it wasn't going to be a space movie.

LS That's right, it's not a space movie, but it *is* science-fiction.

JP What about the director? There have been reports of a row between you and Charles Orson.

LS No comment. I'll just say it was going to be directed by Charles Orson, but now it'll be directed by one of America's best up-and-coming directors, Trevor Inchelstone.

JP Trevor Inchelstone? I've never heard of him.

LS He's my son-in-law. A truly great director.

JP What about the cast? It's been reported here that the leading role will be played by Steve Newman.

LS That was true. It certainly was ... last week. Now we're hoping the part will be played by Lewis London.

JP Lewis London? Isn't he your brother-in-law?

LS Right. Did you see him in *Dracula meets King Kong?* A truly moving performance.

JP Ah, yes. Didn't he play Count Dracula?

LS No, son. He played King Kong.

JP I'm sorry. What about the female lead? I know a lot of newspapers thought it would be acted by Kay Sparks.

LS I thought so, too. Unfortunately, she was too busy. She's on holiday. So, I think it'll be played by Moira Hammond.

JP Isn't she your wife?

LS She is. She is.

JP It sounds like ... a family show.

LS You could say that, James. You certainly could.

JP Jason, my name's Jason.

LS That's what I said.

JP Would you like to comment on reports from New York that financial support has been withdrawn from the film, due to changes in casting?

LS Rubbish. Absolute rubbish. Where's my car?

JP Mr Simon. Mr Sim ... Well, that seems to be all from Heathrow Airport, so back to the studio.

Exercise 1

It's being produced right here in England.

Can you imagine where these films are being produced?
1 *Montezuma – the last Emperor*
2 *Billy the Kid rides again*
3 *The last Samurais*
4 *Love at the Mardi Gras*
5 *Heidi and Hansruedi*
6 *Scherezade*
7 *Montmartre daydream*
8 *The Swinging Sixties*

What do you think the plots might be?

Exercise 2

It will be called 'The Frankenstein Robot'

Imagine you are planning to make a film about one of the following subjects. What will it be called?
1 A film about the Russian revolution of 1917.
2 A western.
3 A horror film based on the original 'Dracula' story.
4 A disaster film about people trapped in a ski-lift.
5 A detective story about heroin smugglers in Miami.
6 A police story about a young motorway patrol driver.
7 A story about a feuding family of ranchers in Arizona set in the present day.
8 A science-fiction film about two rival inter-galactic empires.

What do you think the plots might be?

Exercise 3

It was going to be directed by Charles Orson, but now it'll be directed by Trevor Inchelstone.

Make sentences about these films.
1 produced Lucas Simon/now – not produced at all.
2 directed Jan Houston/now Jim Cord.
3 written J W Simon/now J W Simon, B Felding, A Miller and L Spielman.
4 the part/played Steve Newman/now Simon's brother-in-law.
5 financed several big banks/now Simon.
6 made Hollywood/now Pinewood.

Exercise 4

Choose one of the films in Exercise 1 or 2. Imagine you are the producer.

Look at the class. If you were the producer, who would it be directed by? Who would it be written by?

Who would the male lead be played by?
Who would the female lead be played by?
Who would the villain be played by?
Who would the police chief (sheriff, patrolman) be played by?

Work in pairs and assign roles to the other members of the class. Tell them the story of your chosen film, and the casting.

Exercise 5

One student is a producer. The rest of the class/group are newspaper/TV reporters. Interview the producer of these films:
Battle of Waterloo Station 1995
1001 Nights
The Swiss Connection
Air Crash!
The Last War Film
Curse the Blood of Dracula
Too Much, Too Soon
Romeo and Juliet on Mars

Take it in turns to be the producer who is being interviewed. The reporters will find it easier to think of questions if they decide what type of paper they work for (serious or sensational, British or foreign, a film — or general interest magazine, political or apolitical, conservative or liberal, and so on).

Exercise 6

Write a report for a newspaper using Jason's interview. Then write a report on one of the Group interviews.

Language study

Active	Passive	Reported Active	Reported Passive
He is doing it.	It is being done.	He said he was doing it.	He said it was being done.
I do it.	It is done.	He said he did it.	He said it was done.
I (can) do it.	It (can) be done.	He said he could do it.	He said it could be done.
I will do it.	It will be done.	He said he would do it.	He said it would be done.
I have done it.	It has been done.	He said he had done it.	He said it had been done.
I will have done it.	It will have been done.	He said he would have done it.	He said it would have been done.
I did it.	It was done.	He said he had done it.	He said it had been done.
I had done it.	It had been done.	He said he had done it.	He said it had been done.
I was doing it.	It was being done.	He said he had been doing it.	He said it was being done.

Anything to declare?

Read the text and answer the
questions.

What is the Queen's sewer?
What is the Queen's pipe?
What are the 'traditional goods'?
What is the 'smuggler's eye'?

Write down five tricks that smugglers
use.

Anything to declare?

Once a month a sad ritual is performed at the Queen's Warehouse at Heathrow. Four Customs men open hundreds of bottles of impounded liquor, and invert them into crude wooden bottle racks. The spirit pours directly into a main drain, called the Queen's Sewer, thus foiling anyone who might want to catch and rebottle the evil, eye-watering mixture of wines and strange spirits.

The cloying scent of alcohol is sharpened by tobacco fumes as cartons of cigarettes and cigars are burned in an incinerator known as the Queen's Pipe.

The warehouse is a large basement in the main Customs House on the north side of the airport, conveniently close to the police station. It is stuffed with goods seized by Customs in the Queen's name. The shelves are crammed with bottles, each tagged with the airline flight number and the name of the passenger it was taken from.

Some is sold off at regular auctions. But there are no buyers for the exotic, or for bottles that have export labels or airline stickers on them. It is not worth the expense of relabelling and rebottling for the home market.

So every month the doomed bottles are picked out, Yugoslav Slivovitz, Polish blackcurrant vodka, Thai Mekong whisky, sake and tequila. Occasionally a man will pause from his work before starting a jeraboam of Moet Chandon or a two-gallon bottle of Black Label Scotch on its ignominious trip to the sewage works.

The warehouse reflects the trends in amateur smuggling by passengers, since professionals nowadays often 'smuggle' goods by altering the import tax on invoices. The 'traditional' goods, as the Customs men call them, still stand out in pure volume. In a typical year, 1976, passengers arriving in Britain were relieved of 2,824 proof gallons of spirits, and 1,879 watches. More than 11,000 of them had 20,716 lb of tobacco confiscated. Most of this will pass through the warehouse, together with the expected haul of cameras and photographic equipment.

The amateurs give the Customs men their biggest challenge, for least reward. The professionals, smuggling cannabis by the hundredweight and cameras by the £100,000 worth, are often caught after tip-offs. The small-time returning holidaymaker has to be detected, and all the knowledge acquired at the Customs Training School in Southend is needed.

A good nose, or what the victim might consider sixth sense, is vital. The Customs people call it 'smuggler's eye'. It is indefinable, of course, but it is the quality that makes a really good Customs man as he screens hundreds of passengers pouring past him on a six-hour shift. One man who had it was Liam Sumption, a legendary Irishman who pulled passengers out of the Green Channel at Heathrow for bets with his fellow officers, and is rumoured never to have challenged an innocent traveller.

Every guilty passenger has tell-tale traits. The normally timid become over-boisterous, the placid bite their lips, the domineering are ingratiating, bossy women turn sweet. The 'eye' is mainly a question of feeling who is acting out of type.

'A lot of people look nervous when they walk through the Green,' says a Customs man. 'The art is spotting types who do not seem to be naturally nervous.' The process starts much earlier than most passengers realize – at the moment when they pick their luggage off the conveyor belt. It is there that the Customs men weigh up attitudes. Most people who are stopped in the Green Channel have been earmarked for inspection from the moment they first picked up their case.

Smugglers like to go through Customs in the middle of the queue. If their bag comes up first, they will often let it go round on the conveyor belt and only pick it up after other passengers from the flight have started off through the channels. Likewise, they get agitated if the bag is late and they have to go through at the end.

Some attempts are almost as old as smuggling itself. Passengers are caught with a two-gallon bottle of Scotch, and say innocently that they thought they were allowed a single bottle duty free, irrespective of size. They put old straps on new watches and new cameras in old cases. Fur coats are picked out because they have no labels, or because the shop label that 'proves' the coat was not brought abroad has been sewn in by hand instead of machine and is clearly older than the coat.

'I had one lady who challenged me to look at the Harrods label in her mink. It was Harrods all right – Harrods Man's Shop,' says a Customs man.

Other smugglers show a touching belief that priests, doctors and other respectable men are not searched. A house painter arrived at Heathrow with 300 watches hidden in a woman's girdle round his waist. He was dressed as a Roman Catholic priest with a passport to match. He was fined for the watches, and imprisoned for smuggling when disguised in Holy Orders. Few amateurs have heard of section 73 of the Customs and Excise Act. It provides that anyone either armed with an offensive weapon or in disguise whilst attempting to avoid Customs duty is liable to imprisonment.

From *Airport International* by Bryan Moyahan

Exercise 1
Listen carefully and make a list of all the objects you might expect to find in:
a a businessman's case
b an oilman's case
c an ordinary traveller's case.

Exercise 2
Change the story below into dialogue. Begin:

Customs officer Excuse me. But could I have a word with you?
Woman Certainly.

The Customs Officer called the woman over and asked if he could have a word with her. She agreed. He asked her where she had travelled from and she said she'd been in Paris for the weekend and asked him why he wanted to know. The Customs Officer explained that he was just curious and asked if she had anything to declare. She stated that she hadn't. He requested her, very politely, to open her bag. She said she had only clothes and personal effects in her bag. The Customs Officer repeated his request, but a little less politely, and she asked him why he didn't believe her. Then the Customs Officer ordered her to open her case and threatened to do it himself if she wouldn't. She agreed to open the case but complained that she was in a hurry. He expressed surprise at three bottles of brandy and the woman explained that only one of them was for her and the other two were for friends. He said that it didn't really matter who they were for and that she would have to pay the duty. She said that she hadn't got any English money and the Customs Officers directed her to the bank where she would be able to change it. She thanked him sarcastically. He acknowledged her thanks and explained that he was only doing his job.

Exercise 3
You have been given a new watch for your birthday. You arrive in England to study English for 3 months. The Customs Officer accuses you of smuggling. Construct a dialogue between you and the Customs Officer.

Exercise 4
How would you smuggle a large diamond through Customs?

Doorstep salesmen

Most doorstep salesmen are reputable and you may find their services helpful and convenient, particularly if you live a long way from a big shopping centre, or find it difficult to get about because of illness or old age.
But some are rogues and their activities can cause misery for people who don't know how to recognize or cope with them ... Could you?

Listening

What is the salesman's name?
Which company does he work for?
What is the name of the book?
What is the final price of the books?
How much will the books cost next month?
How much is the deposit?
How many instalments will there be?
What rate of interest will she pay?

What do you discover about:

a Mr Curtis
b the children
c their financial circumstances.

Write down some of the things he says to persuade her to buy the books for her children.

'Good evening . . . I'm doing some market research on how people spend their spare time . . .'
A well-known opening to gain your confidence, get inside the door and see what sort of home you've got.

'I'm carrying out educational research . . .'
Nothing like talking about your children for putting you off guard. How are they getting on at school? What do they want to do when they leave? And so on. And then, suddenly, you're talking about . . . BOOKS!

'I happened to be passing, and I noticed you have a tile loose . . .'
If you're not as agile as you need to be, or you live alone, you're wide open for this approach, because you're hardly likely to shin up a ladder to check. He's banking on doing a quick, very expensive and possibly unnecessary job, and he's almost certain to ask for cash on the spot which you may be tempted to pay to avoid an accident. Look out, too, for a similar approach about 'woodworm in your rafters'.

'I'm a consultant on back ailments/rheumatism . . .' etc.
This one will try to impress, and maybe frighten you with his medical knowledge and sales talk which could be about special beds, massage equipment or some other 'medical' product.

'Congratulations! My company has picked your house to be the showhouse for the area . . .'
Naturally, you'd feel flattered. The next step is to offer you a product or a service 'at a *very* special price' – it's usually double glazing or central heating, but could be anything for the house.

'I'm selling for the blind/disabled/old age pensioners . . .' etc.
He could be selling for himself and making a big profit on goods – often 'seconds' – which you may feel duty-bound to buy; things like all-purpose cloths, felt-tipped pens and oven gloves which, if they have any connection with the old or disabled, are most likely to have been packed by them for very low wages.

'I've been sent by the council/ housing/ social security/ education department, or the gas/electricity board . . .' etc, etc.
A surefire way to rivet you to the doorstep. Who'd blame you for thinking this caller's business was 'official'?

'I can help you to cut your fuel bills . . .'
He's probably done his homework, too, and knows yours is the type of house that's plagued by draughts. He's called to give you the benefit of his 'free' advice on double glazing or central

heating – but this advice could prove very expensive in the end.
For major installations like these, you should always get and compare estimates from other firms; and for central heating, find out about the running costs.

'I'm a student working to win a travel scholarship . . .'
Don't be surprised if this one's got hold of your name and says that he, or she, needs points to win a scholarship which they will get simply by talking to you. 'Lack of understanding in the world today' is a popular subject. There'll be a questionnaire, too, on books that would interest you, and before you can say 'doorstep salesman' you may find yourself committed to a subscription for books and magazines, which could prove expensive reading – if they ever arrive!

'I'm an adviser on security (or fire) precautions . . .'
Here's that 'official' tone again, and this time it's meant to frighten you. You're likely to hear that your home is at risk without a special type of lock on the doors, or a fire extinguisher; you will probably see the word 'SECURITY' in big letters on the card he flashes quickly in front of you.
If you're not sure what protection you need, you can get free advice from your local crime or fire prevention officer.

Points to remember

If you answer the door and it's a salesman (or you think it is), ask yourself:

1 **Do I want to buy anything?** 'Not today, thank you' could be all you really want to say. *So say it.* Don't wait until your caller's foot is firmly in the door. You're wasting your time and his, and getting more deeply involved as each minute passes. Cut him short as soon as you realise you're not interested – and close the door.

2 **Is he who he says he is?** Never invite callers into your home until you are sure who they are. Ask to see a visiting card or other means of identification. Genuine callers will be happy to oblige. If you really think there is something fishy about the visit tell the police.

3 **Am I being pressured?** Even if you are interested in a product or service – you may have sent for information about it – DON'T BE PRESSURED. The salesman may offer you a tempting discount if you buy there and then – he doesn't want to give you time to change your mind! But remember, you've been *taken by surprise*, while he's had *plenty of time* to plan his sales talk. Don't give him this advantage – take time to be as choosy and shrewd as you would be in a shop. You could always say you would like a day or two to think things over – a genuine salesman won't mind calling back.

Remember, if you think a salesman applied unfair pressure or wasn't honest with you, he could do the same with your neighbours. Tell your local Trading Standards or Consumer Protection Officer.

4 **Have I done enough shopping around?** Before you decide whether to buy, find out what the same goods would cost in shops or, in the case of services like building and decorating, get and compare estimates from other firms. If you have a Consumer Advice Centre in your area, they may be able to give this sort of pre-shopping advice. And if you are offered credit, remember that credit charges can vary too, so find out what the total cost will be and shop around – a bank loan or a loan arranged by you with another finance company could prove a better buy.

5 **Can I afford it?** If you're being asked to pay cash, then you will know if you can afford it. But if goods or services are being offered on credit, insist on being told the number of instalments you will be paying and how much they will add up to (including the credit charges), and compare this figure with the cash price. It can all seem so easy – just a few pounds down and the rest over a few years – but you could end up paying a very high price and, even worse, the payments may prove too much after a while. 'Rogue' salesmen often try to conceal the real cost of their goods – *it's up to you to find out.*

Note: If someone calls on you uninvited and offers to fix you up with a mortgage or loan not connected with any goods – or to help you with your debt problems – he could be committing an offence under the Consumer Credit Act. Report him to your Trading Standards or Consumer Protection Officer.

6 **Could I find him again?** Remember, things like domestic appliances are likely to need servicing or spare parts at some time. And whether you buy goods in a shop or in your home, you have certain rights under the Sale of Goods Act. The Act says that goods must be of 'merchantable quality', 'fit for their purpose', and 'as described'. If not, you could be entitled to your money back or to sue for damages. But having rights won't help if you can't find the seller again. *So keep details of his name and address.*

7 **Am I afraid to say 'No'?** While the salesman's talking or when he calls back, you may have second thoughts about the price or suitability of the goods. *Don't be afraid to change your mind.* Most people find it embarrassing to say 'No' – and salesmen bank on this – but remember, it's your home, your money and your right to refuse. A responsible salesman won't make difficulties, and when you say, 'Will you please leave' he should do so. Otherwise he is trespassing.

Exercise 1
Make a list of all the words in the passage above connected with money.

Exercise 2
In Points to Remember, you are advised to 'cut the salesman short as soon as you realize you're not interested'. You could say:
'Not today, thank you.'
'I'm sorry, but I'm not really interested.'
'I'm not in the slightest bit interested in what you're selling.'
'I've got one already.'

'Please take your foot out of the door or I'll break it.'
'I never buy from doorstep salesmen.'
'Buzz off.'

Exercise 3
What might you say in following these pieces of advice:
Ask to see a visiting card or other means of identification.
Ask him if he'd mind calling back.
Find out what the total cost will be.
Insist on being told the number of instalments and how much they will add up to.

Keep details of the salesman's name and address.
Don't be afraid to change your mind.

Exercise 4
Now role-play a householder and a very persistent salesman. (Try this with: encyclopaedias, vacuum cleaners, brushes, a magazine, double glazing.)

The driving test

What makes a good driver?

A good driver has many things in his make-up. Some of these, such as experience and skill, will come only in time. But others—just as important—must be part of him from the start. These qualities are a sense of responsibility for the safety of others, a determination to concentrate on the job of driving, patience and courtesy. Together, these become what is generally known as a driver's 'attitude'.

Not everyone is patient by nature or gifted with good powers of concentration. But because attitude is so important a part of safe driving, every driver must make a real effort to develop these qualities—and this effort must start from the very beginning of his first driving lesson.

Getting into the right attitude will be harder for some people than others. It can be more difficult than the actual business of learning to make the car go or stop. All the things which go to make up attitude are just as necessary for the experienced driver as for the learner. So, before we go any further, let us look at these qualities in a little more detail.

Responsibility

As a driver you must have a proper concern not only for your own safety and that of your passengers, but also for the safety of every other road user, including pedestrians. You can do this only if you pay close attention to the varying traffic situations as they develop. Then you can plan your own actions well in advance so that they do not cause danger or inconvenience to others. At times you may be tempted to make a rash move—don't.

Concentration

With responsibility goes concentration on the job of driving. You must concentrate all the time if you are going to be able to deal with present-day traffic. Nowadays this is usually heavy and fast-moving and there are possible dangers all around you. If you let your mind wander, even for a moment, the risk of making a mistake is increased enormously. And mistakes can cause accidents. If you are tired, upset or unwell, or even thinking about something else, you will take longer to react. It is better not to drive at all in these circumstances, but if you have to, make special allowances for them.

Anticipation

Concentration helps you to 'anticipate'. In motoring, anticipation means acting promptly to fit in with what other road users are doing, as well as being able and ready to alter your own course or behaviour as a situation develops.

To those who do not drive, this quality of anticipation has the appearance of being automatic—and this is what it should become. Experience and anticipation together will enable you to act to prevent possible danger from becoming actual danger.

Patience

It is very easy to get impatient, or lose your temper, when other drivers do something wrong, or you are caught up in a traffic jam. But if you do, you are well on the way to having an accident. Never drive in a spirit of retaliation or competition. If the incompetence or bad manners of another road user cause you inconvenience, don't let your annoyance, even if justifiable, override your good sense and judgment. Attempts to 'teach him a lesson' don't do any good: there is no better lesson than a good example.

Confidence

The degree of confidence a driver has in handling his vehicle is, in a sense, part of his attitude to driving. New drivers will, of course, be unsure of themselves. Confidence grows with experience. But a good driver never lets himself get over-confident. This leads to carelessness, risks, and eventually accidents.

Planned tuition

All the things we have talked about so far—becoming a safe driver by developing a sense of responsibility, concentration, anticipation, patience and confidence—will depend very much on getting good instruction from the start. Drivers often begin to learn with a parent, relative or friend and this allows them to get lots of practice at low cost. But although some non-professional teachers can put over the details of car control and road procedure within a reasonable time, many good drivers are not good instructors. They can ruin a pupil's confidence by leading him into situations he is not ready for. In other words, they often teach him to run before he can walk. And, of course, not all parents, relatives and friends are good drivers anyway.

A planned approach is essential when teaching someone to drive. Ideally, each lesson should be phased to suit the pupil's development. There are no short cuts to being a good driver, either in time or money. There is no doubt that the best way to learn to drive properly is to have good professional tuition—and plenty of it. It will prove well worthwhile in the long run. But you need plenty of practice too.

Mechanical knowledge

So far we have said nothing about mechanical knowledge—how a car works. It is not necessary to know all the complicated details of car construction to be a good driver. But the more you do know the better, because if you know how the different parts of a car work, and what happens when you use the controls, you will develop a sense of car sympathy. This will not only make you a better driver, but add to your interest in driving. It will also prolong the life of your car.

Exercise 1

Read through *What makes a good driver?* and make two lists. In one list write down all the words you would associate with a good driver and in the other all the words you would associate with a bad driver.

Good	**Bad**
safe	rash
patience	impatience

Exercise 2

Change the following verbs into nouns:
judge/allow/behave/experience/
annoy/confide/practise/proceed/
develop/know/sympathize/control/
risk/anticipate/concentrate/act/
instruct/compete/describe/attend.

judge   *judgement*

Exercise 3

Explain the following expressions:

'to teach somebody a lesson'
'to run before you can walk'
'to take a short cut'
'in the long run'

Exercise 4

Go through the examiner's checklist and discuss what the examiner will be looking for. Why might people fail on specific points? What mistakes might they make?

THE DRIVING TEST

Take proper precautions before starting the engine.

Make proper use of/accelerator/clutch/gears/footbrake/handbrake/steering.

Make progress by/driving at a speed appropriate to the road and traffic conditions/avoiding undue hesitancy.

Exercise proper care in the use of speed.

Make effective use of the mirrors well before signalling/changing direction/slowing down or stopping.

Give signals where necessary/correctly/in good time.

Show awareness and anticipation of the actions of pedestrians/cyclists/drivers.

Overtake/meet/cross the path of/other vehicles safely.

Act properly at road junctions.

Allow adequate clearance to stationary vehicles.

Take appropriate action at pedestrian crossings.

Take prompt and appropriate action on all traffic signals/road markings/traffic lights/signals/given by traffic controllers/other road users.

Stop the vehicle in emergency/promptly/under control/making proper use of front brake.

Reverse into a limited opening either to the right or left/under control/with due regard for other road users.

Turn round by means of forward and reverse gears/under control/with due regard for other road users.

Select a safe position for normal stops.

Exercise 5

Traffic accidents and their causes. Explain how this accident might have happened.

APPENDIX

Material recorded on cassette but not included in the text of the units is printed below.

Unit 1

Naseem Aziz
I was only seven when my family came here. I'd never been to school in Pakistan, and I suppose I started learning English straight away when I started school here. I never actually learned it – I was just chucked in with a lot of English kids. I reckon they thought I was really thick at first, but I didn't understand a word. Anyway, I just picked it up. It's weird because I haven't got a Pakistani accent. That's because I didn't learn English there. Some families use English at home in Pakistan, and they'll never lose their accent. Everybody says I sound like a Liverpudlian, because I went to school in Liverpool, and I've always lived here.

Bernard Lefort
I have studied English since . . . for five years in France. We studied at school, and we learned the grammar, and we . . . we translated everything into French. I started at the age of twelve. I think I do not speak well. I am very slowly . . . slow. But I can understand everything I read very good . . . very well. I do not like to make mistakes, so I do not speak too much. I am living in Paris, and I meet English people in my work. I have a very French accent, but this is not important. I am French and I am happy when people know this. Anyway, the English think French accents are very romantic, yes?

Luciana Rossi
I am Italian. I was born in Rome. I studied English at school; I began to study at 13. All our lessons were in English. The teacher only translated some difficult words. I think I had a good basis at school, and then I went to England for the summer. At the beginning, everybody spoke very quickly, and I couldn't understand much, but after a few days it was easier, and everything I had learned came back to me. I didn't go to a school in England, but I met my husband there – he's Scottish, and I thought his accent was very difficult at first. Now it's no problem . . . we live in Scotland.

Jesus García
I didn't study English at school in Mexico, and I started to learn at evening classes when I was twenty-two. It was only two evenings a week, but I enjoyed the lessons. After two or three years I went on holiday to the States, and picked up a lot of expressions. Then I saved up and went to a language school in England for 2 months of 25 hours a week. There were all different nationalities in my class and we had to speak English! Anyway, I reckon my English is OK now. I work in Mexico City and I use English a lot in my job. I'm a travel agent.

Unit 7

1 Well, I really go for posters. I've got five or six in my room. Some of them were really cheap, 75p or something. The most I ever paid was £2.50, but that's not the point. If you get fed up with them, you can always change them. You can get all sorts of posters. There are the old adverts, or photos of rock stars or just beautiful landscapes. I've got a photograph of a seagull flying over some waves with a slogan on it 'Everything is beautiful'. The ones I like best, though, are the old Vogue magazine covers of the . . . the 1920s, I think. There's one marvellous one of a girl. She's very geometric in a . . . yellow kind of dress against a gorg . . . a lovely pale blue background. She's on an ocean liner, I suppose.

2 Yes, we've got a picture. Horses. We bought it in Woolco. It's got a lovely frame, kind of brown cloth with a strip of gold running round it. It was only about thirty quid. I don't know much about art, but I know what I like. They say it's an 'original painting', but I reckon they do them on a production line. We'd just decorated the room, and it . . . it matched the wallpaper. That sounds a bit odd, but why not? Anyway, I've always liked horses.

3 I bought that years ago. It's by Van Gogh. It was pretty reasonable really. About £7 . . . and that included the block mounting. I know it's only a cheap reproduction, but I've always loved that painting. There was a reproduction at school. It's the colours, I suppose . . . and the texture. You can see the thickness of the paint, even if it's only a reproduction. Anyway, I'd rather have a cheap copy of a . . . well, a masterpiece . . . than an original of something that's . . . mediocre.

4 We haven't really gone in for many pictures. You see, we've always been in rented flats, and it hasn't seemed worth it. Well, a calendar in the kitchen with 'Views of Scotland', perhaps, and that collage of family photos . . . maybe a poster over a damp patch on the wall. What I do buy though is books . . . books of paintings. This is from a Beryl Cook book . . . isn't it lovely? There's such a sense of humour. A kind of child-like quality that I really love.

5 That's a screenprint. It's a limited edition, actually. That means they print perhaps a hundred and then destroy the plates. This particular one appealed to me very strongly. There's something so clean and simple about it – photo-realism. I love it. My husband says it does nothing for him – he thinks it's pretty awful, in fact. But then again he hasn't got much taste – not when it comes to art.

Unit 10

1
A You pay over here, Mum.
B All, right, all right. Come on, keep together. One adult and two children, please.
C One ninety . . . Haven't you got anything smaller?
B Er . . . no, no, I'm afraid I haven't.
C Hmm. One ninety . . . two . . . three . . . four . . . five, and five is ten, and ten is twenty.
B Thank you. Er . . . which way?
C Just go through the door on your right. Follow the signs, and you'll see everything.
A Mum, I want a drink and a biscuit.
D Me, too. I'm starving.
B Excuse me, er . . . is there a refreshment room?
C It's just round the corner, on the right.
D I want to see the mummies, first.
B What?
D The mummies. The Egyptian ones.
B Er . . .
C Yes?
B We were particularly interested in seeing the mummies. Could you direct us to the Egyptian room?
C It's the last room you come to.
B Yes, but we'd like to go there first.
C All right. Turn left when you get in. It's the first door you'll come to on the left.
B Thank you . . . sorry.

2
A 'scuse me.
B Yes, luv?
A I think I'm a bit lost. I've been wandering round for ages trying to find the tea.
B The tea? Right love. It's in the . . . let me see, one, two, three, four, five . . . the sixth aisle along from here, or is it the seventh? If you go this way, past the checkouts, you'll find it on the right.
A I've been all around there.
B It's just past the biscuits, on the middle shelf.
A Thank you very much, dear. I'm getting on a bit. I can't see as well as I could.
B Oh, well, come with me, luv. I'll take you there.

3
A One litre of whisky, two hundred Marlboro, two bottles of wine . . . which currency are you paying in, sir?
B Er, do you take Canadian dollars?
A Well, yes sir. But I'll have to give you the change in Dutch guilders, sterling or American dollars, I'm afraid.
B Oh dear. Yes, of course . . . and I've only got a one-hundred-dollar bill.
A Are you in a hurry, sir?
B Not particularly, why?
A Well, you could break your bill at the currency change desk and come back for your duty-free goods.
B That's a good idea, thanks. Where is it?
A It's right in the middle of the concourse. Just turn left out of here, and walk towards C and D piers. You'll see it straight in front of you.
B Thank you very much.
A You're welcome.

4
A Yes, madam? Can I help you?
B I've got a connecting flight to London, BA . . . , let me just find my ticket . . . yes, it's BA208.
A Right. Is your luggage checked through?
B Yes, it is.
A It leaves at 14.30 from Gate 27, on Pier B. Smoking or Non-Smoking?
B Non-Smoking. I'd prefer an aisle seat, if you've got one.
A Yes, that's fine. Seat 5D.
B Is there somewhere to get a coffee?
A Of course. Right over in that corner, between B pier and A pier. Can you see it?
B Yes. Thank you very much.
A It's a pleasure. Yes, sir? Can I help you?

5
A Excuse me! Miss!
B Yes, madam?
A I can't find the pet food. I expect I've just walked past it or something. Can you tell me where it is?

B Er . . . pet food . . . It's opposite the frozen meat cabinet.
A The frozen meat? Where's that exactly?
B It's near the back. Look, just go towards the back of the shop, and it's the . . . let me think . . . the second aisle in from the right-hand side . . . The pet food's about three quarters of the way along, on your right.
A Thank you so much.

6

A Excuse me.
B Yes, miss?
A I particularly wanted to see the Victorian Room, but I seem to have missed it.
B It's in the far corner, miss. Just go out of that door and turn right. Walk through the main hall, and you'll see two doors in front of you. Go in the left-hand one, that's the Roman Room.
A Ah, I've been there already . . .
B Yes, you must have come out of the wrong door. Anyway, once you're in the Roman Room, take the door on the left. That's the Victorian Room.
A Thank you. Thank you very much.

Unit 11

I'm sitting out on the road in front of my own house where I've lived for . . . 13 or 14 years . . . and it's going down in front of me.

The roof's falling in. It's in flames and there's nothing I can do about it. And . . . and the flames are in the roof . . . and, and, ah . . . Goddammit! It's just beyond belief . . . er, my own house. And er . . . everything around is black. There are fires burning all around me . . .

Unit 13

A

Steve Hello, there. My name's Steve Newman – but I expect you know that. I have to entertain a lot, that's one of the problems of living in Beverley Hills, and after dinner, I always give my guests Maxcaffeine Instant Coffee . . .

Raquel Steve, this coffee's marvellous. It's so fresh, where do you get it?

Steve Glad you like it, Raquel. It's my secret.

B

I am standing in a launderette in Bromley, Kent. It's Monday morning, and I have just asked ten housewives to do half their wash in Fizz detergent, with its new XR74 foam booster, and half in another leading brand. Well, all of them agreed that Fizz with new XR74 washed whiter, cleaner and fresher. Fizz with XR74.

'For families use Fizz . . . For families use Fizz.'

C

A country walk . . . a summer's day . . . the man you love . . . somewhere to sit . . . the sky is blue . . . your love is new. Make him happy with a Macbeth cigar . . . Macbeth, with the masculine aroma of carefully selected tobaccos.

D

'Mum, I'm so bored. Do I have to stay in bed?'

'Yes, dear. You've been ill . . .'

Sick children are always a problem. Help to give them energy and vitality again with 'Glucozone', the sparkling health drink with added vitamins and minerals.

E

Waiter Did you enjoy your meal, sir?
Man Thank you. May I have the bill?
Waiter Here you are, sir.
Man Hmm . . . I see . . . er . . . do you take credit cards?
Waiter Well, sir, that depends . . . which card is it?
Man It's an International Streamline Platinum card.
Waiter Oh, in that case, of course we do. Thank you very much, sir . . . and madam. Do come again.

F

Are you looking for a car that's prettier than a Polo? Faster than a Ford? Mightier than a Maestro? Cheaper to run than a Renault? Then you're looking for the new BM Calypso. Phone your local dealer for a test drive, and if you buy a Calypso this month he'll give you a free radio, a full tank of petrol, one year's road tax and free number plates.

G

All right, I went up the pub last night. They didn't have my favourite beer. 'Run out,' they said. 'Have some of this Burgomaster Lager,' they said. 'What?' I said, 'Lager? Not for me.' 'Go on, try some,' they said. Well, I had a glass. Didn't think much of it but I had another. 'Load o' rubbish,' I said. 'Try another,' they said. I did. 'Awful,' I said. 'I don't believe it,' they said, 'Try another.' 'This is the worst beer I've ever had,' I said. 'Try another; we'll pay,' they said. 'No, it's rubbish,' I said and staggered off into the night. I was laughing. Five free glasses of Burgomaster – and it's not that bad.

H

Don't forget. Johnson's January Sale starts Monday the 28th December in Johnson's stores in Bournemouth, Southampton, Portsmouth, Brighton and Canterbury. Johnson's January Sale – 9 o'clock on the 28th.

I

I want to talk to you tonight about a very personal problem. Foot odour. Do you suffer from smelly feet? I did. Until I discovered Malcolm's Talcum Powder. Now I don't walk around smelling like a piece of old cheese. Remember: For Talcum – say Malcolm
For Talcum – say Malcolm.

J

Ann Hi, Sandy. I love your hair.
Sandy I've just washed it.
Ann Mine is always so dry and unmanageable. Yours looks so clean and natural.
Sandy That's because I use Ariel conditioner. It's naturally balanced for dry hair. It's been tested for years – and it's safe enough even for a child.
Ann I'll try some . . . can I borrow yours?
Sandy Buy some . . . you'll be surprised: it's the cheapest on the market.

Unit 15

Salisbury

Salisbury was one of the earliest 'new towns'. The city was founded in 1220 to replace the town of Old Sarum, 3 miles to the north. Old Sarum had been founded by the Romans and developed by the Saxons, and was already an important town in the 11th and 12th centuries. The water supply was poor, though, and so the town was moved to its present site where smaller rivers join the River Avon. The most striking feature is the cathedral, which was founded at the same time as the town. It was built between 1220 and 1258 and is thought to be one of the most beautiful in Europe. The spire is 404 feet high, making it the tallest church in Britain, and was added in 1334. The cathedral is 473 feet long. Salisbury is a market town for the surrounding agricultural area, and a shopping centre for the large numbers of military bases to the north of the city, on Salisbury Plain. It is also a tourist centre, because of the cathedral and old town, and because of Stonehenge which is 10 miles north-north-west of the city. It's situated in central Southern England, about 30 miles inland from the south coast, and 83 miles west of London. The city centre is particularly pleasant, as a ring road takes heavy traffic away to the East.

Caernarfon

Caernarfon is the usual spelling, that is C-A-E-R-N-A-R-F-O-N, nowadays, although older maps use the English spelling C-A-E-R-N-A-R-V-O-N. As it is the centre of the area of Gwynedd, which is 75% Welsh-speaking, the Welsh spelling is preferred. Gwynedd, by the way, is G-W-Y-N-E-D-D. It is situated in North Wales, and has always been an important strategic and military site. The Romans built a castle here in AD 78. The present castle was started by King Edward I in 1283, and completed in 1322. His son was born here in 1284 and became the first 'Prince of Wales'. Prince Charles was invested as Prince of Wales at the castle on July 1st 1969. The castle, at the top left, is one of the finest surviving castles in Britain. The old town wall is still in good condition. The population is 10,500, and the town is a market centre and a tourism centre for the Snowdonia National Park. There is no railway, the nearest station being at Bangor, 9 miles away. It is famous for sailing and fishing. Sea and river fishing are both excellent, which adds to the town's attractions.

Durham

Durham, in County Durham, is in the north-east of England, about 14 miles from Newcastle, and 260 miles from London. It is built on a bend in the River Wear, and it grew around the Norman castle, which was built in 1072 to protect England from the Scots. A wall blocked off the peninsula. The cathedral was begun in 1093, and has been called the finest Norman building in Britain, if not in Europe. The religious schools developed from the 15th century onwards, eventually becoming the University of Durham in 1832. It is England's third oldest University, after Oxford and Cambridge. Durham is an administration and market centre, and although it is surrounded by coal mining villages, it has remained reasonably quiet and beautiful. The present population is 24,777.

Liverpool

Liverpool is one of Britain's largest cities. The city population is 605,600, but the population of the Merseyside conurbation is more than 1¼ million. Its most famous inhabitants are probably John Lennon, Paul McCartney, George Harrison and Ringo Starr, and Liverpool has built a 1 million pound 'Beatles Museum'. Its fame in the world of football is as widespread as its fame in pop music, with Liverpool Football Club being the most successful European team of the late seventies and early eighties, winning the European cup three times. However there's a lot more to Liverpool than just music and football.

It developed very quickly in the 18th and 19th centuries as Britain's major Atlantic port. It was a centre for the cotton trade and manufacturing industry, as well as a centre for ships taking part in the infamous slave trade. At one time, there were seven miles of continuous docks along the River Mersey. The river is crossed by two tunnels, a railway tunnel built in 1886 and a road tunnel, the Mersey Tunnel, in 1934. For many years ferries were the main way across the river, which has no bridges at this point. There are also two 20th century cathedrals: one Church of England, the other Roman Catholic. The Catholic cathedral, one of the few in the world built with an underground car park, can be seen in the lower right foreground of the picture. The famous Lime Street station can be seen just right of the centre.

Liverpool is a cosmopolitan city and, to the anger of both the Irish and the Welsh, it has been called 'the real capital of Ireland' and 'the real capital of Wales', because of the large number of Liverpudlians of Irish and Welsh descent. Today it is well-known for the wit and humour of its people, and its high unemployment figures. There are plans to attract tourism to the area, and to the north west generally, by converting areas of dockland into leisure areas, parks and museums.

Unit 16

You can take either the Caerdowy route or the Llanevy road. Caerdowy's the better road, but the Llanevy way's shorter. It's up to you, really. I'll tell you the short way, anyway. Go about 2 miles up this road until you get to Llanevy. Just after you leave Llanevy, you'll see a turning on the left, the B4007. Keep going along here for about two miles or so, past the Tredowy Mine on your left. Go down the hill into the town and you'll come to a roundabout. Turn left, past the post office and go on to the next junction . . . you'll see a church on the other side of the road. Bear right and carry on to the next fork in the road. Take the right fork, and look out for a little road . . . it's a track really . . . on the right. It's easy to miss it. Go a hundred yards or so up the track, and look at the field to your left. That's the site for the reactor.

Unit 17

Good afternoon and welcome to another edition of *Collector's Corner*. For this afternoon's programme we've come to visit 16-year-old Adrian Shaw. We're in Adrian's room at the moment and we're completely surrounded by bottles . . . yes, bottles. Big ones, small ones, blue ones, green ones. In fact it's difficult to see the walls at all, there are so many bottles. How many bottles are there, Adrian?

Adrian 1,429.
Interviewer 1,429? Have you counted them?
Adrian Yeah. This morning. I thought you might ask me that question.
Interviewer And are they all different?
Adrian Yeah. I keep my spares in a box in the shed.
Interviewer How did all this start?
Adrian About three years ago. I was fishing in the river and I found a bottle, this one here, and I'd never seen one like it. So I took it home, cleaned it up, and showed it to my grandad. He said all the bottles were like that when he was my age.
Interviewer I've never seen one like it.
Adrian No. My grandad's nearly 70. It's an old beer bottle.
Interviewer Hmm.
Adrian Anyway, grandad said it might be worth a bit of money, so I took it along to this shop my mum knew, where she'd seen old bottles in the window.
Interviewer And how much was it worth?
Adrian Well, the bloke in the shop offered me six quid for it. It's a pretty rare one, 'cos it's got the name of the brewery on it, and it was only a small brewery.
Interviewer Weren't you tempted to sell it?
Adrian No, not really. I told him I'd think about it. I saw one in a catalogue the other day. I could get fifteen quid for it now, but I wouldn't sell it. Anyway, I like it.
Interviewer And where did you find all these other bottles? Not all in the river, surely?

Adrian No, though rivers are good places to look. 'Specially near bridges where people chuck them in, and they get stuck in the mud.
Interviewer Where else, then?
Adrian Rubbish dumps, usually the ones out of town, you know, where they used to bury all the old rubbish.
Interviewer And do you know where to find these dumps? A lot have been built on, haven't they?
Adrian Some have, but not all. You can look at old maps in the library, or you can ask old people. They can often remember where people used to chuck rubbish.
Interviewer And of course it doesn't cost anything, does it?
Adrian No. I've never spent a penny on a bottle. Though you can buy them in shops. A lot of people do.
Interviewer Do you ever sell a bottle?
Adrian Oh, yeah. But only if I've already got one the same. You know, I sell one and keep the other.
Interviewer What did people keep in all these bottles?
Adrian All kinds of things. Medicine, you find a lot of old medicine bottles; they're usually blue. But there are all sorts, really: beer bottles, ink bottles. All shapes and sizes.
Interviewer Tell me about that green one over there. What was it used for?
Adrian Oh, that was . . .

Unit 21

A Right, well . . . um . . . my name's Don Crabtree and I come from Headingly in Leeds. I'm an insurance salesman working for the Ribble Mutual Widows Benevolent Society and I travel over four hundred miles every week in my work which doesn't leave me much time for a hobby but I do like em . . . I do like a drop of real ale.

B Hello, my name's Dora Entwhistle and I'm from Liverpool and I work in a factory like and I've got three kids and a husband.

C Hello there. I am Angus McPherson from Glasgow which is in Scotland, of course. Morag, my wife and I have eight children. So it's quite a large family. And I have a general medical practice in the town; so I keep pretty busy.

D My name's Gwyneth Jones. I live in Gwent, which is South Wales. I'm a housewife with two children and my husband's a miner.

E My name's Wayne Roberts and I come from Birmingham in the Midlands. I work in a car factory and I like to play football at weekends. I got married last year and we've got a little girl aged four months. We'd like to have a boy next time.

F Well, I work as an assistant matron at Budleigh Salterton Infirmary, that's what the locals call it. I live in Exeter which is in Devon. Oh, my name is Jill Carpenter and I've got three children. There's not a lot of work in the area so most of my cases are . . . well . . . some of the lads from the farm with agricultural injuries, that sort of thing.

G Hello, my name's Laurie Morrison and I'm from Whitley Bay, which is up near Newcastle in the north-east of England. I'm unemployed at the moment but me hobby's playing football and watching it on the tele like.

H My name's Tracy Sparrow and I come from Hounslow in London . . . em I work in a shoe shop in Richmond High Street . . . um . . . I never really go away on holiday, 'cause . . . well I just think London's the greatest city in the world and I wouldn't want to leave it.

Unit 22

Jenny Macpherson is the Managing Director of GB Electrics. She's talking to a Marketing meeting.

JM Now we come to the most important item on today's agenda, that's Item 7, the GB Express coffee maker. I think all of you have reports for the meeting? Yes? Well, we'll hear them in a moment. I have not seen them yet, and so I'll make my remarks as brief as possible. I'd just like to point out a few problems. Over the years coffee consumption in Britain has been increasing rapidly, and is now around the same level as tea consumption. That's the good news – if you're selling instant coffee. During the same period coffee has become a weak, warm liquid with little flavour or taste. In other words coffee has become more and more like English tea. You know the joke about our canteen here, 'How do you know which is coffee and which is tea?' 'The tea comes in blue cups.' When we began selling filter machines our initial sales were low. On the other hand, the profit per machine was high, and what is more, sales have doubled in almost every year since then. The British public are slowly beginning to develop a taste for real coffee, by which I mean filter coffee. Our new machine, or so I've heard, is a great improvement. Imported machines from Italy and Holland are beginning to sell well, and unless we make a positive move, we'll be too late. The public will identify espresso coffee with imported machines. After all, they are an Italian invention. From another point of view we could say that a British manufacturer will not do well in this market, and that we might be safer to promote our filter machines, which of course are considerably cheaper. The last thing I want to say before hearing your reports is that I still have an open mind. It's up to this meeting to come to a conclusion, either way.

Unit 25

1 Charles Orson
Well, of course, I started in Hollywood right in the middle of the Hays Office days, and you know, we had to show them scripts before we started filming. I'm not sure how carefully they looked at them, but it was a good thing for us. You see, it's pretty expensive to film a five-minute scene which you later have to throw away because of one wrong word. It was much easier to discuss it beforehand. Sometimes it was pretty absurd. I remember a script in . . . oh, '48 or '49 . . . where the Hays Office sent it back and said, 'You can't use this. There are three "damns", two "hells", and one "blast" in this scene.' We got back to them and said something like, 'It's essential to the story,' so they say, 'OK, but you'll have to cut it down a bit. You can have two "damns", one "hell", and scrap the "blast".' I thought that was pretty silly, I mean, either it's wrong or it isn't. Mind you, some of the things they said were sensible. You weren't allowed to show how to pick a lock, and you weren't allowed to show how to kill yourself, for example. No, we often laughed at them, censors are never popular, but the Code gave us a discipline. I mean, some beautiful images came on to film because of it. You were forbidden to show something on screen, so you'd have to use an image instead . . . butterflies whirling round, or waves on a beach . . . you know the kind of thing. Nowadays it's all too direct, too obvious. There's no mystery left in the cinema. I was against censorship all my life, but when I see some of the stuff little kids are watching, I think maybe it's gone too far in the other direction. I mean, you have to draw the line somewhere. You really do.

2 Bourne Hall

Julie is a new student at Wessex University. She has just arrived at her Hall of Residence, Bourne Hall. She's talking to Tricia, a second-year student.

Tricia Hi, I'm Tricia Lambert. I think we're going to be neighbours.

Julie Oh, hello, I'm Julie Morgan. Yes, I suppose we are.

Tricia Are you new here?

Julie Yes. I've just been looking at these regulations. I don't suppose it was worth bringing my cassette player.

Tricia Why not? Everybody's got one. Oh, I see. You've been reading the rules. Well, look, Julie, it's a matter of common sense. Nobody's going to stop you playing it, it's not like that. It's just that you mustn't stop other people working.

Julie No, I wouldn't want to do that. I won't play it late.

Tricia You don't have to worry. All you've got to do is check with the others on this floor. Usually, they won't mind a bit of music.

Julie But it's not allowed after eleven.

Tricia You're not supposed to play it late, of course. But I'm sure you'll find it's all right sometimes.

3 On the bus

Annette's on a bus.

Conductor Oy! You can't stand there.

Annette Sorry?

Conductor I said you mustn't stand there, luv. You're in the driver's way. Go on, move back.

Annette I'm terribly sorry. I didn't realize. But there's no need to be rude about it, is there?

4 On the beach

Micky C'mon, Sam . . . kick it over here . . . c'mon . . .

Beach inspector Oy! You two lads! Stop that!

Micky Stop what?

Beach inspector Stop kicking that ball around. It's against the regulations.

Micky Eh? What regulations?

Beach inspector Can't you read, son? No ball games on the promenade. It's not allowed, see.

Micky Why not? We're not doing any harm.

Beach inspector It's a regulation, that's why. You can play football on the beach. That's all right.

Micky There's no room on the beach.

Beach inspector Well, you can't play here. Go on, get a move on.

Unit 26

Voice 1 Hello . . . hello? Is anybody there? Oh, lord, my head's splitting. Ah, Mary. There you are. Bring me some coffee. Some black coffee.

Voice 2 You should be in bed, ma'am. That's what the doctor said. He did.

Voice 1 Bed! How can I sleep with all this going on? Bring the coffee, Mary.

Voice 3 Ah, this is a surprise. We haven't seen you at breakfast for years. What's happened? Summer sale at the off-licence?

Voice 1 That's enough! You're just like your father, you know. Just like him.

Voice 3 But a bit brighter, eh? Just a bit brighter.

Voice 1 I sometimes think you're worse. You're not like me. Not at all like me.

Voice 3 Thank goodness for that.

Voice 4 Hello, nice to see you up so early . . . good morning. Has anybody seen my husband yet?

Voice 3 Why? Has he left you?

Voice 4 Very funny. No, I just thought he'd be here. He said he was going straight down to breakfast.

Voice 3 Perhaps he's run away. (It wouldn't be the first time for you, would it?)

Voice 4 What do you mean? Come on, what are you trying to say, exactly?

Voice 1 Yes, leave her alone. There's no reason to start on her.

Voice 5 Hello, everybody. What's all the fuss about, eh?

Voice 4 It's nothing, darling. Just your delightful brother, as usual.

Voice 3 Just my sense of humour, that's all.

Voice 5 I thought I told you to leave her alone.

Voice 3 Do you often have to say that to people?

Voice 5 Why, I'll . . .

Voice 6 What's going on here? Can't we have breakfast in peace for once? Sit down, both of you. I won't have squabbling in the house. Why, when I was a lad, I'd done two or three hours' work before breakfast. I didn't get where I am today by squabbling. Where's my scrambled eggs? I've got a meeting at 9 o'clock.

Voice 3 A meeting? You didn't tell me about . . . a meeting.

Voice 1 He's been having private meetings for years. What's her name?

Voice 6 Leave it out. I haven't got the time . . . or the patience. I suppose that layabout isn't up yet?

Voice 1 That's no way to talk about him. After all, he is your . . .

Voice 7 Good morning, everyone. Hello, darling. (kiss) I'm sorry I'm a little late. I couldn't find my eye-liner.

Voice 3 Hello, darling. You look splendid. By the way, I might be late tonight. I've got to see somebody.

Voice 7 That's all right, my sweet. Milk, dear? Oh, you must let me introduce you to my hairdresser, dear. You've been neglecting yourself since . . . since . . . well, you know.

Voice 4 (sob, sob)

Voice 7 Oh, I am sorry. I did promise not to mention it again.

Voice 5 Come on, love. It's nearly a year now.

Voice 6 It was his own bloody fault, anyway.

Voice 1 There's no need, you oaf . . .

Voice 8 (huh, huh, huh) Help! Everybody! Come quickly! She's in the pool . . . the swimming pool . . . I think . . . I think she's dead!

Unit 28

This is Craig Walton of Southern Radio Sport, here at the Inter-city Athletics Championship at Wembley Stadium. I've just heard that they're ready to begin the draw for one of the week's most popular events, the Men's 4 × 100 metre relay, so we're going over to the Committee rooms.

Official

Phew – phew . . . testing one-two, testing one-two . . . Can you hear me? Right. We are going to begin the draw. The first four teams out of the hat will be in the first heat, and they are: South London, on the inside track, Brighton, Bristol and York, on the outside. In the second heat . . . testing one-two, I think there's something wrong with this microphone – one-two, Oh it's OK . . . we have Exeter on the inside, Newcastle, Dover and Swansea. And in the third heat we shall have Leeds on the inside, Liverpool . . . quiet please, quiet . . . and (crackle, crackle) Which switch? Oh, it's on again, sorry about that . . . one, two . . . Liverpool, Cambridge and Nottingham. And in the fourth heat . . . one, two, one, two . . . the teams will be Oxford, on the inside, Glasgow, Birmingham and finally Manchester. That completes the draw for the (crackle, crackle) . . . one, two, testing one, two . . .

Now listen to the heats.

1

They're lining up now for the first heat, they're ready. (On your marks . . . set . . . (pistol).) They're off to a flying start, Waters from South London's taken the lead as they round the bend, then Gates, Tankard, Bell, Singh's taken the baton, Minster's in hot pursuit for York, then the Bristol boy as they come up for the third stage, and it's Marley for London . . . really moving there, and Riding . . . these two are well ahead, into the fourth stage, Minder's stumbling and the York boy is moving through . . . yes, it's Rowntree in front, then Minder, straining to catch him . . . and that's it! Rowntree of York is first, Minder from South London second, then Bristol with Brighton at the rear.

2

If you've just joined us, we're at the start of the second heat in the Men's 4 × 100 metres relay. In many ways, this is the weakest heat with none of the favourites in it. They're on the blocks, Exeter in the orange on the inside, then Terry from Newcastle, Castle from Dover and Llewelyn from Swansea in the green vest. (On your marks . . . set . . . (pistol).) Oh, something was wrong with the start, there. They're going back to the blocks . . . very nerve-racking when that happens. (On your marks . . . set . . . (pistol).) Oh, and Castle's surging into the lead, going like a rocket, the other three bunched together . . . and at the baton it's still Dover, nothing to choose between the others as they come to the second change . . . and it's Dover well in front in the yellow, Moor of Exeter making a challenge . . . is he moving! Round to the last change, and Ferry's blocking Penbern of Exeter, Penbern can't get through . . . What is Ferry doing? And at the tape, it's Ferry of Dover, from Penbern, Exeter and D F Jones of Swansea and North limping home for Newcastle. Of course he injured his foot in the hurdles. But wait . . . Ferry has been disqualified for pushing. What a pity for Dover! After a great race . . .

3

Well, many would say that this was the strongest heat, perhaps the one most likely to produce the champion team. Cambridge must be the outsiders here, with Liverpool the clear favourites. But you can't write off teams like Leeds, and Nottingham who were so narrowly beaten last year. Sharp of Liverpool is just looking at his shoes – no trouble, I hope, for the Jamaican lad who's run so brilliantly for Liverpool . . . no, they're getting ready (On your marks . . . set . . . (pistol).) . . . and Sharp explodes into the lead, with Clough just behind him and Lomax pounds ahead of Jones, but they're all keeping together at the baton, and Nottingham takes the lead after a clumsy change by Liverpool, now falling back into third place behind Leeds as they come up for the next change . . . that was better for Liverpool, Harrison is forging ahead . . . but Lawrence is keeping up for Nottingham . . . Chatterly takes the baton from Lawrence just ahead of Lenton, but these two are neck and neck and going like the wind, and at the tape it's a photo finish, but I think Liverpool just ahead there. Yes, that's confirmed . . . and Liverpool have set a new British record of 38.12 seconds . . . in fact the first three have all bested the previous record.

4

Lining up for the final heat. (On your marks . . . set . . . (pistol).) It's Bob Bruce in the lead, from Vic Aston and Billy Kramer . . . what an athlete Bruce is, marvellous runner, and Macbeth's going to take himself into a good lead now for Glasgow . . . then Birmingham, then Manchester, with Oxford trailing as we come into the bend and Campbell's off to a bad start . . . look at Thomson! He's making a strong challenge . . . going past them all for Oxford, he's ahead of Glasgow at the change and Hartley just has to run home . . . yes, they can't catch him now . . . he's over the line, with McLeish taking a good runners-up place for Glasgow. A great run from Thomson, there.

Now listen to the semi-finals.

1

There's a tremendous atmosphere here at Wembley as we wait for the first semi-final in the men's 4 × 100 metre relay. The first runners are getting prepared, and who can predict the result? York are the surprise semi-finalists and a lot of people are shouting for them. On the other hand Nottingham must be the logical choice, just beaten by Liverpool in that record-breaking third heat. Then again Glasgow seemed unlucky in the fourth heat. They're on the blocks (On your marks . . . set . . . (pistol).) It's Clough into an early lead in the white and red for Nottingham, with Bruce and Gates fighting for second place, coming up to the change – and Forrest keeps the lead for Nottingham, running beautifully, then Minster in the all-white strip for York, Macbeth . . . into the second change, oh, and Campbell's chasing Lawrence of Nottingham – it's anybody's race, York's just behind as they go for the change . . . but Chatterly has dropped the baton! Chatterly has dr . . . York are well ahead . . . and Glasgow run into second place . . . what a turn up for the book! York are in the final for the first time, and Chatterly is on the ground . . . utterly dejected . . . but over now to the javelin . . .

2

Perhaps the second semi-final is a little more predictable. We have four good teams, but Liverpool must be unbeatable. That's Sharp talking to Waters . . . both men of course in the Olympic team, but that doesn't mean they won't be doing their best to beat each other today. They're getting ready . . . Oxford in dark blue, Liverpool red, South London white, and Swansea green . . . we're ready . . . (On your marks . . . set . . . (pistol).) And it's Sharp . . . Hornby in the blue, then Swansea in green with Waters trailing for South London . . . they're coming . . . they're into the change . . . beautifully taken for Liverpool by McCartney and Cole of Oxford fighting Singh for second position . . . Bryn Jones lagging for Swansea . . . it's a race for second place surely now as Harrison races ahead . . . he's nearly 20 metres in front now as he comes up to pass the baton to Lenton . . . oh, he's well ahead . . . maybe this could be a record breaker again . . . Lenton's across the line! Then Hartley for Oxford just a touch in front of Minder for London . . . let's get the time . . . 38.09 seconds . . . Liverpool have just beaten their new record!

Now listen to the final.

Well after yesterday's semi-final there can't be much doubt about who's favourite for today's 4 × 400 metre relay. Liverpool are on top form, and the less experienced teams from York, Oxford and Glasgow must realize the fight is for the second place. But no race can be a 100 per cent foregone conclusion, as we line up for the final. Sharp as usual takes the start for Liverpool, Oxford have changed the running order with Thomson opening and Hornby taking the third stage. (On your marks . . . set . . . (pistol).). Gates for York first off the line, but Sharp's with him . . . Thomson passes Bruce . . . they run for the changeover . . . smoothly taken . . . they're all together . . . not much to choose between them . . . McCartney edges to the front, but Cole's going like a steam engine . . . they're into the second change and it's got to be Liverpool. Harrison pulls away from Hornby, Riding and Campbell and both close . . . very cl . . . the third . . . and . . . Lenton! Lenton is . . . Lenton's down . . . he's down . . . and Oxford fighting to catch York desperately . . . Lenton's up, but . . . at the line it's Oxford! Oxford by a hair's breadth from Rowntree of York.

Unit 31

Pilot We came alongside and looked into the cockpit hoping to see . . . or wondering whether we were going to see . . . the crew or a hijack in progress or whatever. And we looked in, and on the first pass we weren't sure, er . . . John thought that he saw somebody in the front cockpit. Second time we came round we managed to stabilize with the aeroplane in a close formation position and er . . . we looked in and were able to see that there was nobody sitting at the controls.

Navigator In many ways it was a good thing that they were probably dead or unconscious at that time in that if there'd been somebody in the rear waving at us, I mean there was nothing we could do, er, to resolve the problem so it made things a bit easier for us, if you understand what I mean.

Unit 36

Timothy Old . . . that was the latest record from Computer, 'Space Travel'. Eleven o'clock on Tuesday 17th September here on the Timothy Old Show on Radio Wessex, 206 metres medium wave, and it's time for our Medical Advice spot. Today's guest is Dr Guy Lines from the Common Cold Research Unit. Dr Lines, could you briefly describe your work?

Guy Lines Yes, Tim. We ask volunteers to stay with us at the Research Centre for two weeks . . . and we give them a cold.

Timothy Old You give them a cold?

Guy Lines That's correct. Actually, we give half of them a cold. That is we infect them with a solution of cold germs. The other half are given clear, plain water. They're a control group. Our researchers don't know which volunteers have been infected.

Timothy Old How do you get volunteers?

Guy Lines By word of mouth. It's like a holiday hotel, really. And of course only half are infected. We can then study the effect of different cold treatments.

Timothy Old So, have you found a cure yet?

Guy Lines Not yet, I'm afraid. Although I'd like to get rid of a few old wives' tales. You get a cold from germs. Not from wet feet, or cold air or sitting in a draught.

Timothy Old What advice would you give to cold sufferers, then?

Guy Lines The oldest of all. If you treat a cold, it takes about a week to get over it. If you don't treat it . . . then it takes about a week to get over it.

Timothy Old What about aspirin . . . or hot whisky and lemon?

Guy Lines Of course aspirin, or a drink of spirits helps the symptoms. It makes the sufferer feel better, especially if they just go to bed and wait. It doesn't cure it, though.

Timothy Old What about your research?

Guy Lines We're finding good results from vitamins – large doses of vitamin C . . . and I mean 5 or 6 grams a day . . . do seem to help some people if taken at the very first sign of a cold. Once it's started though, it seems much less successful. Vitamins A and B6 also seem to help, but we have a lot more research to do. Interferon does give good results, but of course it's wildly expensive, and we can't really waste the limited supplies we have on cold research. Most of it is being used for cancer research at the moment.

Timothy Old Interferon?

Guy Lines Yes, I'm sure you've heard of it.

Timothy Old Wasn't there a programme about it on TV recently?

Guy Lines There was.

Timothy Old What's your final advice then?

Guy Lines Basically, go home. Take plenty of liquid. Vitamin C certainly won't do you any harm, and it may help. Aspirin will make you feel better, but the best advice I can give is rest. Plenty of rest.

Timothy Old Thank you, Dr Lines. We'll be coming back to you after our next record, it's Daisy Barton singing 'You broke my heart', . . .

Unit 40

(The first three sections, 1 Introduction, 2 Cinema and 3 Fashion are also recorded.)

4 Pop music

Perhaps the classic example of youth culture is pop music. There has always been 'music which is popular', but until 1950 or so, popular music meant the music of the working classes. Since 1955, or thereabouts, we have had 'pop music' which is classless. A musician might tell us that the causes of 'pop culture' are complex. He might say modern pop music is the result of a mixing, a blending of Black American rhythm and blues with White American country and western music. We are interested in the effects of pop music, and no account of its origins can explain its worldwide popularity. This is almost certainly due . . . once again . . . to changes in technology. I would say that pop music as we know it is a direct consequence of the invention of the transistor. The transistor gave teenagers their own source of music, which was cheap and portable, that is to say the transistor radio. As a result teenagers were freed from the family radio, broadcasting bland music for a family audience. A demand was created for specifically teenage music, and as usual, industry responded. At the same time, the invention of the 45 r.p.m. vinyl record, which was almost unbreakable, led to greatly increased record sales.

5 Other entertainments

The new youth audience were too young to go to the traditional British pub, because of British drinking laws which forbid the sale of alcohol to under-18s. In the United States, the drinking age was 21. This was a result of the Prohibition era, between 1919 and 1933 when alcohol was totally forbidden. So again there was a market, kids looking for somewhere to meet, and again there was a response. Coffee bars and Milk bars began to open all over the country in the 1950's on account of this demand. Like pop music, an American model forms the basis. The pubs were left to the older males, the tea-shops to the older females. Another effect, a side effect, of this Americanization was increased consumption of coffee. In 1945 tea was the normal British drink. By 1965 tea and coffee consumption was almost equal.

6 Summing up

So the main areas we shall look at are the cinema, next week, fashion, the week after, pop music, the week after that, and finally, other entertainment in the last lecture in the series. There are some other manifestations of youth culture, most of them a consequence of industry's response to a group with surplus money. I shall just mention a few of them. Motor scooters became popular here, as British kids, unlike their American contemporaries, could not afford cars. The scooter was not really suitable for Britain, on account of our weather and the resulting slippery roads. Thousands were sold, another reason being that you could ride a scooter at 16, a year before you could apply for a car licence. A huge cosmetics industry grew up, with massive advertising to make girls buy cosmetics which became very cheap. Why? As usual, the price resulted from new technology and synthetic ingredients. Magazines directed at the youth market were published in large numbers, too. The same forces, as ever, were at work on this, the first TV generation. Because of their spending power, the concept of 'teenager' – in inverted commas – was developed. However, in the 1950's their spending power was still controlled by traditional industries. In the 1960's things changed, but that's the subject of another lecture.

Unit 45

Ground crew Come in Tango-Alpha-Charley. Do you read me? Over.
Pilot We read you loud and clear. Over.
Ground crew What is your altitude? Over.
Pilot We are holding steady at 4000 – repeat 4000 feet.
Ground crew I can hear you, but I can't see you yet. Over.
Pilot Please check on ground conditions. Over.
Ground crew There's a slight breeze down here. Nothing to worry about, though. It's only about 4 or 5 knots, blowing south-south-west. You'll pick it up as soon as we light the smoke flare. Look out for the telephone line to the north of the field. Also take care not to get near the sports pavilion. Over.
Pilot The sports pavilion? Over.
Ground crew Yes. There's a telephone line running from the north-east corner to the north of the field. I reckon they should avoid that whole sector . . . just in case. Over.
Pilot Right. We're going to turn in for our approach. Over.
Ground crew Please give check-list. Over.
Pilot Right. We throttle back the engine and slow down. Once the door is open I shall count down, and cut the engine right back as they jump to avoid any turbulence. Over.
Ground crew I'm going to light the flare. Over.
Pilot Watch you don't burn your fingers this time. Over.
Ground crew Very funny. Over.
Pilot I can see it. OK. Door open. Counting 5-4-3-2-1, one out, two out, all out. Over.
Ground crew I can see them. One, two, three. All chutes open. Here they come . . .

Unit 52

Cross examination by the prosecution

Prosecution Lady Wyatt. Would you describe yourself as an intelligent woman?
Lady Wyatt I would never describe myself as anything . . . I'm not stupid.
Prosecution Do you not think it was stupid to put that scarf in your bag and walk away without paying?
Lady Wyatt I intended to pay. There was nobody *to* pay.
Prosecution You couldn't have looked very hard, could you?
Lady Wyatt Look, I've told you. I had an appointment . . . I was in a hurry.
Prosecution Surely not in such a hurry that you couldn't find someone to pay. Surely you could have spent a few minutes. Surely your friend would have waited.
Lady Wyatt I don't like keeping people waiting. I'm never late.
Prosecution Couldn't you simply have put the scarf back and collected and paid for it later?
Lady Wyatt I suppose so. I just didn't think. I intended to pay for it later.
Prosecution But you didn't pay for it, did you?

Lady Wyatt I've told you ten times already. I simply forgot.
Prosecution Every shoplifter says that, Lady Wyatt.
Lady Wyatt I am not a shoplifter.
Prosecution Hmm, hmm. Now these pills. How long have you been taking them?
Lady Wyatt Four or five years. They calm me down.
Prosecution And in those four or five years have you ever suffered from loss of memory or forgetfulness?
Lady Wyatt Not that I know of.
Prosecution And have you walked into shops, taken things, put them in your bag and walked away without making any effort to pay?
Lady Wyatt No, no, no.
Prosecution But you did on this occasion. You took a scarf, put it in your bag and made no offer to pay. That is theft, common theft. If we accepted your claim that you simply forgot, then every Tom, Dick and Harry would be walking in and out of shops, taking whatever caught their eye. No, no, no Lady Wyatt. 'I forgot' is no excuse at all. I maintain that you intended to steal. I believe many people do that . . . just for 'kicks' . . . it gives them a thrill.
Lady Wyatt That's not true.
Prosecution But it is true, Lady Wyatt . . . No further questions, your honour.

Cross examination of the defence

Defence Lady Wyatt. You're a very wealthy woman, aren't you?
Lady Wyatt Wealthy, yes. I don't know about 'very'.
Defence But you don't need to work.
Lady Wyatt No.
Defence How often do you go shopping at Hall's?
Lady Wyatt I don't know exactly. I suppose once or twice a week.
Defence So in a year you would probably spend hundreds of pounds there.
Lady Wyatt Yes.
Defence So there is no reason why you should want to steal anything – a scarf worth £10 maybe.
Lady Wyatt Of course not. It's quite ridiculous.
Defence Have you ever been in trouble with the police before?
Lady Wyatt No, never.
Defence Not even a traffic offence.
Lady Wyatt No.
Defence And you're a well-known figure in the community.
Lady Wyatt I suppose so. I do a lot of work for charity.
Defence And you say that you just forgot to pay.
Lady Wyatt Yes.
Defence That's easy enough to do. I've done it myself and I imagine many people in this court have. And of course you would have returned to pay as soon as you realized.
Lady Wyatt Yes. I would have realized when I got home.
Defence Thank you, Lady Wyatt. No further questions, your honour.

Unit 54

Message 1 10.42

Suzy Greyson Worldwide Trading Ltd.
Man Er. May I speak to Mr Greyson, please?
Suzy I'm afraid Mr Greyson's out. Can I take a message?
Man Oh, dear. When are you expecting him back?
Suzy Um . . . I'm not sure. Who's calling?
Man It's Mr Jackson, from the Midland Bank. Can you ask him to call me?
Suzy Certainly, Mr Jackson. Goodbye.
Man Goodbye.

Message 2 10.56

Suzy Gre . . .
Man Greyson? Is that you?
Suzy I'm afraid Mr Greyson's not here at the moment. Who's calling?
Man It's . . . er, tell him it's Mr Smith. Mr John Smith. He'll know who I am. Can I speak to him now?
Suzy I told you he wasn't in, Mr Smith.
Man Come on. He'll speak to me.
Suzy I'm sure he would, but he really is out.
Man Who are you?
Suzy I'm . . . his secretary. Is there any message?
Man Secretary? Greyson with a secretary? Don't make me laugh, sweetheart.
Suzy Look, do you want to leave a message, or not?
Man Yeah . . . Just say . . . Can you meet John Smith at 8.30? The usual place. Say it's important, very important. Say . . . say . . . I want to know whether he's got the papers. Have you got that?
Suzy Yes. Thank you, Mr Smith. Goodbye.

Message 3 11.02

Suzy Greyson Worldwide Trading . . .
Woman Hello? Hello? I'm phoning about my order.
Suzy Could I have your name, please?
Woman Oh, yes. It's Brown. Mrs Brown from Leeds.
Suzy I'm afraid . . . I'm afraid the person who deals with orders isn't here. Can I take a message?
Woman Oh, dear. I've tried to phone several times, and this is the first time I've had a reply. It's about the order, you see.
Suzy What order was that, Mrs Brown?
Woman The complete set of kitchen knives. I saw the advert in the paper, and I sent my cheque months ago. Well, the order's never arrived, you see.
Suzy Could I . . . Could I take your number? Someone can phone you back.
Woman I'm not on the phone. You see, I'm using a neighbour's phone. Perhaps you could phone her, if that's all right. I'm getting worried, you see. I've written twice, too.
Suzy Shall I take your number?
Woman Oh, yes. Yes. It's Leeds 178432.
Suzy Thank you. I'll pass on the message.
Woman Yes, yes. They were expensive, you see. Yes, goodbye, then.

Message 4 11.19

Suzy Greyson Worldwide Trading.
Man Where's Greyson?
Suzy Mr Greyson's not here, can I . . .
Man Are you sure?
Suzy Yes. Who's calling?
Man My name's Evans. Evans Printing Company.
Suzy Er . . . would you like to leave a message?
Man Yes. Where's my money? He owes me £2,700, and he'd better pay up . . . soon.
Suzy I see. Anything else?
Man Yes. What's he done with all the letters I've sent him? I've written every bloody week. You tell him . . .
Suzy I'm just a temporary secretary, here.
Man Yes. Well. Sorry, luv. It's not your fault. Tell him he'd better phone me back. All right? I'll be waiting. Goodbye.

Message 5   11.26

Suzy   Greyson Worldwide Trading.
Woman   I'd like to speak to Tim Greyson, please.
Suzy   I'm afraid he's out at the moment.
Woman   Who am I speaking to?
Suzy   I'm. . .I'm a temporary secretary.
Woman   Is that what he calls you?
Suzy   Sorry. I don't know what you're talking about. Can I take a message?
Woman   Yes. Ask him where my car is, why he hasn't called me for two weeks, what he's done with my cheque, when I'm going to see him again . . . and what the hell he thinks he's doing. Did you get all of that, dear?
Suzy   I think so. Who shall I say called?
Woman   There can't be many people who would leave a message like that. He'll know. Goodbye.

Message 6   11.34

Suzy   Greyson Worldwide Trading.
Woman   Can you put me through to Mr Greyson, please?
Suzy   He's not here at the moment. Can I take a message?
Woman   Yes. This is the Toptype Secretarial Agency. I'm phoning to enquire about our bills, which haven't been met.
Suzy   Bills? What were they for?
Woman   For? He's had three temporary secretaries, and we haven't received a penny.
Suzy   I've only been here an hour . . . I'm from the A1 Agency.
Woman   Really? Well, I'd just leave him my message . . . and not waste any more of your time!

Unit 58

Simply put, the average traveller is very average. He has two cases and the things in those cases accurately reflect his position in life and his journey.

Let's say he's a businessman back from Europe. He may have had a rather complex journey, been to a few capitals over there. His cases will have a fair bit of paperwork in them. He'll have a couple of pairs of shoes, good shoes, and a Brooks Brothers suit or whatever, three or four silk ties, and a good selection of shirts and socks, all neatly laundered by a hotel. There will be a little stack of laundered handkerchiefs and a couple of hard-cover books.

Now, if he's an oilman, even a fairly senior one, he'll be very different. If his travels have taken him to the North Sea, he'll have bought a couple of tartan rugs, for certain – they all do! He's going to have slacks, maybe a plaid jacket, and sports shirts and a pair of boots. He may have a paperback and a shooting or hunting magazine. And, almost certainly, a couple of bottles of straight malt whisky. Don't ask me why oilmen have dirty laundry; maybe Scottish hotels won't do it.

When we get somebody whose luggage doesn't match his appearance or his story or his route, then we get curious. Like with Pan Am 800. Why should people carrying light clothes, slacks and short-sleeved shirts, be coming from Tokyo in February? Why should they have sun-tan oil in their toilet kits? Because they started out from Colombia. They may claim to be students. What is a student doing in Tokyo in February? He's surely not on vacation. So where is he studying? Or a businessman. So how come he's not carrying lots of papers, commercial samples, sales aids?

Smugglers never accumulate all the rubbish in their cases that an ordinary traveller does – phrase books, torn street maps, half-filled-in postcards, used rolls of film, hotel receipts, book-matches, curios, presents for the children. And they can make real fools of themselves. They'll say 'Colombia! Where's that?' And then you point out that their shirt wrappers, back to shirts again, are labelled 'Bogota Hotel' or that their toothpaste or shaving cream is Colombian. You get some who are so stupid that they don't even fill their suitcases. They seem to think that we won't find it odd that they're travelling with an empty case. Those who fill them often get the mix wrong. There will be masses of clothes but not heavier shoes or books. The clothes themselves are often suspicious: shirts of different sizes, trousers that don't seem they would fit the passenger, labels with little give-aways: 'Ind Col' (Colombian made) or all the other clothes will obviously be new or they don't suit the personality of the owner. We had one, a 'macho' type, and he had all dull gabardine trousers and chunky sweaters, totally out of character. Though the cocaine we found wasn't!

It takes a lot of skill to fool a man who's been looking at suitcases for 15 years.

Unit 59

Mrs Curtis   Yes?
Salesman   Mrs Curtis?
Mrs Curtis   Yes.
Salesman   You don't know me. I'm an educational consultant.
Mrs Curtis   Oh!
Salesman   And I wonder if I could talk to you about your children's future.
Mrs Curtis   My children's future. Well . . . er . . .
Salesman   Could I come in for a moment?
Mrs Curtis   Well. I don't . . .
Salesman   Thank you. I won't take much of your time . . . I'm sure you're very busy.
Mrs Curtis   No, no. I was just making a cup of tea.
Salesman   That's very kind of you. I never say no to a cup of tea. Just one sugar.
Mrs Curtis   Hmm. Hmm. There you are.
Salesman   Thank you. Is Mr Curtis at home?
Mrs Curtis   No. I'm afraid he isn't. He's at work. He won't be home till late.
Salesman   And the children? They're at school, I suppose.
Mrs Curtis   Yes, that's right.
Salesman   Which school do they go to?
Mrs Curtis   Worlsden Primary . . . just up the road.
Salesman   And how old are they?
Mrs Curtis   Gary's eight and Julia's ten.
Salesman   How are Gary and Julia doing at school?
Mrs Curtis   All right. About average, I suppose. They seem to be very happy there.
Salesman   Only average, eh? Hmm . . . do you think they could do better?
Mrs Curtis   I don't think so. I'm sure they're doing their best. Anyway we leave that up to the teachers.
Salesman   But I'm sure you want your children to do well, don't you, Mrs Curtis? I mean it's only natural to want the best for one's children, isn't it? I suppose Gary and Julia read a lot at home.
Mrs Curtis   Well. Not a lot. They watch the 'telly' a lot . . . And they bring books home from school.

Salesman   Hmm. But that's not the same as having your own books at home, is it? Research has shown that children who read lots of books at home do better at school, you know. Reading's very important.
Mrs Curtis   I'm sure it is. We sometimes buy them books for Christmas.
Salesman   Yes, but what kind of books! Let me show you this. Just look at that for a moment and tell me what you think of it.
Mrs Curtis   Hmm. It's beautiful . . . the pictures are lovely.
Salesman   And it's not just the pictures, Mrs Curtis. All human knowledge is there. Everything your children might want to know on every subject under the sun.
Mrs Curtis   All in this book.
Salesman   No, no. That's just one volume. There are forty volumes. It took over twenty years to produce it.
Mrs Curtis   It must be very expensive.
Salesman   Well they are usually. But this month, I'm in a position to offer very generous terms. Just for this month, I can give a 20% discount. Those books will never be so cheap again.
Mrs Curtis   Well, I don't know . . . I'm sure we can't afford it. Things are a bit difficult at the moment.
Salesman   But these books are an investment in your children's future. You can't really put a price on that, can you, Mrs Curtis?
Mrs Curtis   No, I suppose not. I don't know . . . I . . .
Salesman   I mean, you want your children to do well, don't you?
Mrs Curtis   Yes, but we haven't for that kind of money, you see.
Salesman   Not many people have these days, Mrs Curtis. But I can make payment very easy for you. You just pay a small deposit and then a small payment every month. That's how other parents pay.
Mrs Curtis   Oh, I see.
Salesman   And the terms are very reasonable, I can assure you.
Mrs Curtis   Well, I just don't know. The books are very nice, I'm sure, and the kids would love them . . . but I usually let my husband deal with . . .
Salesman   Yes, I understand that, Mrs Curtis, and I would never dream of asking you to commit yourself finally. You just sign this form, we send you the books and if you change your mind, you can always send them back.
Mrs Curtis   Well, I don't know what to do. I really don't.
Salesman   You wouldn't regret it, you know. I can give my word. An offer like this will never come along again. And I know the price is going up at the end of the month.
Mrs Curtis   All right. Where do I sign?
Salesman   Just there, Mrs Curtis. That's right. It's the best investment you've ever made.